To Michael,
Thanks for your support!
Todd Overgard

Escaping the Flames

Chronicles of a Jet Crash Survivor

Todd Overgard

Escaping the Flames: Chronicles of a Jet Crash Survivor

EscapingTheFlamesFlight575@gmail.com

Cover photo: Larry Stoddard, Associated Press
Design and layout by Robert Goodman, Silvercat™, Encinitas, California

ISBN: 978-0-578-53303-2 (print)
　　　978-0-578-53304-9 (ebook)

printed in the United States of America

TO MY LOVING AND

SUPPORTIVE WIFE, MYRA

CONTENTS

AND SO IT BEGINS

It was a bit before midnight when I arose from my university dorm room bed where I had just been with Debbie. I had been seeing her off and on since the summer. Debbie was just over five feet tall with long blond hair. I liked her, but we were not exclusive. We wouldn't be seeing each other for the better part of a month as I was headed home for the Christmas holidays. Home was where my folks lived in Madison, Wisconsin. Our dorm rooms consisted of two individual twin beds separated by a dresser, two desks against the opposing wall next to the entrance door, a closet, and a bathroom shared with the dorm room next door. This was a male-only dormitory. My roommate was not around at this time. He had probably left for the holidays already.

Oklahoma City University (OCU) is a Methodist University that had roughly 1,500 students at the time. The school had some pretty strict dorm rules, including not having women in the men's rooms. This was, after all, the Oklahoma of the 1970s. The sexual revolution of the 1960s had not reached them yet. At that time, there were four men's dormitories and a women's dormitory tower on the campus. The men's dormitories were three stories each and had what was known as a "house mother." These were older women who had been hired by the university to live

1

in a lobby level apartment and monitor the male students. Monitoring was a next to impossible task as we had external stairwells leading to the second and third floors. Therefore, the house mothers had little control over us. Frankly, they weren't looking very hard to catch anybody. We just needed to be a bit discreet.

The plan for my trip to Madison was to catch a ride with Ralph, a student from my dorm. He lived in Chicago, Illinois. Ralph was going to drop me at O'Hare International Airport in Chicago where I could catch a flight to Madison. We would share the driving and gas expenses. The trip would be about 800 miles, taking 12 hours. We were in for a long night.

CHAPTER 2

MY FOLKS

My family heritage was primarily European. There was a lot of German and Norwegian in my background. Dad's original first name was Evlyn which was the same as his father's first name. My Grandpa went by Ev for short, but Dad never liked the name and had it legally changed to "E." He liked to be called Ted. He was born in 1926, in Eland, Wisconsin which is a small town in the northern part of the state. Dad had a sister, Dido, who is six years younger, and a brother, Jerry, who is eleven years younger.

He went to high school in Viroqua, Wisconsin, another small town in the west central part of the state. Dad played sports in high school. He played football and was an undefeated boxer. Yes, they boxed in high school back then. I think Dad only fought in his senior year. He told me that he faced another boxer who had never been beaten in high school and Dad beat him. Dad told me that the guy came up to him after the fight and said he had never been hit that hard in his life.

Mom and Dad were raised during the depression. Dad was so poor in high school that one of his coaches actually bought him some clothes. About the only thing that made poverty any better was that most Americans were suffering as well.

My father was also to go through his own close calls with death. He enlisted in the Marine Corps in 1943. Dad had skipped a grade in elementary school, so he was 17 upon completing high school. In October, he headed by train to Camp Pendleton in Southern California for basic training.

During basic training, he not only shot "expert", but was the best shot of the five platoons that had tested at the same time. After completion of basic training, Dad was asked to go to a 15-week radio/telephone school in San Diego. He did well enough to then be sent to Omaha, Nebraska for a 14-week advanced radio/telephone training school.

Back at Camp Pendleton, Dad and his fellow Marines boarded ships for the Big Island of Hawaii. They would be stationed at Camp Tarawa, which is located in the highlands, to train and await orders to a war zone. Dad was assigned to the 28th Marine Regiment. On the first payday, Dad did not get paid and it turned out that the Marine Corps had lost the records necessary to pay him. While this was being straightened out, Dad had to borrow money. He borrowed three dollars from four of his fellow Marines. Before he was to leave Camp Tarawa, he was transferred to the 27th Replacement Battalion. Nobody ever told him why. He thinks they did this because his radio skills were in short supply and so he was not required to be on the front lines.

One frightening experience happened while he was swimming in the ocean off one of Hawaii's beaches. He got caught in a rip tide that pulled him out about half a mile. Luckily, Dad was a very good swimmer and was able to swim back to shore.

In early 1945, the Camp Tarawa Marines boarded ships for destinations unknown. At least it was unknown to them upon leaving port. They were to find out on the way that they were going to invade a small island called Iwo

Jima which was Japanese territory. This island is about eight square miles shaped like a two-mile by four-mile pork chop with Mt. Suribachi located toward one end of the island. The plan was to invade the island beaches under Mt. Suribachi and then sweep the island within a few days. It would not turn out to be nearly that easy.

The Battle of Iwo Jima became very famous because of the second flag raising on Mt. Suribachi that was captured by Joe Rosenthal in his iconic photo. That photo was the basis for the Marine Corps War Memorial statue in Washington, D.C.

The U.S. started bombing Iwo Jima on June 15, 1944 and it went on for a full nine months. The U.S. Marine Corps landings on Iwo Jima did not start until February of 1945. This bombing turned out to have had little effect since the Japanese had gone underground. Lieutenant General Tadamichi Kuribayashi, who was commanding the Japanese troops, knew that he could not win the upcoming battle, but hoped to inflict massive casualties in order to get the Allies to reconsider an eventual invasion of the Japanese home islands. The black lava sand apparently could make good cement, so Kuribayashi built an underground network of caves, passageways, and rooms. The bunkers and defensive arrangements on the north side of the island were all connected so that bunkers that had been vacated could be reentered later. This strategy was very inventive and was the cause for so much difficulty and death for the Marines.

The U.S. sent in the 3rd, 4th, and 5th Marine divisions. Dad was a part of the 5th Marine division. He had a last-minute assignment change as a radio/telephone man for the 13th Artillery Regiment and landed on day two, February 20.

This was another factor which probably saved his life. The battle was so horrific that his memory shut down in order to protect him. The battle was severely traumatizing.

Dad ended up near one of the two completed landing strips not too far from Mt. Suribachi. He tells the story of being ordered to fix what was an apparent broken radio line. The radio/telephone lines ran from the artillery location near the runways to the front lines where fighting was the fiercest. The center of the island, where the wires ran, was relatively flat and open. This open space was several miles long. These radio/telephone lines were on the surface and were being cut daily. I assume this was due to mortar fire, hand grenades, or other explosive weapons. Only Dad and one other radio operator were authorized to do these repairs. A bodyguard was sent out with Dad for protection while he was doing the repairs. Dad was to follow the radio line until he could find the break and repair it.

Passing through open territory was never safe. Although this was behind the front lines, the network of tunnels built by the Japanese allowed them to pop up at various locations behind these front lines. This made the task especially dangerous. On one occasion, Dad and his bodyguard went out to find the break. His memory of what occurred next was filled in by other Marines that watched his progress. Two of the Marines back at the artillery location could see Dad and his fellow Marine out on the flat open space. They told Dad later that shots rang out and Dad's bodyguard fell. Dad immediately rolled and came up with his rifle ready to fire from the prone position. There were six Japanese that moved in toward the downed Americans. Dad fired back and over the next 15 minutes, he would shoot at them as they came out of their tunnel exit points trying to finish off the Marines. The two fellow Marines who saw the whole thing go down tried to get to Dad. By the time they got there, they had watched Dad take out all of the Japanese. These men did not know who Dad was until after the battle ended. When they found out, they told him what they had seen. That was pretty amazing and another example of my dad's escaping death!

Even where the artillery was located, the Marines were in their foxholes, but not completely safe. The Japanese launched a mortar that struck the foxhole next to Dad's. The Marine in that foxhole was severely injured but survived after spending many months in hospitals. Still another close call where death was avoided.

Iwo Jima was also to become the scene of some of the bloodiest and fiercest fighting in the history of the Marine Corp. There were 27 Medals of Honor awarded for actions taken during the Battle of Iwo Jima. This is more than any battle in history. The US had over 26,000 casualties. Of these, 6,991 US servicemen were killed and almost 20,000 wounded. There were about 21,000 Japanese who died. Only 216 Japanese were captured. In the Japanese, we had an enemy that was defending their homeland and who was resigned to fight to the death.

As mentioned earlier, Dad had borrowed three dollars from four fellow Marines at Camp Tarawa. He found out that all four had been killed on Iwo Jima. There was a 5th Marine Division Cemetery that had been set up on Iwo Jima. Dad found his four friends and said a word over each of their graves. This was very emotionally difficult for him.

After the Battle of Iwo Jima ended, the runways were used for planes that had attacked the Japanese mainland and had been struck by anti-aircraft fire. Many lives were saved because these planes avoided having to ditch in the ocean. At the conclusion of the battle, Dad and his fellow Marines traveled back to Hawaii and Camp Tarawa on the Big Island of Hawaii. Their arrival on the Big Island would have been in late April of 1945.

The Camp Tarawa Marines continued to train in anticipation of the invasion of Japan. Dad was given a radio jeep when he got back to Camp Tarawa. He said this was good because he didn't have to go on the 15-mile hikes that the other Marines did. Instead, he would be driving right past them chauffeuring his Captain around.

The invasion of Japan was expected to be much bloodier than any of the battles leading up to it. It was expected that millions would die in a Japanese invasion due to the likelihood that every Japanese man, woman, and child would be told to fight to the death. The Marines boarded ships headed to Okinawa where they would be staged for the final invasion of Japan. This situation was preempted on the way to Okinawa by the atomic bombs that were dropped on August 6th on Hiroshima, Japan and August 9th on Nagasaki, Japan. This resulted in the unconditional surrender by Japan and the end of the war. As you can imagine, the ending of the war was a great relief for my dad and his fellow Marines.

Dad's ship was diverted to the Japanese island of Kyushu where he was assigned to the post-war occupation of Japan. His ship went to the city of Sasebo, a Japanese naval base. This Sasebo location is less than 50 miles from Nagasaki. Dad arrived in September of 1945. He was to spend the next ten months in Japan. Shortly after his arrival, his Captain wanted Dad to drive him to Nagasaki to see the damage. So, in early September of 1945, he drove the Captain to Nagasaki, where Dad said that it was very devastating to see.

Dad was convinced, as am I, that radiation was still an issue in that area of Japan at that time. The Captain died later of cancer. In Dad's later years, he developed a blood cancer that was treated with a chemo pill. Granted it was over 60 years after his visit, but the doctor had indicated that Dad's blood cancer was likely due to exposure to radiation. That cancer did not kill him, but the pill's side effects were uncomfortable.

After the War, he came home to where his family was living in Hawkins, which is in the North central part of Wisconsin. From 1946–1947 he went to Superior State Teachers College in Superior, Wisconsin. It would go on to be renamed University of Wisconsin—Superior. He played football as a fullback while he was there. He continued to be in the Marine Corps reserve and was not discharged until June 19, 1948 with a rank upon discharge of Sergeant. From 1947–1948, he remained living with his folks who had moved to Potosi, Wisconsin. Potosi is a small town in the southwestern corner of Wisconsin. He continued his college education at Platteville State Teachers College in nearby Platteville, Wisconsin, which was about 15 miles from Potosi. This college was also renamed in 1971 to the University of Wisconsin—Platteville. In Potosi, he met my mother.

My mother was born Joyce Julia Hoffmeister in Potosi, Wisconsin, in July of 1928. She went to Potosi High School and graduated as valedictorian of her class of three. She was only 16 when she graduated high school in 1945. I think she started school a year early. She had a sister, Elizabeth, who was two years older, and a brother, Fred, who was eight years younger.

While in high school, Mom and Elizabeth took summer school classes, so they had at least one year of college credits behind them upon graduation. Starting in 1945, Mom attended Platteville State Teacher's College. She graduated in 1948 at the age of 19. From 1948–1949, she was teaching high school in Cuba City, another small town, about 18 miles from Potosi. Mom once told me the story that she was teaching high school at age 19 and had a boy in one of her classes who was older than she was.

Mom was quite a talented piano player. She played for her church. This was the precursor to my years of being required to take piano lessons. Thinking back on it, it was surprising that Mom didn't teach me herself. She was a working mother which was somewhat unusual in the 1950s when stay-at-home moms were the norm. I spent five years taking weekly lessons from ages six to eleven. I was required to play for half an hour a day. It was torture to come home from school, wanting to go out to play, but being forced to practice piano instead. It should have been enjoyable, but it wasn't. I'm sure my parents didn't want the lessons to go to waste, but they pretty much did anyway.

As this book will point out, my life was also filled with instances of danger and near death. I created many of these situations, but a surprising number of them were just plain happenstance.

ON THE ROAD

My driving companion, Ralph, and I left Oklahoma City around midnight. Early on we ran into fog. This was not a light fog, but a very dense, heavy fog. Ralph and I traveled switching drivers every couple of hours or so. The driving was difficult due to that fog. We were averaging close to 70 miles an hour, but the fog created a strange phenomenon.

I remember sitting in the passenger seat and freaking out because I could not see more than 20 feet in front of the car. I assumed that we could run into another car or fly off the road at any moment because the lack of visibility was so great and we were going so fast. Or, at least it felt like that. When we switched positions and I drove, I could suddenly see well down the road and traveling at 70 miles per hour didn't seem too fast at all for these treacherous conditions. This was definitely weird.

Obviously, it was dark during the first half of the trip, which might have made matters worse. The route was to take us from Oklahoma City through Tulsa on Route 44. That night is a bit of a blur to me, due to the fact that 46 years have passed. The foggy landscape contributed to a continual grayness during the drive. Since Ralph lived in Chicago, I left the route to him. I suspect that we continued up through St. Louis and then onward toward O'Hare, most probably using Route 55.

The fog continued from early on in our lengthy trip, and was still dense when he dropped me off at O'Hare. Neither of us got much sleep because the fog created a high level of tension. We seemed drawn to watch for potential problems while sitting in the passenger seat even though we couldn't prevent an accident. All we could do would be to alert the driver to something that he may not have seen. As morning approached, I am sure we felt better, but the visibility was still very poor. I am surprised at the fact that we had not driven out of the fog. A large swath of the middle of the country must have been blanketed during the time we were driving.

Another disturbing issue was that cold air was blowing up through the driver's side door. Ralph told me that his car door had been hit a month or so previously and no one had left a note. I realized at that moment that I was the culprit.

I was at Oklahoma City University on a full tennis scholarship. I had grown up in Sunnyvale, California, to conservative parents. I went off to school at the age of 18 in 1969. The 60's were a drug-fueled time where rebellion against the status quo was normal. The Vietnam War was taking young men and sending them off to a foreign land where they would fight in the midst of another country's civil war. Many of those young men died. I was lucky to have had a draft deferment based on my college attendance. Further cultural divides complicated matters when situations like the Kent State crisis arose.

On May 4, 1970, Kent State University in Kent, Ohio, was the scene of anti-war protests. A crowd of 2,000 protesters were on the march. The prior days of protest had gotten out of control and the local officials didn't think they could handle it. The Mayor of Kent had called the Governor of the state of Ohio to ask for help. The Governor in turn had called out the Ohio National Guard which arrived on the evening of May 2nd. The city and the university had both seen destruction during demonstrations on prior days. Beer bottles had been thrown at police cars and downtown store windows were broken. There were rumors that the local water supply was going to be poisoned and that stores would be destroyed. A reliable informant told police that the Reserve Officers' Training Corps (ROTC) building, the local army recruiting station, and the post office were all targeted for destruction. Local businesses were threatened with destruction if they did not put anti-war posters in their windows. The arrival of the Ohio National Guard was too late as the university ROTC building had been set on fire and later students had been bayonetted when a curfew was being enforced. This set the stage for the May 4th events.

On that fateful day, the students did not obey orders to cease and disperse, and the National Guard used tear gas, but that was ineffective due to wind. At one point, the Ohio National Guard, feeling threatened, fired upon them. Four students were killed and nine others injured. This was a national story that stirred up huge resentment against our federal and state governments on college campuses throughout the United States. The publicity at the time focused on the National Guard firing on unarmed students. There were photos like that of a distraught young woman screaming while kneeling over a dead student that appeared in Life magazine. A cropped version of the same photo received a Pulitzer Prize. Crosby, Stills, Nash, and Young sang a song written by Neil Young called "Ohio." This song became an anti-war anthem with its iconic refrain "Four-Dead-in-O-hi-o." Students around the country felt that the government was out to kill them if they expressed a negative opinion of the Vietnam War.

Having grown up in a conservative household and going to a liberal arts college, I had my own sort of culture shock. The 60s and early 70s were a time of great social unrest and rebellion. This included the drug culture. Timothy Leary touted the use of psychedelic drugs as a path to enlightenment. His books and philosophy of "turn on, tune in, and drop out" and "think for yourself and question authority" captured the imagination of the youth of America. The "Establishment" hated him. Using psychedelic drugs such as psilocybin and LSD, Leary and others of this counter-culture drug revolution believed that our parents and the establishment had lied to us. President Richard Nixon once described Leary as "the most dangerous man in America."

Some popular musicians were strongly pushing the drug culture and rebellion. Although in hindsight, many top musicians died from overdoses. Jim Morrison of the Doors, Janis Joplin of Big Brother and the Holding Company, and Jimi Hendrix all fell victim to drugs in the early 70s. Nonetheless, the obvious inconsistencies that were supported norms of the Establishment led many of us to rebel. For instance, marijuana was portrayed as evil and as the gateway to hardcore drugs such as cocaine and heroin. At the same time, the smoking of cigarettes and drinking of alcohol were treated as acceptable. These positions did not sit well with my generation.

Athletes in particular were supposed to take care of their bodies, but we were just as susceptible as other students to the changes that were happening around us. Like others in the 1970s, I experimented with drugs. Initially, it was drinking alcohol and smoking marijuana. After smoking marijuana, I was surprised that there were no major repercussions that were obvious. It became clear to me that marijuana was no more harmful than alcohol. That was a big revelation. There was no addiction to marijuana, so I decided that experimenting with other drugs in social settings was fine. This drug usage was most prevalent from my sophomore year of college forward. I never used drugs consistently or used needles. To me these were fast tracks to addiction, so I only used recreationally. I am not advocating that anyone should use drugs. It is not that they were good for us, only that they were not what our parents had portrayed them to be.

Sometime in the fall of 1972, I ended up taking a couple of Seconal pills, as did two of my buddies. That was quite a dose and the barbiturate had an effect like alcohol where we were quite high. We came back to my dorm room where we were literally throwing each other off the walls. We could feel no pain. At some point, I left the dorm, climbed into my car, and drove. When I returned, I tried to park my car in the angled parking, but instead I backed into the front door of an already parked car. After striking the door, I immediately became concerned about the potential of having the police involved. I couldn't afford to get arrested for driving under the influence. It could affect my scholarship and even my status with the University. If I was out of the University, I was potentially eligible to be drafted. I decided to park elsewhere and deal with the accident the next day. At least then, I would be sober and hopefully would only be responsible for the accident. The next day I came back to the parking area and went looking for the car. It was no longer parked in front of the dorm.

There was nothing left for me to do unless I saw the car again later which I didn't.

I realized that night on the drive to O'Hare that Ralph's car was the car that I had hit. I debated what to do about this situation. I should have told him as soon as I realized that I was responsible for the cold air blowing on the driver, but I didn't. I felt bad about it, but couldn't bring myself to admit to him what I had done right then and there.

MY EARLY YEARS

I was born Todd Howard Overgard on April 29, 1951 in Iowa City, Iowa. My dad was getting his master's degree in Education at the University of Iowa at the time. After my birth, my parents and I lived in a trailer park which was part of the housing arrangement set up for veterans. After Dad's graduation, we moved to Albert Lea, Minnesota. We were only there for a short while and I do not know the circumstances of my dad's employment at the time. I knew that he had taught school prior to moving to Iowa City. He may have started his career of selling books to schools.

When I was three, we moved from Albert Lea to Webster, South Dakota, where we lived for a couple of years. This is where I remember my dog Tippy. Tippy was a cocker spaniel that I loved very much. When we left Webster a couple of years later, my folks told me that Tippy had run away. The truth, which I did not find out for many, many decades, was that they had given him away to the farmer across the street. I think they knew that I would take it very hard and would have vehemently argued to take Tippy with us. Clearly, they didn't want to deal with that situation.

Also, in Webster, we lived on the outskirts of this very small town. There was a huge field behind us and to one side of us. One day, I was out playing with a couple of friends. We were hitting golf balls. I don't know where we had gotten the clubs. Perhaps we had taken them from my dad's golf bag, but I don't remember if he had clubs at that time. I was standing behind one of the kids when he went to hit the ball. I think he got me on the backswing, but it was a pretty solid blow to my forehead which left me screaming and bleeding. I still have a scar to this day.

At the age of five, I moved from Webster to Aberdeen, South Dakota. Aberdeen was one of the larger cities by population in the state of South Dakota. Aberdeen was interesting for me. Here I first learned to ride a bike. There was a large field across the street from our house that was either part of a public school or Northern State University. Dad took me over there to learn, so that if I fell, at least it would be on grass.

I was living in Aberdeen when my Grandpa and Grandma Overgard took me to a lake. I must have been about five years old. I remember walking along the very steep bank when I lost my balance and plummeted into the water. There was a torn-up tin can in the shallow water near shore, and it was just my bad luck that I fell directly onto it. It cut deeply into my right hand as I held my hands with my palms out to brace my fall. The cut was about two inches long, running from my palm down onto my wrist around the base of the thumb. I was lucky that it missed my wrist artery, which might have been the end of me. My grandmother completely soaked two dishtowels in wrapping up my wound on the way to the hospital. Frustrating for me was that my grandmother told everyone that I dove into the water. I am pretty sure I wasn't wearing swimming clothes, but I wouldn't have been diving into that shallow water in any case. I was to find out later that my Grandma

Overgard often lied when it was expedient for her. The injury left me with a prominent scar on my right hand.

This was not the only scar that I was to get in Aberdeen. It seemed that at least once a month, over several months, I was headed for stitches. One happened in winter when I slipped while pushing a sled on snow or ice. I hit my chin hard on the handle that extended across the back for pushing. Yes, another scar that I have to this day.

Then there was my attempt at whittling. My knife skills were not the best. I cut my right forefinger to the bone between the two knuckles closest to the tip. I am right-handed, so I assume that I was trying to control the knife left-handed. I have no idea why I might have been wielding the knife in my left hand instead of my right. I have a scar there as well.

Aberdeen is where I got into my first fist fight at the age of five. A larger boy, perhaps older, started the fight, but I only remember that I grabbed his legs, lifted him up and threw him down. Then I got on top of him and started hitting him with my fists. He had a bloody nose and he was crying, so I figured the fight was over and I got off of him. He got up still crying and wildly angry. I took off and he came after me. He was so angry that I ran from our backyard where we had been fighting to our front door with him chasing me. I pounded on the door which must have been locked. My mother answered before the boy caught up to me and she let me in. I think she was mightily confused because of this boy crying and angry and bleeding, yet I had been the one fleeing. I still count this as a victory although my actions at the end may make it seem otherwise.

Another adventure in Aberdeen was my first encounter with hornets. We had a detached garage at the back of the lot next to an alley. The garage was at right angles to the house. We used to play "Annie Annie Over," which was a game where kids throw a ball over a low roof. Our garage was good for that game with one side facing our backyard and the other side facing the alley. One day when I was playing in the back yard by myself, I discovered that on the back side of the garage, hornets had built a ground level nest. As a five-year-old, I clearly didn't have the right understanding of the situation. My thinking was that these hornets had built a nest on our property. They shouldn't have done that and I was going to defend our property. I picked up mud and started throwing mud balls at their nest. You can guess what happened next. They came after me in great numbers and I ran like a demon for our house. I actually got into the house very fast, but I was stung five times. I learned my lesson and have never thrown mud at bees, hornets, or wasps since.

In 1956, my folks moved just for the summer to Greeley, Colorado. I don't remember too much about this time. I do remember Dad recounting that he took us on a roller coaster somewhere in Colorado. He said that he spent most of the ride trying to keep me safe, as my mother was too busy hanging on for dear life to be concerned about her five-year-old son.

As you can tell, I had a lot of adventures and misfortunes during my Aberdeen years. I also went to school for the first time there. I attended kindergarten, 1st grade, and part of 2nd grade before we were to move again. Shortly after I turned seven in 1958, my sister Jayne was born. I loved it. Having been an only child for seven years, I thought that I would finally have someone to play with. Well our age difference really made that difficult. Nonetheless, I was thrilled to have a little sister.

Aberdeen was where I had a precognitive experience. I had a dream one night that I was walking to school, which was just a few short blocks away. As I walked along a sidewalk with a nicely manicured lawn separating the per-pendicular sidewalk which would meet mine at the corner, I saw across the lawn a boy heading for the same corner I was, and at about the same distance. Suddenly, he bent down and picked up a rock. He turned and threw it at me. He hit me squarely in the head, causing much pain and bleeding. I didn't know why he would do this. I had never seen that boy before.

Well, the morning after the dream, I was walking to school, and there was that very same boy approaching that very same corner. I was watching him like a hawk because I was now wary that he might follow through with the rest of my dream. Sure enough, he stops in the same place, picks up a rock turns and throws it at my head. Having been forewarned by the dream, I was ready. I ducked and the rock sailed over my head. This whole situation freaked me out and I ran as fast as I could back to my house. I do not remember ever seeing this boy again. I also became a believer that the future could be seen in certain instances.

I was not really aware at the time, but my father had been invited to become a Mason. The Masons are a world-wide brotherhood that was historically somewhat of a secret society. Dad went on to take their tests and advance. By the time we left Aberdeen, he was a 32nd Degree Mason. That is the highest level attained via testing. There is a 33rd Degree which cannot be applied for. The 33rd Degree can be conferred upon 32nd Degree members for outstanding service to Freemasonry and/or community leadership as selected by the Deputy of his state and confirmed by unanimous secret ballot vote of the members present at the Annual Meeting of the Supreme Council. Reaching the 32nd Degree level is one hell of an achievement, but my sisters and I were not aware of this until we reached adulthood. Even then, we did not really know what it meant. Dad stopped going to Masonic meetings upon leaving South Dakota.

CHAPTER 5

SHAWANO, WISCONSIN

In 1958, when I was seven, we moved to Shawano, Wisconsin. Shawano (pronounced "Shaw-no") was the largest city and county seat of Shawano County. Shawano is located in northern Wisconsin and really wasn't very big. It had a population of about 6,000 people at that time. The name "Shawano" comes from the Chippewa language meaning "southern." I was to live here for the next four years. We had now moved four times in my first seven years. This was due to my dad being assigned to different territories in his work selling books to schools.

At age seven, I had a lot of energy and freedom. It was as if my folks never bothered to watch me. I was pretty much free to wander the neighborhood and play with friends as I could find them. Our house was a couple of houses from the Wolf River on West Green Bay Street. It was located on the northwest corner of W. Green Bay St. and N. Bartlett St. It was a two-story house with a detached garage that faced Bartlett. North on Bartlett, across the street but on the same block, was a funeral home. The funeral director had a son, Mark, who was about one year younger than I was. He and I would often play together. A couple of blocks further north was W. 3rd Street and heading west for a few blocks on that street led back to the river. Here during the summers, a public beach was set up. There was a lifeguard

23

and boundary buoys with ropes to identify the safer swim zones. There was also a very large raft set out near the boundary.

As kids, we loved going there to swim. We would play a game where between four to ten kids would get on the raft. One of us would have a small plastic toy soldier which could fit in the palm of your hand. That person would dive off of the raft and take the toy soldier to the bottom which was maybe 15 feet down. There, we would release the toy which would begin a very slow rise to the surface. The rise was slow enough that the diver could surface and climb back onto the raft to join the other kids. On the raft, we would closely watch the water trying to gain sight of the rising toy, which could typically be seen a few feet down before it reached the surface. Once the toy was spotted, that person would jump or dive in the water trying to be the first to retrieve the toy. Typically, when one person went for the toy, so did all of the others in a mad free-for-all. Once one person had secured the toy, we would all return to the raft where the person with the toy would repeat the process. It was a lot of fun.

The only problem with our swimming hole was that the river had a very soft black muck bottom. After swimming for a while and coming out of the water, there would always be leeches clinging to our toes, feet, or legs. We would have to pull these bloodsuckers off.

Shawano was also the place where I remember taking piano lessons and being restricted by required daily practice. That doesn't seem so bad now, but it sure did then.

In July of 1959, our family went to Potosi, Wisconsin, to visit my Grandma Pearl Hoffmeister. Potosi is 239 miles to the southwest of Shawano. My grandma lived in a two-story house on the main road that went through the very small town of Potosi. In the late 1950s, it had a population in the high 500s. My grandma had lived there all of her life. She still had her son Fred living at home in those days.

Uncle Fred had a small fishing business. I think he was doing this to earn money for college. He did go on to eventually get his doctorate. Uncle Fred took my dad and me out on his boat to show us his operation. He had a small aluminum boat of about ten feet in length and it had a motor on the back. He operated the boat on the Mississippi, which was only a few miles from Potosi. He would put out set lines with many hooks, maybe even hundreds of hooks. He would follow the set line and check each of the hooks individually. When he caught fish, which were primarily catfish, he would bring them into the boat and put them in a fresh water container to keep them alive. When he got back to his home, he would transfer them to a fresh water spring that was set up to contain them in the backyard of the house. He would then sell the fresh catfish to the local restaurants. Today, Potosi is known as the "Catfish Capital of Wisconsin" with an annual Catfish Festival and Fireman's Fish Fry held every August.

On the particular occasion of this trip, Uncle Fred took us out onto the mighty Mississippi and along his route of set lines. Periodically he would lift a catfish out of the water, unhook it, and put it into the aforementioned fresh water container. Once we had completed the route, we started back up the Mississippi toward his docking location just outside of Potosi. Dark clouds had begun to move in. These were actually clouds from a very heavy thunderstorm that had suddenly appeared in our path. The Mississippi was about one mile across at this location and not terribly deep. To complicate matters, there were tree stumps throughout the river which caused Uncle Fred to have to go pretty slow. In a matter of minutes, the thunderstorm was upon us and it was a doozy.

Uncle Fred lost much of the visibility that he had because the rains were so heavy that they prevented us from seeing more than ten feet in front of the boat. This torrential downpour was about the heaviest that I have ever seen in my life. Dad and I were in the mid-section of the boat with Fred in the back. Fred was steering the boat and controlling the direction with the steering handle which allowed the engine to swivel. Fred was going very slow since the visibility was so bad. The storm brought lightning and we quickly realized the great danger that we were in. Here we were, in the middle of the Mississippi in an all metal boat, with lightning striking every two to three seconds. The stumps were the recipients of the lightning strikes. Each time a lightning strike would take place, the entire river lit up. These strikes were close to us too. It was extremely frightening.

Dad kept me close to him. Oddly enough, I was not terribly frightened, although I should have been. I think that I realized that there was nothing I could do. Uncle Fred had to go slow and we just prayed we would make it through. We must have been in this storm for about ten minutes, although my judgement of the time involved is not great. The storm was moving fairly fast, so we eventually came out the other side. As we completed the last mile or so approaching the docking area, the skies cleared and we were greeted with brilliant sunshine. It was practically a spiritual awakening to the fact that we had survived.

This adventure on the Mississippi was something that the family talked about very often. Uncle Fred vouched for just how the dangerous the situation was and how lucky we were to have made it through. Dad said that he had never been so scared, even on Iwo Jima during that deadly battle. This was simply amazing. My life has been filled with so many completely unusual events like this that I don't know if I have been cursed or blessed. Here I was, at seven years old, already having survived a number of situations that could have cost me my life!

While in Potosi, I remember playing baseball with the local kids, so there were things to do. Next door to my grandma's place there lived a family named the Krepfles. There was a patch of land where planting was done between the two houses.

The Krepfles had a son named Keith who was about nine months younger than I was. He was a burly kid. There was a fairly steep hill set back behind my grandma's house. Just before the land began sloping upward, there was a creek. At times, this creek was polluted with discards from a cheese factory. The hill was good for sledding. Keith and I would take sleds to the top of the hill and ride them down to the creek at the bottom. There was one area where the hill dropped off directly to the creek. We would have to veer away from that small cliff in order to avoid being injured. One time we were coming down the hill fast. I veered away from the cliff, but to my amazement, Keith just kept going. I don't think he did it on purpose, but he went right off that cliff. It had to be an eight to ten-foot drop directly onto the frozen creek. I was pretty sure that he had gotten hurt badly, so I hurried over to find him still sitting on his sled and laughing hysterically. That was when I realized that Keith was one tough kid.

Keith became a star football player, first for Potosi High School, and then for Iowa State University. He grew up to be 6'3" tall and weighed 227 lbs. He was drafted in the fifth round of the 1974 National Football League (NFL) draft by the Philadelphia Eagles. Keith became the first ever Eagle to catch a touchdown pass in the Super Bowl, which was Super Bowl XV. In 2002, he was inducted into the Iowa State Cyclones Hall of Fame. I was right about Keith. He was one tough kid!

Back in Shawano, I remember walking to houses in costume one Halloween when I was eight. Yes, my folks sent me out to trick or treat by myself. As I walked south along Bartlett St. and into some of the nicer neighborhoods, an older boy befriended me. He must have been at least 12 but could have even been in high school. We went to one house together and once we had reached the sidewalk that ran along Bartlett, he came from slightly behind me and stole my bag of candies right out of my hand. He quickly ran off leaving me stunned and crying. I went home and reported the theft to my folks. Halloween has never been the same for me since.

I attribute many of these problems to my folks letting me roam freely. I truly enjoyed it for the most part, but I did not always use the best judgement. I was very lucky that I did not suffer permanent damage or death. The next couple of incidents will illustrate just how lucky I was.

At one point while in Shawano, my folks bought me an air rifle popularly known as a BB gun. I am sure my folks talked to me about being careful, but I was not. I knew guns were used for hunting and so I went hunting. I killed several birds, but I felt bad about it. I remember that my folks had told me that using sling shots or BB guns could put an eye out. I was in the basement, one winter and shot at a wooden saw horse from close range. The BB ricocheted off of the saw horse and stuck in the tear duct of my eye. It had lost most of its momentum, so it didn't hit terribly hard and I was able to pick it out without a problem. Clearly that was not a safe way to use the gun.

My friends and I used the air rifle for other dangerous games. The force that the gun would shoot with was increased by the number of times that the rifle was pumped, increasing the air pressure in the rifle. We must have figured out that the rifle could fire a BB that would not enter the skin if it were to hit one of us. I remember playing a game in which we would go down a path through lots of trees that wound along a rather steep bank of the Wolf River. We found a place where we could jump from above the path and land on the bank below the path. There were trees and brush above and below the path. The one of us that had the rifle was positioned down the path a bit where that person could see the pathway. The game was to wait for the person on the bank to jump across the path, thus becoming visible while passing over the pathway. The person with the gun would then attempt to shoot them. We did end up hitting each other, but no one ever got seriously hurt. I am sure that it stung quite a bit. Still, that was not the smartest thing to do.

One winter, my friend Mark, and I went down to the Wolf River where the swimming pool was set up during the summers. We walked out onto the ice. In Northern Wisconsin, lakes would often freeze over. Often, fisherman would drive their cars out onto the ice and drill holes in order to ice fish. Being aware of this and thinking the river was solid ice, Mark and I walked out further. We walked all the way to the other side of the river which was about 1,000 feet across. Then we walked back. As we got very close to shore, where the summer swimming hole would have been, the ice was thinner and we broke through. It wasn't any deeper than my waist and it may have been no deeper than my knees. We scampered out of the river, very wet, and headed for Mark's home. Mark lived in the funeral home where his dad was the funeral director.

When we got to his house, we went to the basement where there was a furnace going. It was warm there and we took off our wet pants and socks, hung them up and let them dry. It was warm enough that it didn't take too long for our clothes to dry. Once we were redressed, our parents never knew what had happened. Looking back, I am a bit appalled by many of my actions as a kid.

In hindsight, this could have been extremely dangerous. What I didn't realize at that time was that there is a significant difference between ice on a river and ice on a lake. Since a river has moving water, it will typically not freeze as well or as deep as a lake. Now the Wolf River in that spot is referred to as the Wolf River Pond. I assume this is due to the fact that as the river is flowing, it stalls a bit in that area where it is wider than it is downstream. Nevertheless, the river is moving. If the ice was thinner due to the moving water, Mark and I could have fallen through. I have no doubts that falling through out in the middle of the river would likely have resulted in our deaths. Moving water could quickly pull a person under the ice. In any case, it was not particularly smart to walk across the river. Another potential disaster was averted!

Another unusual incident in Shawano happened while I was in school. I was in the 5th grade, but the class was a combined class with half of the kids being 4th graders. I believe that my female teacher was irritated with me, probably for talking during class. One day, I raised my hand and was allowed to go the restroom. Shortly after I came back to the class, it was time for the lunch period. I remember being outside when at least five or six of my younger classmates surrounded me and began to attack me with their fists. I didn't know why they were doing this. I fought back. For maybe 20 minutes, I would fight, and run to a new location, always with multiple kids trying to beat me up, and I would have to fight again. Each time they closed in, I grabbed the one closest to me and started beating him with my fists as hard as I could. Finally, I was able to get into the school. I was standing by the lockers outside of my classroom and crying. I was not hurt physically, but I was hurt that these kids would just attack me for no good reason. Then, our teacher came out of the classroom. She and I were the only ones in the hallway. She asked me what happened and I told her about the attack. She looked totally shocked. She said "I told them that someone should teach you a lesson, but I didn't mean like this.."

I could not believe that my teacher had told the kids to teach me a lesson. What did she think was going to happen? Now I was pissed. When I got home, I told my parents. They were highly upset. They scheduled a meeting with the school principal. The principal, whom Dad knew, decided to move me to the other 5th grade classroom under a different teacher. Following my pattern, that didn't go as smoothly as it could have either. On the first day in my new class, the teacher announced that the capital of South Dakota was Pierre, but she pronounced like the name "Pee-air." Having lived in South Dakota, I knew that wasn't the correct pronunciation. I raised my hand and told her that it was pronounced "Peer" with a long "e" sound. The teacher took my correction very poorly, so I kept my mouth shut after that.

Shawano had Shawano Lake, that was connected to the Wolf River and was on the outskirts of the town. The lake was actually bigger in size than the city. Dad had bought a boat, which we used to cruise the lake and/or to fish. One day, Dad and I were out fishing. Fishing in Wisconsin often consisted of casting, rather than just sitting with bobbers. We would cast out our lines using bait, which could be a lure or live bait. During one of my casts, the fishing pole slipped out my hands and flew into the water. In my household, I was used to a lot of yelling and I fully expected that I was going to receive an earful. To my surprise and delight, Dad did not yell. He started to cast his lure in the direction that my fishing pole had gone. He would let the bait drop to the lake floor which was no more than 10–15 deep with a sandy bottom. He would then reel the line in hoping that the hooks on his lure would snag my fishing pole or line. After several attempts, he hooked it. I was amazed that he was able to bring up my fishing pole. So little damage was done, and I was sure to hold on to my fishing pole tightly from then on. I was always grateful that Dad kept his temper in check that day.

I mentioned the yelling in my home as I was growing up. Now, over half a century later, I understand that it is because both of my parents were predisposed to alcoholism. They would drink to excess and then their emotions would get the best of them. Long after I had reached adulthood, both of my parents would abstain from alcohol for the rest of their lives.

In the summers, the city would cut the trees along the streets flat on top. This turned out to be another great way of having fun. I would climb the trees, sometimes with Mark, and we would sit on the flat tree branches, which were pretty large. They would create a circular seat that in most cases was at least six inches around. From 10 to 15 feet in the air, we could see over the top of the tree we were in and get a good view of the surrounding area. We would also be shielded from people being able to see us from below if they were close to the tree. It was like having a fort in the sky.

We would climb other trees in the neighborhood as well. The only accident that I remember happened when I was not present. Mark's younger brother had been climbing one of the trees at the funeral home when he fell and broke his arm. I guess that could have happened to us since we would sit on those stools at the top of the trees with nothing to hold on to. Maybe we were just lucky…again.

My sister Nancy was born in 1960 in Shawano. Jayne was two years old at this point and I was nine. Nancy was to be the last of my siblings and I was happy to have the addition to our family. When she was a one-year-old, she was admitted to the hospital with bruises all over her body. I remember Mom telling me that she had to convince the hospital staff that she was not beating her child. This turned out to be a serious situation and we were worried that she might die. They finally did get it under control and she was released from the hospital.

When I was ten, Dad had a friend name Roger, who owned the local Shell Service Station. Roger and his wife got my folks to buy season tickets to the Green Bay Packers home games played in Green Bay, Wisconsin, for the 1961 NFL Season. This may not have been as expensive as it seemed. Although there were 14 games in the regular season that year with seven home games and seven away, Green Bay always played some games in Milwaukee. In 1961, they played three games at Milwaukee County Stadium leaving only four home games to be played in Green Bay's City Stadium. This was informally referred to as the New City Stadium which had replaced the old one in 1957. It was renamed in 1965 as Lambeau Field after Curly Lambeau who was the founder, player, and longtime head coach of the Green Bay Packers.

Roger and his wife had a son about my age and we were given season tickets as well. Roger and my folks were seated on the 50-yard line. Their son and I were seated in Row 1 at the goal line end of the field. The only game that I remember from that season was a 24–0 shellacking of the Chicago Bears. The stadium, at least in my memory, was like high school stadiums are today. I believe that it was open ended at both end zones and the seats did not go up terribly high on each side of the field. There was snow on the ground surrounding the field and in the stands. The Packers and the Bears were hated rivals and we certainly knew that.

The Bears were coached by the legendary George Halas. Halas was quite the character. He played college football at the University of Illinois. He went on to become a founder of the Chicago Bears and a co-founder of the National Football League (NFL). He was also an NFL All-Pro player for the Bears.

Vince Lombardi was the Packers coach and was not yet as famous as Halas, but was to become an equally dominant NFL figure. Halas was a cantankerous old man at the time of the game against the Packers in 1961. At age 66, he was as feisty as could be. At one point, he had moved down the sidelines where he was relatively close to me. Well, we Packer fans didn't like him. I rolled up a snow ball from the accumulated snow and threw it at him. I hit him, although I am sure it wasn't very hard. Shortly after that, he was yelling at fans in my section. Something really ticked him off because he came charging into the stands and went up about 20 rows to go toe to toe with one of our Packer fans. They were yelling at each other. I thought a fight would break out for sure and I wasn't positive that I hadn't caused it. But, after a minute or so, Halas moved back to his sidelines. No punches had been thrown.

This was all pretty exciting for us kids, and maybe the rest of the fans as well. The Packers went 11–3 that season and finished first in the Western Conference ending 15 years of not reaching the playoffs. They capped their season with a 37–0 win over the New York Giants in the NFL Championship game. This was the first championship played in Green Bay. All of this preceded the advent of the Super Bowl. Mom and Dad along with Roger and his wife had tickets to that Championship game, but there were no tickets for us kids. I presume that these tickets were more expensive. In any case, it is always fun to tell people that I had season tickets to the 1961 Green Bay Packer home games.

CHAPTER 6
1961–1962

THE PAPER ROUTE

My folks had instilled a strong work ethic in my sisters and me. This probably came from their having grown up during the Great Depression. Poverty and the struggle to better oneself were a way of life. Even as a child, I wanted to earn money. I thought that a paper route would be a good way to do this. Shawano had only one newspaper, the Shawano Evening Leader.

In order to get the paper route, I had to pay the current carrier. I don't remember clearly, but my folks may have helped me out with this. In any case, they would have expected me to pay them back. The paper route was in my neighborhood, which was good. It was a rather large route consisting of 81 papers to be delivered in the evening.

I would fold the papers, usually into a trifold from the top half page format that the papers were delivered in. This fold secured the paper into a roughly 4" by 12" paper. When all of these papers were folded, then I could start on the deliveries. I would be carrying them in a canvas bag that was slung over my head and onto one shoulder.

In the summers, I could use my bicycle. I remember getting that bicycle around that time and being ecstatic. Anyway, in the warmer weather, the papers could be flung into the driveways. I could complete the route in 45 minutes on my bike.

Collecting was another problem. Most people paid their bills when I would come around to collect once a month. The community was generally poor, so I would get stiffed by maybe five percent of houses that I delivered to. By that, I mean that the payments were either delayed or never made. My folks did not help me with folding my newspapers, nor did they help with deliveries or collections. It was totally my responsibility. I was the one who had asked for and wanted the job, so it was all up to me. If a delivery client didn't pay, the Shawano Evening Leader did not take the loss. The paper boy did. There always seemed to be something funny about the fact that if a new person signed up for having the paper delivered, the newspaper couldn't lose. The Leader's position was that they sold the newspapers to the paper boys and the paper boys resold papers including handling the collections. At age ten, this was a hard lesson to learn because we didn't set the prices. Nonetheless, we could and did make money despite delays in getting paid and customers who never paid at all.

I went through one winter and delivering papers in the cold was the worst. Northern Wisconsin isn't called the "Frozen Tundra" for nothing. First, I could not use my bike. The roads were slick and often carried quite a bit of snow particularly on the sides of the road where I would have been likely to ride. Second, I could no longer throw the newspapers into the driveways since they were usually covered with snow and even when they weren't, the newspapers could potentially get wet. This meant that I had to stop at every house and go up to the front door and put the paper inside the screen door where the paper would be protected.

It was not unusual for me to have to hand-carry the 81 papers while trudging through three feet of snow. Because this was an evening paper, I was delivering after it was dark in the winter. The temperatures had dropped rapidly by that point. I remember that it would take three hours for me to complete the route. It was tough work. I did not have winter clothes made to withstand three hours of fighting the cold while walking through snow drifts. In the winter, I would come home after finishing my paper route and quite often I could not feel any of my toes. They were all numb and in the early stages of frostbite. Mom would bring down a pan of hot water for me to put my feet in. That was agonizing because as the feeling came back into my feet, my toes were feeling like a thousand pins were pricking the skin. This painful ritual went on throughout that winter. To this day, I do not have great circulation in all of my toes.

I looked up the temperatures for that winter. I knew it was not unusual for the temperature to dip below 0°F. Sometimes the temperatures would go quite a bit lower than that. One March day in 1962, the low temperature in Shawano was -28.7°F. If you can imagine going through three-foot snow drifts for three hours as a ten-year-old kid and doing this in inadequate clothing, you can see why I consider Wisconsin winters so bad. I never did understand why my folks weren't more concerned about this situation. I know they grew up with the same kinds of clothing that I wore. Typically, that would be a winter jacket, galoshes, and maybe ear muffs. When I look back on the situation, I realize that these clothes were designed to be good enough to keep someone warm enough for 15 minutes. I don't believe they were ever designed to keep a child warm for three hours. I would have thought that my parents would have applied more thought to the clothes that I wore on my paper route. As a parent today, I would not have let my child go out into what was a potentially deadly situation. Even though I may have added layering, I now realize that keeping me warm on those cold winter nights would have been a very difficult task in 1962.

This experience was a primary factor for my selecting warmer climates to live in when I reached adulthood. But I still spent several winters in my adult life in the upper Midwest. I will recount those choices later, but suffice it to say that I never wanted to see temperatures like I experienced on my paper route again. This would not turn out to be the case.

The paper route taught me responsibility. It taught me about managing money. It taught me that some people will cheat you in this world. The winter taught me that I was tough. Tough enough to withstand that bitter cold. I do believe that my ability to persevere, which applied to so many things later in life, was enhanced by my trudging through those cold winter evenings. Of course, perseverance initially came from my parents' set of values. They believed that if you are going to start a job, you need to finish it.

ESCAPE FROM WISCONSIN

In 1962, my dad had still another change in job locations. He announced that he was going to move the family to California. I was ecstatic. After the awful winter that I just gone through, the idea of moving to a warm, sunny climate where movie stars could be seen was very enticing. In August of that year, Dad and I left for California by car. Mom and my sisters were going to fly out later. Driving to California is not a short trip. It took us four and a half days to reach our destination. We were headed for the San Francisco Bay Area. There would not be movie stars on the streets, but it would still be warmer than Wisconsin.

We would most likely have driven southwest from Shawano until reaching I-80, which is the transcontinental highway that runs from the East Coast to San Francisco. We would have crossed Iowa and then Nebraska. After that, we would have headed into Wyoming and the cities of Cheyenne and Rock Springs. It then drops down into Salt Lake City, Utah. It runs past the Great Salt Lake and on through northern Nevada until reaching Reno, which is close to the western border of Nevada and the eastern border of California. The landscape after leaving Nebraskan farmlands becomes very bleak. It is high desert with minimal vegetation pretty much all the way until Reno. Our trip took us about 2,300 miles which meant about 500 miles and eight hours of driving a day. That is averaging around 60 miles per hour which is not too bad. Of course, we had to stop for food, bathroom breaks, and motels at night.

I remember entering California and seeing the bright blue sky. There was not a cloud to be found. In the Midwest, I was used to seeing the puffy cumulus clouds floating overhead at most times. Now the skies in California were a new and wondrous experience. I was thrilled! With those brutally cold winter nights and the pain of my feet in hot water behind me, California was looking to be glorious.

Sunnyvale was a good city to grow up in. It has good schools, great weather, and a low crime rate. Sunnyvale is the second biggest city in Santa Clara County behind San Jose. It's population is estimated at just over 150,000 people as of 2016. Many people don't know that San Jose is the largest city in Northern California. As of 2010, Los Angeles is first with more than four million people, San Diego was second with close to 1.4 million, San Jose is third with a little over one million. San Francisco, is fourth on the list with a little over 850,000 in population. San Jose was preordained to surpass San Francisco because of the very limited amount of undeveloped land in San Francisco. San Jose had quite a large area to grow into, and was in the heart of Silicon Valley. Much of the expansion came from high-tech's growth in the Santa Clara Valley.

At one point, when I think I was high school, I went to Santa Cruz where there were beautiful beaches. I loved to swim and the ocean was inviting. I particularly liked the idea of riding the waves, but I didn't own a surfboard. My way of riding the waves was to body surf. As in surfing, you go out into the ocean to the point where the waves begin to rise up on their way to the shore. You had to watch the waves and try to swim fast enough that the wave will lift you up. There is a sudden acceleration when you have caught the wave. You straighten out your body with your arms out in front of you in order to ride the wave until it drops you. The longer the ride, the more fun you have. The typical waves in Santa Cruz would break at three to five feet. This day, the waves were about that same height when I entered the water. I looked around and there were maybe 100–150 surfers spread out over a few hundred yards next to the wharf. The wharf extended well out into the ocean and when I looked to my left, I could see it. I was one of the very few body surfers that day. During the next half hour or so, the waves got bigger and bigger until they were topping out at about 15 feet. These waves could be dangerous. I looked around and saw that most of the surfers were gone. I counted five surfers plus me. Now I knew that trying to ride these waves was not for the faint of heart. I looked to the left and the wharf was packed. I think people realized there could be some huge wipeouts and they wanted to see them. I remember riding some of these waves in. They were faster and I was riding a lot higher. At one point, the wave broke underneath me and I was driven straight down. The water was shallow, so I tumbled off of the sea floor, but recovered without too much difficulty. I didn't stay out there for too long when there were just a few of us. The waves were tough to body surf and my toes were numb from the cold waters. Northern California waters are not warm since the ocean currents come from the North. Nevertheless, I attributed the numbness to those cold days delivering papers in Wisconsin.

CHAPTER 8
WEDNESDAY, DECEMBER 20, 1972

CONTINUING TO O'HARE

The drive from Oklahoma City to Chicago's O'Hare International Airport was grueling. The fog was there through much of the evening. As dawn broke, I estimate that we had traveled close to 500 miles and were in the vicinity St. Louis, Missouri. Unfortunately for us, the fog was still there once daylight had broken around 7:20 AM CST. It seemed very unusual to me that the dense fog would last so long. We had been blanketed for some time. Ralph and I continued northward alternating the driving and putting up with the cold air blowing through the door on the driver's side. This was definitely not fun.

However, we only had 300 miles to go. That was both a good and a bad thing. We knew that there was light at the end of the tunnel. We would reach our destinations and the horrific drive would be over. The bad side was that we still had close to 5 hours of driving left. There was more light as the day wore on, but not better visibility. We continued the monotonous and difficult trek to O'Hare, where destiny was waiting for me.

CHAPTER 9

1962–1965

JUNIOR HIGH, SPORTS, & FIGHTING

We had arrived in Sunnyvale in time for me to start 6th grade at San Antonio Elementary School that September. San Antonio was a block from my new home. During that year, I alienated many of my classmates by bragging about my many skills. I felt that my classmates didn't know how wonderful and unique I was, so I told them. This had the opposite effect than what I was trying to achieve. I was treated badly until I learned that this was a very poor way of making friends and influencing people. I actually read the book by Dale Carnegie "Making Friends and Influencing People" to change the way my classmates were treating me. I don't remember if I ever made much progress that year, but I stopped boasting and started working on my people skills.

In the summer of 1963, I tried out for one of the local Little League teams. In Shawano, I was eleven and nothing special in baseball. I warmed the bench. In the much larger state of California and the city of Sunnyvale, I didn't know exactly what to expect. There was a tryout and I remember that I asked one of the other guys how he thought that I did. "Would I make it?" I asked. He simply said, "Yes, with flying colors."

He was right. I had a rather spectacular Little League season. I went 18 for 36 which was a .500 batting average

44

with two home runs while playing first base. I remember playing against Lee Pelekoudas. Lee's father was Chris Pelekoudas who was a major league baseball umpire. Lee was eventually to be drafted right out of high school by the Montreal Expos in the 48th round. He elected instead to play baseball for the Arizona State University Sun Devils. He went on to have a 30-year career as an executive for the Seattle Mariners. Anyway, on the day in question, Lee was pitching for the opposing team. I remember that he threw the ball right over the plate and I launched it. Our fences were about 180 feet out. In center field was a flagpole that was about 20 feet high. I hit that ball about 20 feet over the top of the flagpole. I loved being able to hit the ball with that kind of power.

At the end of the season, there were All-Star selections. I was one of two players selected from my team. Lee also made the team. Of the All-Stars, three of us played first base. I ended up starting. We were to play other leagues' All-Star teams with the eventual result of reaching the Little League World Series if we could win all of those games. I thought we had a really good chance to go pretty far. We had Marty, who was already 6'1" as a 12-year-old. He towered over the rest of us. He was a very good pitcher, so we figured we would win when he pitched. Our first game was against a Santa Clara, California, team. Santa Clara is another Santa Clara Valley city located right next to Sunnyvale. Our little league team was actually the Cupertino Pacific Coast Little League since we played our games there and the players were from the surrounding cities. Cupertino is just south of Sunnyvale. In any case, we lost our first game 4–1. I did get on and advanced to 3rd base. There was a throwing error, so I broke for home, but I was thrown out at the plate. Oh, well! The Santa Clara team went on to win something like 4 games before eventually losing to a Nevada team.

Another interesting event occurred when my father decided to take my Grandpa Overgard and me to a San Francisco Giants baseball game in famed Candlestick Park. I had changed allegiances from the Milwaukee Braves and their superstar Hank Aaron to the Giants and their superstar Willie Mays. Grandpa didn't really know baseball very well as I remember it. This was a day game and a pitcher's duel between the Giants ace Juan Marichal and Houston Colt .45's Dick Drott. The great Willie Mays had gotten a single in the 1st inning, but there were no other hits by either team until the 8th inning, when a couple of doubles by Jim Davenport and Chuck Hiller finally scored a run for the Giants. Marichal completed the top of the ninth without a hit and the Giants had their 1st no-hitter in 34 years and their 1st since moving from New York to San Francisco in 1958. This was a very special moment for the three of us and a big moment in Giants history. Grandpa really didn't understand what everyone was so excited about. The game only lasted 1 hour and 41 minutes and there wasn't a lot of action. I loved the newspaper headline the following day: "JUAN TO NOTHING WAS THE SCORE!"

In September of 1963, I entered Cupertino Junior High School. We were no longer in elementary school with the same teacher and classmates for the entire year. Also, we were enrolled with other elementary school students who were fed into this junior high school. I still had some problems with fellow students who were picking on me. This is not unusual for that age bracket. Teasing, bullying, and being bullied were all too common.

I was not part of the "in" crowd at Cupertino Junior High. I was an athlete, which gave me a certain status, but I was not popular by any standard. As far as social interaction goes, Dad had always told me to be different. He didn't want me to blend in with the crowd. His reasoning was that I should be a leader and not a follower. I am not sure that he was aware of the consequences of "being different." So how was I different? My dad always used a brief case. These are the older style brief cases that held a lot of books and folded up from the sides to latch. Using this at school was a very uncool thing to do. Only I and a few others knew the pain of not fitting in by bringing our books in brief cases. It actually was a pretty good way to carry our books, except for the teasing.

One of the students at Cupertino Junior High was Steve Wozniak. Steve was in eighth grade when I was in seventh. Steve entered and won first place in the Santa Clara County Science Fair where students would bring in science projects and compete with other students to see whose was the best. Steve also won a special award for his electronics project at the Bay Area Fair. And yes, this is the same Steve Wozniak that went on to invent the personal computer and help found the Apple Computer Company.

Getting picked on in school never amounted to anything severe. It would be teasing like when a group of students made fun of my name by chanted chanting "Toad", "Toad", "Toad", or kids grabbing the baskets on my bike when I would ride through the orchards, which caused me to stop and then they would run off. Numerous incidents put me in a position of taking it and being bullied or fighting back.

In eighth grade, I was terrified of fighting. Very often, the fear of fighting is worse than the fighting itself, particularly if one backs down. Males have it very tough. If you back down from a fight, you are labeled a coward. Thinking of myself as a coward was horrible for me. We had a family tradition of standing up for ourselves. My dad had told me the story of my Uncle Jerry being challenged to fight three boys when he was young. Somehow, he got them to fight him one at a time and whipped all three. My dad was an undefeated boxer in high school and a war hero by virtue of having survived The Battle of Iwo Jima. None of this helped me to feel OK about not defending myself. In fact, when I felt fear, this just made me feel that I wasn't living up to the Overgard name.

I talked to Dad about this. He took me in the back yard and gave me boxing lessons. That put me ahead of most kids my age. I wasn't smaller than other boys for an eighth grader either. I was 5'8" and 125 lbs. sprouting up from 4'11" in 6th grade. That meant that I was now taller than a lot of kids. In eighth grade, I competed in a lot of sports, such as flag football, wrestling, basketball, track & field, and baseball. What I didn't realize then was that the wrestling was great training for fighting. That is what it is based on and I was very good at it. There was one wrestler, who had been held back a year in school, that could beat me at 125 lbs. and under. The coach left him there and had me wrestle at 135 lbs. I went on to six wins and no losses for the season while giving away ten pounds when wrestling other schools. The wrestler who was able to beat me finished second in our large county.

I ended up getting in a lot of fights that year and it helped to curb my fear. There was no fear greater than to have to meet someone at a designated time under "the old oak tree" at the edge of the campus. The waiting seemed interminable. We were young and never tried to severely hurt someone else. A bloody nose and bruises were usually the extent of it. There were also the kids we termed "hoods" which was short for hoodlums. They typically wore leather jackets with their hair slicked back. Often, they wore boots. There were a number of them at Cupertino Junior High and I had also heard of at least three of them at Kennedy Junior High in Cupertino. These schools were in the suburbs which should have made them significantly less dangerous than schools in the inner cities. At Kennedy, there were two boys whom I will call the Italian Brothers who had a vicious reputation. I know that one of them had kicked a friend of mine in the groin ending that confrontation. It was also alleged that during a fight which may have happened a few years later in high school, a teacher had tried to break it up. They turned on the teacher and beat him up. Supposedly there was an even tougher guy at that school named Arturo. Apparently, even the Italians didn't want to mess with him.

At Cupertino, we had a student who was called Rocco. Rocco had hurt two of my friends in fights sending both of them to the hospital. One of them was kicked so hard in the groin that he was having urinary bleeding problems. The other one was kicked and ended up with a broken finger. I didn't see any of this, but just heard about it later via the rumor mill. One day, I was on the school grounds near the open corridors which were next to a tarmac area with basketball standards. Rocco at 5'10" weighed about 175 lbs., so he was two inches taller and 50 lbs. heavier than I was. A friend of mine, Dave, was standing with Rocco. Just having noticed the situation,

I watched to see what was going to happen. It appeared that Rocco was trying to intimidate Dave. It wasn't working. Dave was smiling at Rocco and Rocco was getting angrier and angrier. This was actually quite funny. Dave was about five feet tall and Rocco towered over him, but was failing to scare him. I started laughing. Apparently, I was too close to both of them. Rocco turned and punched me straight in the nose. My instincts kicked in. I immediately went for a two-leg takedown. I dove down and wrapped my arms around his legs, picked him up and threw him down. Immediately, I was sitting on his stomach punching his head repeatedly. After a number of punches, I somehow noticed our gym teacher standing about 15 yards away with his arms crossed. My thinking was "now I'm in real trouble." I stopped punching Rocco and let him up. He spotted the teacher also. As he was leaving, he said, "Later!"

The gym teacher walked up to me and asked "Why'd you stop?" I told him because I had seen him and thought that I was in trouble. That is when I realized that he had no intention of stopping it as long as I was winning. Apparently, Rocco was not one of his favorites which in hindsight was understandable. Nevertheless, I was shocked by his presence and I had stopped fighting. I knew now that my wrestling skills were likely to make a big difference in any one-on-one fights.

Rocco wanted to finish our fight several days later and off campus. I agreed even though I knew that he would likely have his friends there. I was trusting that they would not interfere. Well, the next thing you know, this is all over the school. Literally hundreds of kids were intending to go watch the fight. I think Rocco's reputation and our initial confrontation had a lot of the students excited about the fight. As usual, I was nervous about it, but I had gotten the better of him earlier and felt that the continuation would end up with the same result.

As the day of the fight came, both Rocco and I were called into the principal's office. I had been in here before for fighting. In a previous fight, the principal had asked us whether we wanted the paddle or should he call our parents. I did not want my folks involved, so I took the paddle. My opponent had not decided because I think he didn't want either. I had to bend over and received something like five swats. The wooden paddle had holes throughout to minimize wind resistance. When Rocco and I got in front of the principal, he said, "I have heard that you two are getting ready to have a fight. Whether you fight on or off campus, I will call in the Sheriff's Department and you will both be expelled from school. This fight is off. Now, I want you two to agree not to fight, shake hands, and walk out of here." Reputation was a large part of the reason for fighting, but now that the principal had threatened us, we had a really good reason not to fight. We agreed, shook hands, and left his office. There would be no fight.

This set of circumstances had me labeled as the toughest, or at least one of the toughest kids at Cupertino Junior High. The school only had seventh and eighth graders, so my class was the oldest there. The buzz both about the fight and my new-found reputation continued. I heard rumors that some kids were going to Arturo at Kennedy to set up a fight. I had no interest in that. Arturo had never done anything to me nor I to him. I had started fighting that year to stop getting bullied, and it had worked. I was not trying to be the toughest. I had many fights sometimes without a definitive winner. I will say this: I never lost a fight. That is probably just luck, but it also had to do with the combination of my dad's boxing lessons and my wrestling skills.

Emotionally, these junior high years were extremely hard. The stress of having to uphold the Overgard name and defend one's honor was not just my burden to bear, but many young boys go through similar situations. In today's world, many boys are worried about being beaten up or even killed by gangs. The fear of being attacked day after day is horrible, not to mention the physical injuries that can occur. At least all of my confrontations were one-on-one and weapon-free.

ARRIVING AT O'HARE

Ralph and I continued our journey during the daylight hours from St. Louis, Missouri to Chicago, Illinois. Traveling during the daytime was better than the nighttime driving due to the increased light, but it was still extremely foggy. The visibility was minimal. The hours of driving had been harrowing and we still had about five hours to go.

I don't remember much about these five hours. I was very relieved upon arriving at O'Hare International Airport and not having to drive any further. Ralph lived in South Chicago, so he still had some distance to travel, maybe 30 or 40 minutes' worth. For Ralph, the worst of the traveling was over. For me, it was just beginning.

After being dropped off at the airport, I went and checked on outbound flights. I found out that there were no flights arriving or departing and there hadn't been all day. It was around noon on December 20, 1972. Chicago's O'Hare International Airport is located 14 miles northwest of the Chicago loop district and is the primary airport for the Chicago area. Also, since Illinois is toward the middle of the country, that makes O'Hare a prime place to transfer planes if you can't get direct connections. O'Hare today is typically in the top six airports in the world in passenger traffic and the top three in the United States behind Hartsfield-Jackson Atlanta International Airport and Los

Angeles International Airport. However, in 1972, O'Hare was the busiest airport in the world.

The airport was very crowded as people waited for flights. Making it all the worse was that this was close to the Christmas holidays. Lots of people were traveling to, from, and through O'Hare. Chicago has a secondary airport called Midway International Airport. It is located about 8 miles southwest of the Chicago loop district. Midway is a smaller airport compared to O'Hare. O'Hare is a primary hub for both United Airlines and American Airlines. In 1972, it also catered to smaller airlines that served regional airports throughout the Midwest and East.

Based on the status of O'Hare being completely shut down, I had no choice but to just wait. This was the worst fog that I had ever seen. Clearly, it had covered a good portion of the middle of the country and it had lasted a long time. There was no telling how long it would be before O'Hare would reopen.

MY FIRST THREE YEARS OF HIGH SCHOOL

There were a couple of unusual and potentially dangerous stunts that I did during my high school years. Teenagers often do dumb things and I think these qualify. Our house was a ranch style home whose front faced the west. The house where I lived as a teenager had a slanting roof line that created a narrow porch-like area covering the front door, sidewalk, and kitchen window. On one occasion, I challenged myself to jump off of the roof. This was just another activity that would have driven my parents crazy had they known about it. The roof was between eight and ten feet off of our lawn. Our lawn created a softer landing than cement, so jumping onto it and rolling allowed me to avoid injury.

The other stunt took place sometime during my junior or senior year of high school. Several of my friends and I were riding around in one of their cars. We got on the freeway and opened the front and back windows on the passenger side of the car. Then I held on to the center post between the front and back passenger windows, swung my right leg out of the back window, ducked my head out of the car, and brought my right leg up and through the open passenger side window. Now I was sitting with my body outside of the car, my left leg was in the back window, my right leg was in the front window, and my arms are wrapped tightly around the window frames/center post with my head just above the roof of the car. The driver spotted a car in the right lane. He moved to the left, one lane over, and sped by them at about 80 miles an hour. He moved back into the right lane and then took the next exit. After leaving the freeway, I climbed back into the back seat. We drove a couple of miles east of this freeway, which ran north and south. Then we turned around and drove back toward the freeway. At this point, we were pulled over by the police. The officer told us that he had pulled us over because there was a report of some crazy incident having occurred on the freeway. Our driver must have told him that we were headed to one of our houses. I think it helped that we were moving toward the freeway appearing to have come from the opposite direction. We got lucky and he let us go.

In 1965, I had graduated from Cupertino Junior High School. In the fall, I would be a freshman at Homestead High School. Homestead was about a mile from where I was living in Sunnyvale. It was just over the border to the south and located in Cupertino. The high schools in the South Bay were noted for their excellence. Homestead in particular was noted for both its athletic and academic prowess.

I should mention that I only got into a couple of fights in high school and nothing very serious. I was being treated with respect and didn't feel the need to defend myself. All of the gossip about eighth grade fights and who was the better fighter had faded away.

We called Homestead 'the prison' because of its brick walls and completely enclosed fencing. It was a closed campus meaning you couldn't leave the school grounds in between classes. There were other rules of the 1960s. Long hair on males was just starting to come into vogue in

1964 when the Beatles broke through to become one of the greatest bands ever. The schools hadn't gotten the message that freedom should apply to students. If a male student's hair touched either his collar or his ears, he would be suspended until the hair was cut back to school standards. I am pretty sure that the females had restrictions such as absolutely no cleavage showing and dresses had to be at or below the knees. Shorts were not allowed, either. By today's norms, Homestead was a prison. My understanding was that Homestead was a closed campus because of its size. The size of the school peaked with my senior class in 1968–1969 at well over 2,000 students.

I think it was in high school where I developed my philosophy of a positive mental attitude or PMA. This probably comes from my sports experiences. If you don't think you can win, you probably won't. You simply need to have PMA to be a winner. Clearly in sports, superior technique and talent may be required to be the victor, but often, your opponent will have these characteristics as well. Avoiding negative thoughts is paramount when your opponent has gained the upper hand and you are seeking to come from behind. Interestingly enough, this is also the time where negativity is trying to force its way in because you are behind. The evidence that you are on the way to losing is right in front of you. Mentally, you need to project a picture of what your come-from-behind victory will look like, then believe that you can do it. Since many sporting events, but particularly individual sports, often have a situation where the lead goes back and forth, keeping a PMA is vital.

This philosophy, of course, applies to many things. It is the essence of the Law of Attraction. Our viewpoint determines where we end up. As we approach life from either a positive or negative perspective, we reap the results of that thinking. When I see people struggling with life, I usually see just how negative they are. When I see people succeed, I typically see just how positive they are. Keeping positive thoughts leads to positive results.

At Homestead High School, from as far back as I can remember, I started eating lunch in the quad. The quad was, as you might assume, a large open square. There were plenty of short walls where we could sit, have lunch, and talk. Friendships were built there. Among the folks that would show up for our lunch sessions were Jeff, Steve, Matt, Carter, Clark, Bob, Gloria, Dan, and others. Most of us would bring our lunches and eat there. I remember that at least two of us had a contest to see whose paper bag could be used day after day and last throughout the school year.

Jeff was a very good friend. He and I had wrestled back in junior high when he went to Kennedy. We know the outcome because I was undefeated in wrestling against all other junior highs. One day, Jeff and I started whistling at exactly the same time and, oddly enough, exactly the same song. It was not a popular song but one from the musical My Fair Lady in 1955 called "I Could have Danced All Night." Jeff and I felt that this was a sign of some sort of psychic connection. We stayed in touch as the years went by, and are still in contact today.

As we all know, beginning high school is a big step. It is usually the last school before one reaches the age of 18, when independence usually happens. At that age, we all wanted independence. I now had two years of success playing sports. As a freshman, I played Frosh Football, Frosh Basketball, and Varsity Tennis. The structure for some sports at Homestead was that there was a Freshman team, a Frosh-Soph team, and a Varsity team. For Tennis, there was a Junior Varsity and a Varsity team.

I first played football. I was playing quarterback, halfback, and defensively, I was a starting cornerback. I don't remember much about our freshman games. I do remember that I was brought up to one of the Frosh-Soph games to be the 3rd string back-up quarterback. This was a rough game and the starting quarterback was knocked out of the game. The 2nd string quarterback took over. As the end of the game neared, we had the football and the 2nd string quarterback also got knocked out of the game. The Frosh-Soph coach put me in the game. He called the play, something like "527 pitch left." Not only was the pressure on me, but I had no clue what that play was. I should have called a timeout and asked the coach what the play was. You see, the problem was that the coach for the freshman team was using a completely different play calling system than the coach at the Frosh-Soph level. All of our plays on the Frosh team were two-digit plays. As soon as I heard three digits, I knew I was probably screwed. I thought to myself, it has the word "pitch left" in it. I'll get the ball and swivel to pitch the ball to a halfback or fullback or whoever looks like they might be ready to catch it. Well, the ball was hiked and I swiveled, but there was no one there to catch it. "Crap!" I had already started to pitch it and I tried to hold the ball, but it squirted out of my hands. I ran after it and dove on it. The opposing team piled on to me with one of them spearing me in the leg with his helmet causing great pain and an inability to walk without limping. I did have the ball and mercifully, the game ended. One of our sophomores, Dick, who would go on to play football beyond college, helped me off of the field. I never did tell the coach why I had screwed up. I knew it was not my fault, but theirs.

In the winter, I played basketball. I was on the starting team there as well. I had a real affinity for basketball, but I was still short at 5'9'. I wasn't short for high school, but I wanted to play professional sports and I definitely did not fit the professional basketball mold. Based on my size, I figured my best chances would not be in football or basketball. I had played basketball at a friend's house in Shawano where he had a basketball hoop set above his garage. I would practice even in the winter, and to the point where the skin on my fingers would split. Nevertheless, I thought I played well. At Homestead, I would start making baskets in practice and would think that I was playing well for that day. But it seemed that I shot that well almost every day. I also remember throwing a ball the length of the court and swishing it. I don't even remember if I was aiming at the basket or just returning a ball to the players practicing on the other end of our court. Still, it was pretty awesome.

Baseball was a game that I had played and that I was good at. However, baseball was played in the spring. I had started playing tennis when I was 13. Dad loved the game and wanted to get me involved. Tennis was also played in the spring, so I couldn't join both the baseball and the tennis teams. I chose tennis. I thought I was pretty good, but I had a tough time winning on the Northern California junior circuit, which I started playing in the summer of 1965 when I was 14. The United States Tennis Association (USTA) had two year age brackets for junior players, such as 12 and under, 14 and under, 16 and under, and 18 and under. After age 18, you played adult tournaments. Even though I wasn't beating anybody on the 14 and under tournament circuit, I knew that most of these kids had been playing a lot since they were 10 and quite a few of them had started when they were around 5 years old. At those very young ages, they could not serve very powerfully and they were too short and too slow to attack the net. So they learned to hit groundstrokes from the backcourt. My biggest problem was that I never had that solid basis in hitting groundstrokes. I learned to volley and then tried to get to the net as quickly as I could. This was a pretty big problem because it meant that my return of service, or ability to break my opponent's service, was limited.

I thought that I was an average player when I started playing tournaments, but I didn't know enough to know how bad I really was compared to other kids who played tournament tennis. By the time they were my age, they were miles ahead of me. I played the Boys 14s National Hardcourt Championships in 1965. That is for those 14 years of age and younger. I played the #1 seed Jeff Austin. I believe that I won a game or two, but it was no contest. Jeff did go on to play in the pros and you may know of his sister, Tracy Austin. Tracy was world-ranked #1 and won the US Open twice. She is the youngest player inducted into the International Tennis Hall of Fame. I also played Erik Van Dillen the following year in the Boys 16s National Hardcourt Championships, and I think I got one game. Erik was the top junior in the country for his age while growing up. He went on to a professional career reaching 36th in the world in singles. He had wins over John McEnroe, Stan Smith, Arthur Ashe, Jimmy Conners, Guillermo Vilas, and Ilie Nastase. He also reached the Doubles Finals at the Australian, Wimbledon, and U.S. Opens. The bottom line was that it would take me years to become as good as I thought I was early on. At about the point where I was getting very discouraged, I started winning. And nothing provides encouragement like winning.

At Homestead, I thought that I still had a chance to make the Varsity tennis team as a Freshman and I ended up playing #4 singles. In high school, we played five singles matches and two doubles matches using nine players for each team. I practiced hard and got better and better. The summer between my freshman and sophomore years, I played in the 16 and under age group since I turned 15 that year. I was finally able to win maybe one out of three matches. I didn't get ranked in Northern California that year, which was my current objective. Nevertheless, I was rapidly improving.

I continued to play football my sophomore year. At the beginning of the year, I was the starting halfback on offense and the starting cornerback on defense for the Frosh-Soph team. I was a good enough athlete to play Varsity football as a sophomore at most high schools, but not Homestead. Homestead had one of the best Varsity teams in the state of California. The Santa Clara Valley Athletic League, also known as the SCVAL, had the top ranked Varsity team in the state, Los Altos High School. The Homestead Varsity team, made up largely of juniors, was ranked number three in California.

In the second game of the season, Homestead was playing our archrival, Fremont. The Frosh-Soph game was played before the Varsity game. On one play, I flared out from my halfback position on offense and headed down field. Our quarterback threw the ball and I was able to catch the pass in stride. Once I caught the ball, I was too fast and eluded the defenders. I went all the way in for a 65-yard touchdown. Later, we had the ball on the Fremont 17-yard line. My number was called and I was supposed to run up the middle. I took the ball, started up the middle, but saw that it was clogged. I stopped, cut to my right and sprinted around the defense for another touchdown. Coach H., the Frosh-Soph coach, seemed upset that I had not gone up the middle which was the play that was called. In my view, that was very short-sighted. We ended up losing that game 29–18. The following week against Santa Clara, I ran a short yardage play into the end zone for my 3rd touchdown in three games.

Practice with Coach H. was always an adventure. For instance, there was the time that he was teaching all of our backfield players how to take a handoff from the quarterback. He had asked us to swim with the arm closest to the quarterback to leave a big space in the stomach area. This swimming motion would result in keeping the arm bent and moving the elbow up to about head level and then bringing it down to close on the ball. What could possibly go wrong? Well, shortly after being taught this technique, I took the ball as a halfback swinging my elbow up to our quarterback, Dan. Dan was a freshman and a big kid. He must have been at least six feet tall. I felt my elbow connect with Dan, as I got the ball. Dan went down, unconscious. He recovered quickly and was rotated out and then back in. He was still affected though when he came back in because he couldn't remember the plays. He was done for the day.

Another interesting occurrence was when Coach H. wanted us to practice cutting, meaning change direction at a certain location deep in the backfield. I ran the play and he was very unhappy that I was not as deep as he wanted. There was a lot of screaming from all of the coaches in those days. Coach H. angrily threw down his hat and told me to cut beyond the hat. We ran the play and the Coach went ballistic. I had no idea what he was angry about. I must have shortened the route yet again without realizing it. My friends, who were teammates, were very gleeful about this situation. They weren't any happier than I was with the dictatorial screaming from the Coach. They told me that when I made my cut, I stepped on his hat and sent it 15 feet into the air. They thought that my cut was absolutely great and laughed hysterically, although the laughing probably had to wait until after Coach was not around.

I remember getting the wind knocked out of me. I was rolling on the ground groaning in agony, unable to breathe. Coach S. came up to me and stared at me for a few seconds as if I should just get up. He reached down grabbed the front of my waist band and pulled up on my midsection, which opened up my airways. Suddenly, I could breathe again. That was such a relief.

On another occasion, I was blocking incoming defensive players in practice as I slid to my hands and knees. One of the guys stepped on my left hand. I looked down and there were two deep cleat marks in the back of my hand that started to bleed. I went to Coach and told him I needed to get this taken care of. I ended up with stitches to close both wounds, which went down to the bone.

Another interesting practice drill was what the coaches called the suicide drill. This actually had some value, as the depicted situation happened often to cornerbacks. In the suicide drill, four players representing the offense would huddle up with a football. The lone defensive player would be located ten yards away between two blocking pads that would represent the goal line. The players in the huddle would give the ball to one player. Usually this player followed the other three, who would block the defender. Almost all of the time, the defender would just get wiped out by the three players blocking him at the same time, while the ball carrier would just stroll into the makeshift end zone. This drill was very painful, but in games, the cornerback would often have to move up to the line of scrimmage and try to tackle the ball carrier, who often had two or three blockers in front of him.

There was an athletic banquet every year, and for my sophomore year in Frosh-Soph football, I was awarded the Scholar Athlete Award. As far as football went, I was not happy at all with the coaches. I felt that they just wanted to run roughshod over the players. I know a lot of my teammates felt the same way. I decided not to play football anymore after the season ended. I also quit playing basketball in the winter. I wanted to devote more time to tennis, and basketball would take up a lot of time.

In the spring, I became the number one player on the varsity tennis team. There was a junior who was very good and I would struggle to beat him, but I usually did. When the season came, I won most of my matches against other SCVAL team's number one players. During the season, I practiced diligently. I was actually more interested in the Northern California Junior tennis circuit.

The summer of 1967, I started to win more consistently on the NorCal junior circuit. I was winning about two out of every three matches. I had a very good result at the National 16 and Under Hardcourts, which happened to be played in nearby Burlingame. There, I had lost my first match, but they had a consolation tournament where all of the first-round losers would play. In that tournament, I got to the finals before losing. I was surprised to see that I got my picture and name in the 1968 National 16 & 18 and Under Hardcourt brochure.

Just as I might have been getting discouraged by the extremely tough competition, I had started winning. I was starting to beat some seeded players. Seeded players are players that the tournament committee thinks are the best for a particular tournament. It used to be based on the prior year's results and also the current year's play. In terms of tournament wins, I finally got a few of those under my belt. I went on to play in the Boys 16s and 18s at a tournament in Fresno and won both of those titles. I finished with a ranking of #20 in Northern California for 1967 in the Boys 16 rankings.

My junior year came and I was determined to eventually become a professional tennis player. I was sitting in my Speech and Debate class when Coach Ron U. pulled me out of class and into the hallway to talk to me. He was the Varsity Head Football Coach and he had the number one ranked team in the state of California. He wanted to know why I wasn't going out for football. I told him that I needed to devote more time to tennis in order to make the professional ranks. He said that Homestead was not in the business of making professional athletes. He couldn't talk me into going out for football, but I guess he felt that he had to give it a try. I must say that I was flattered.

That 1967 Homestead Varsity Football team went on to 9–0 record. Back then, there were no playoffs, only the regular season. The closest game was 26–0. The team went on to score 322 points to only 32 for the opposition. Fifteen players received full four-year National Collegiate Athletic

Association (NCAA) Division I football scholarships. At least two of these Homestead students went on to play in the National Football League (NFL).

Getting back to my tennis, I was practicing very diligently. I would play about 40 hours a week during the summer. Eight hours in a day was not unusual and seven days a week was the norm. I loved it. A lot of my practicing was against Fremont High School's number one player and my good friend, Steve Sharp. Steve was a year older and a lefty, but he could not beat me. Still, hitting with him was great practice. When I didn't have anyone to play with, I would hit tennis balls against our garage door until the slats started to fall off. It must have driven the neighbors crazy.

By my junior year, my tennis was so good that I was only losing to one player in the league, Tim Vann. Tim played for Los Altos High School, and he was a year younger than I was. During his junior and senior years, 1969 and 1970, he was the number one ranked 18 and under player in Northern California. NorCal did have some players who were not ranked in the section, but were at the top of national rankings. They were better than Tim. These were players like Erik Van Dillen and Mike Machette. Mike was a big kid and an excellent player, who already ranked nationally in the Men's, as well as near the top of the Juniors, by 1969. Still, Vann was really good, and he seemed to have my number, as he beat me in both of our head to head meetings in the spring of 1968. The SCVAL was not a small league. It contained 13 teams from the northwest section of Santa Clara Valley. I am sure that Tim and I must have met for the SCVAL singles championship in 1968, and I didn't win that one either.

Also, Steve Wozniak was in the graduating class of 1968. He has a sister, Linda, who was in my graduating class of 1969. I had known Steve from my 7th grade time at Cupertino Junior High School, but I always thought that he was a bit of a nerd. I may have been, too, but I could always fall back on my jock status at school. I did have a lot of friends. From that standpoint, I was better off in high school than I had been in either elementary school or junior high. Steve was very much into electronics and the electronics club. To me, that was just for hobbyists that were interested in tubes and transistors used in old style radios. It did not interest me. Clearly, it should have. Steve was on to something big. About eight years later, he invented the personal computer and, with Steve Jobs, founded Apple Computer. It would have been better if I had become close friends with Woz. Well, hindsight is 20/20.

Steve Jobs, who has gotten the majority of the credit for Apple Computer, was a freshman at Homestead High School in 1969. He had skipped a grade, so he was actually about 5 years younger than I was. I did not know him, and there was nothing during that year to bring my attention to him.

One day, Woz and I, along with some of the smartest juniors and seniors, were in an advanced math class. It could have been Geometry or a second-year Algebra course. What I haven't told you is that my mother tried to teach high school when we got to California. She couldn't get hired because with her Master's degree, she commanded a higher salary than most other teachers. She had to settle for being a substitute teacher. Well, one day our math instructor was out ill. I looked up and in walked my mother. She announced that she would be teaching the class for that day and that she was Mrs. Overgard. I was mortified. Because I was well known around campus, everyone immediately knew that it was my mother teaching the class. Somehow, I survived.

In early May, my folks received a letter from the principal of Homestead, Warren Bryld. It said that I had been elected by the faculty to the Homestead Chapter of the National Honor Society and that the induction ceremony would be held toward the end of May. I was surprised because I thought of it as a strictly academic achievement award and I didn't have much more than a "B" average. I found out later that in addition to scholarship, the criteria of leadership, service, and character were also considered. There were over 100 other juniors who received this award out of over 550 juniors, and I felt honored.

SUMMER TENNIS CIRCUITS

The summer of 1968 was another breakthrough year for my tennis. I played on the Pacific Northwest Circuit, the Northern California Sectional tournaments, and I even went to Colorado to play in the Intermountain Championships.

The Pacific Northwest Circuit was a group of five tournaments whose adult matches counted toward the adult national rankings. Although the adults were the centerpiece, there was a strong junior contingent as well. Players from Northern California, Southern California, and Arizona would go up there to play. For a high school kid, this was one hell of an adventure. The Northern California Section arranged for housing for the juniors during these tournaments. The housing accommodations were with local families who were almost universally members of the tennis club where we were playing. Among the tournaments on the circuit were the Oregon State Championships and the Washington State Championships. The circuit finished with a tournament in Canada.

I did quite well by beating Steve Stefanki in Tacoma. Steve was another top NorCal player who was to go on to win the 1970 California Junior College Singles Championship while playing at Foothill Junior College. He also played number one for the University of California at

Berkeley after he finished at Foothill. His brother, Larry Stefanki played on the pro tour and became a rather famous tennis coach.

There was one humorous incident on the Pacific Northwest Tennis Circuit. I played doubles with a very good Canadian junior player named Mark. Mark and I fit together extremely well as a doubles team. I remember, we were playing against two good Northern Californians. Mark and I used hand signals. In doubles, if you are not familiar, there is one player serving diagonally from one side of the court to the opposing service box on the returning team's side. The server's partner is typically stationed close to the net and on the side of the net directly across from the service box where the server is going to serve. A difficult thing for the player attempting to return the serve was to know if the net player would dash across the net to intercept the return. If the net player could intercept the return, the serving team would usually win the point because a volley (ball hit in the air) could easily be placed where the returning team could not get it. Our signaling was designed to coordinate where the server would go, either straight forward to cover his side of the court if the net player stayed where he was, or to cross behind the net player if the net player was going across. Typically, an open or closed hand behind the back displayed by the net man would tell the server if his net man was going to cross or stay.

Well, during this match, an unusual situation occurred. I noticed that our opponents would hit behind me whenever I went across and thus win the point. I figured out that one of the adult players, who was sitting in the stands behind us, was stealing our signals and passing them on to our opponents. This was an unwarranted advantage because the receiving team would now know where to hit the ball to avoid the net player which increased their chances of winning the point. This is very unethical. I was pissed, but I didn't show it. I talked to Mark about it. I told him that we would continue to provide signals that could be intercepted, however to fool both the adult in the stands and our opponents, if I let my racquet touch the ground, then the signal was reversed. With this method, I could signal to go and either go or cancel it. So we proceeded with this change. I would signal to go and touch my racquet to the ground. This meant that I was staying. As I suspected, the adult passed the signal that he saw to our opponents. The player returning the ball was sure I was going. He hit it right to me and since I wasn't moving, I put it away for a winner. We tried signaling that I would stay then I would reverse it and go. We were now winning points in spite of our original signals being stolen. After a few of these easy winners, one of our opponents started yelling at the guy in the stands to which the guy yelled back "HE SIGNALED THAT HE WAS GOING!" I started yelling at the guy in the stands and he left. I had innovatively used the unethical interference in our match to our advantage and we were able to win that match. The adult seemed to avoid me from then on.

I also beat Chip Fisher 6–3, 6–4 in the semi-finals of the Washington State Junior Championships for 18 and under players. Chip was only 15 at the time, but rated highly in the country in the 16 and under category. Later, Chip was to go on to play for Stanford University and on the ATP circuit. This win allowed me to reach the finals of the Washington State Junior Championships at the age of 17. I had been the 5th seed. In the finals, I played the 3rd seed,

Bruce Kellock from Richmond, California, where I lost after splitting sets. We were playing in a very large stadium at the Seattle Tennis Club. The stadium was nowhere near full but might have had 500 spectators.

I had a successful tennis season on the Northern California circuit that year. After returning from the Pacific Northwest Circuit, I played in the Marin Junior Hardcourts where I was seeded 7th. In the quarterfinals, I upset the number two seed. I got my picture on the front page of the San Francisco Examiner. Under the picture was the caption "Spoiler in Marin Tennis." In the semifinals, I defeated the number four seed, but I lost in the finals.

A week later, I went to the Denver area to play in the Intermountain Section Championships. I lost in the quarterfinals to a tough nationally renowned competitor.

I ended up getting ranked #13 in the Boys Northern California 18 & Unders. My leap from 20th in the 16s to 13th in the 18s was a testament to the improvements that I had been making. Considering that it was my first year in that division with another year left, I was happy with my ranking and results.

SENIOR YEAR OF HIGH SCHOOL

We were the last high school graduating class of the turbulent 1960s. I was extremely serious about my tennis. I was getting up early and going over to Los Altos Hills to play with some of the Foothill Junior College players at 6:30 AM. We would hit for an hour or so before I had to head off to school. Around 2:30 PM, the tennis players would get out of classes because after school sports fulfilled the gym requirement, so gym was made the last class of the day allowing us to get out earlier than we otherwise would. I had made plans to practice in the afternoons on some days with college players instead of my high school teammates. As much as I liked my teammates, they were no longer providing much competition. I was able to beat the Junior College (JC) players at Foothill and De Anza. De Anza JC was actually the JC for the district that I lived in.

During my senior year, I felt I was playing tennis at a very high level. I had beaten some very good collegians and at least one junior player who was in the top 30 in the country. The juniors were extremely tough. Tim Vann, my nemesis at Los Altos High School, ended up ranked #26 in the country in juniors in 1969.

The De Anza JC coach was Bob Potthast. He offered to play doubles with me in the Fremont Country Club Champagneships, which took place in Los Altos Hills in October

74

of 1968. Yes, I said "Champagneships." This tournament had quite a few of the best adult players in Northern California playing. Potthast had been playing national tournaments for many years. He had won the 1968 Mountain View Open, which was a tough Northern California tournament, beating Whitney Reed in the finals. Whitney was ranked 2nd in Northern California Men's Singles and 23rd in the US in 1968. Whitney had been ranked #1 in the country in 1961, and although past his prime, he was still very formidable. Bob played in the US Open in 1957, 1959, 1961, 1969, and 1970. In the summer of 1969, Bob went to the US Open. In the 2nd round of qualifying, he played Jimmy Connors, who was a 17-year-old phenom at the time. If you know tennis, then you know that Jimmy went on to become one of the all-time great tennis players, winning eight Grand Slam Events. Although Bob was nearly 34 at the time, he prevailed over Connors 6–4, 5–7, 6–1. In the 1st round of the US Open, Bob played another all-time great, Ricardo "Pancho" Gonzales, and lost in straight sets. Bob was one hell of a good tennis player.

Bob was born in Wisconsin and had gone to the University of Iowa in his collegiate days. He had played football for the Hawkeyes and was the starting safety on Iowa's 1957 victorious Rose Bowl team. He was about 6'2" and 210 lbs., so he easily fit the mold of a collegiate football player.

Bob and I won our first-round match, and then we played and beat Mark Elliott and Felix Ponte. These two had a strong doubles reputation. They had a Men's Doubles ranking of #10 in NorCal. Felix was from Peru and went on to an Association of Tennis Professionals (ATP) high world ranking of 174 in 1974.

I think we won one more match before reaching what was being termed a semi-final match. We played Karl Hedrick and Mike Machette. Karl had played in the 1960 and 1961 US Opens. Mike, mentioned earlier as a top junior and adult player, was my age. He went on to play on the ATP circuit for many years, and reached a world ranking high of 92 in 1976. At the time we played them, Mike was 44th in the 1968 U. S. Men's Open Rankings. Bob and I won this match also.

We were then in the finals, along with two other teams, both of whom were from Stanford University. This tournament had deviated from normal scoring by using a 21 point, must win by two, system to win a set. It was the best two out of three sets. Three teams in the final is also not conventional. A round robin where each team played the other was how this was to be resolved. We beat one of the teams, but lost to the other. All three teams ended up with one win and one loss in that round robin. The tournament organizers then added up the points won and lost. Bob and I were awarded 2nd place. It was still a good result, and I had played very well.

In March of 1969, I played in the "B" category of the Northern California Men's Sectional Singles Championships. This was a second tier of players who were not ranked at the time in the Men's Northern California Open Section rankings. It was a new category and ended up with a very large field, which I think exceed two hundred players. There was also a "C" category tournament that was played as a new third tier. These tournaments were held at Golden Gate Park in San Francisco. I always liked the park. Between matches, we would go out into the park, which would be filled with people enjoying the warming weather. In the 1960s, the park was also often filled with hippies and the beat of music traveling across the wide-open expanses of grass.

The B tournament that I played in had many good players despite it being a second tier. I struggled to win a number of matches before getting to the finals. In the finals, I played top-seeded Jaime Collaco, who was a former University of Wyoming tennis star. He won the first set 6–1, but I rallied to take the second set 7–5. Collaco won the first two games of the deciding set and was up 40–0 in the 3rd game, but I came back to win that final set 8–6. This match was reported in quite a few newspapers.

The spring of 1969 arrived and the high school tennis season began. In high school, I played Tim Vann in our first meeting with Los Altos High on the Homestead courts. Tim won that match 6–1, 6–1. Upon reviewing the match with my dad, he thought that I was pressing too much and trying to hit too good of a shot on every point. I may have been giving Tim too much respect and not giving him a chance to make his own errors. I would have to change my strategy for my next match with Tim. I won the rest of my matches in league play against the other 11 schools' number one players pretty easily. Usually, I would only give up a game or two per set.

Near the end of the high school tennis season in May, the league would hold the Santa Clara Valley Athletic League Tennis Championships with a singles and doubles tournament. Tim and I, also as expected, easily defeated the other players prior to the final. Since my first match with Tim had gone badly, another strategy needed to be implemented. I would avoid trying to hit too hard or too close to the lines. The strategy worked, but I still didn't win. The match was very close however, and the score was 6–4, 6–8, 6–3. I wasn't happy about losing my last chance to win a league title, but I was encouraged that I had played a much better match.

About a week after my SCVAL Championship loss to Tim, Homestead took on Los Altos on the Los Altos courts. I was going to play Tim for the last time in my high school tennis career. I used the same strategy that I had used in the League finals. This time it worked. I beat Tim 7–5, 2–6, 6–3. I was ecstatic! I think that was the only SCVAL high school tennis match that Tim ever lost. This win wouldn't count for my NorCal Junior Rankings, but it sure helped my ego. Tim had a win over Bob Murio, who in 1968 had a ranking of 46 in the US Men's Singles. I really felt that I was on my way to the pros!

I started getting a fair amount of recognition with the results of my tennis matches showing up in Tennis Magazine and the local papers. I was the Cupertino Courier's Athlete of the Year for Tennis in both my junior and senior years. This was for the five Fremont Union High School District high schools. I was the Homestead varsity tennis team's Most Valuable Player in both 1968 and 1969. The Homestead Epitaph, which was the school newspaper, did a story on me in April with a very good drawing of how I looked at the time. My friend, Steve Sharp, wrote a very nice article on me for the Sunnyvale Standard. It had a picture of me with a caption, "Overgard Dreams Big— Center Court at Wimbledon", and a fairly lengthy article. I also had a picture and caption on the front page of the San Francisco Examiner. My tennis future looked bright.

Needless to say, I was very devoted to my tennis. I was, however, somewhat shy and inexperienced around girls.

I do remember going solo to a dance or two, but I went out on only one date that I can remember. I never had a girlfriend in high school. I was never asked to a Sadie Hawkins dance where the girls ask the guys. I never went to a prom of any kind. Looking back on it, I missed out. I know I was devoted to my sports and maybe I was not so approachable. I had girls in classes that I would talk to, but my impression was that they were not interested in me as anything other than a friend. So I never pressed. After a couple years of college, I started to make up for lost time.

TENNIS CIRCUITS

In May, I played in the California State Tennis Championships. This tournament was loaded with top flight players, including the 1968 U.S. Men's #8 ranked player, Jim Osbourne, and the #9 ranked player, Jim McManus. Erik Van Dillen was ranked #16 in the US in 1968 and he ended up winning the tournament over #35 Paul Gerken. I played Gil Howard, who was #11 in NorCal, in the first round and lost 6–3, 10–8. Gil was another very good player with a big serve and volley game. I played in quite a few of these Men's Open events before the tennis world broke the amateur lock and became a truly professional sport. However, this was the only match that has gotten me internet recognition via www.tennisarchives.com. There are many players listed on that site that I have beaten, and many tournaments that I have played where the results weren't recorded, but at least I am listed.

Dad had been working diligently to get me an NCAA Division 1 tennis scholarship. That would take care of my college expenses and hopefully set me up for a professional tennis career. He seemed enamored with the South-Central part of the country, meaning Texas, Oklahoma, Louisiana, and Arkansas. From a strictly tennis standpoint, this was not a bad place to look for top level tennis teams in the early 1970s. There were many, many universities offering full tennis scholarships in the late 1960s, often as many as nine scholarships total per team. This meant that every year, schools would have to replace any graduating seniors. Soon, Dad had a number of scholarships lined up. This was very important for me. Dad and Mom had grown up poor during the Depression of the 1930's. They had to work their own way through college and expected me and my siblings to do the same. Getting a scholarship would help me avoid having to work while going to school in order to pay for tuition, books, room, and board.

One of the tennis scholarships that my dad had gotten for me was to Lamar Tech, formally known as Lamar State College of Technology at the time, which was located in Beaumont, Texas. Today, it is known as Lamar University. Lamar is about an 85-mile drive east of Houston, fairly close to the Louisiana border. I seem to remember that the University of Texas provided one of the scholarship offers as well.

Dad and I flew down to Arizona to have me try out for the University of Arizona team. Often when teams had not seen a player's ability, they would have them play a match against a known entity to test the player's ability. At the University of Arizona, I played a match against Eric Evett. who had played #6 for Arizona the year before. He was from Southern California and had been ranked #8 in 1967 and #14 in 1968 in the Southwestern Men's rankings. I expected to beat Eric, but lost 6–3, 6–2. The coach of the University of Arizona, Dave Snyder, offered me a half scholarship. I already had some full scholarship offers, so I politely declined.

I also went over to nearby San Jose State University in San Jose, California, whose coach was Butch Krikorian, a well-known player and coach in Northern California. Carlos Kirmayr was going to be headed to San Jose State, so there would be some strong competition. Although Butch was most likely aware of my playing ability, he invited me out to the San Jose State tennis courts to play a match with King Van Nostrand. King was to end up as the #2 ranked 35 and over player in the U.S. for 1969. I knew that he was very good. We played and I lost something like 6–4, 6–3. Butch offered me a half scholarship indicating that he didn't have full scholarships available. Again, I politely declined.

Dad arranged for at least one scholarship by telephone. He spoke with Emmet Paré, the coach of the Tulane University tennis team. Emmet Paré was one of the stars of the early days of professional tennis. He traveled with Bill Tilden in 1931. Tulane had won eight NCAA singles titles and two NCAA doubles titles. Paré arrived in 1933 and was the coach for six of those singles titles and both doubles titles. Dad told Paré of my successes and Paré offered me a full scholarship on the spot.

Another scholarship opportunity came our way when Dad spoke with Ray O'Keefe, the coach of Oklahoma City University (OCU). OCU had a foreign-dominated team with a strong contingent of Australians and a sprinkling of players from the U.S. Ray said that his #1 player, Colin Robertson, was out in Northern California. He would arrange for us to play and then he would speak with Colin. Dad and I drove to the club where we would meet Colin, who was an Australian. The Australians had a long heritage of excellent players. We played four sets and I played very well winning two of them. What I didn't find out until the advent of the internet was that Colin had played in the 1967 U.S. Open Men's Championship. Coach O'Keefe came back with a full scholarship offer.

There were another couple of scholarships offered, but OCU seemed the best. The competition was surely going to be tough, but I thought that was what I needed in order to improve. I signed a letter of intent to accept the Oklahoma City University scholarship offer.

During the summer of 1969, I played the Pacific Northwest Tennis Circuit once again. In one of the Men's tournaments, I played the #1 seed in the Oregon State Championships, Robyn Ray. He had played #1 for the University of Arizona. We had a very close match with Robyn winning 6–4, 7–5. The next day, I received a telephone call from Coach Snyder of the University of Arizona saying that he had changed his mind and was now offering me a full scholarship. I am sure that Robyn Ray had contacted him after our match and that was the reason for the offer. Robyn went on to win the Oregon State Championships that year. I felt that OCU still had the strongest team, but also, I had already signed a letter of intent. I declined the University of Arizona offer.

I often wonder if I should have accepted the offer to the University of Arizona. If I could redo my college selection, I think Tulane University might have been the better choice. In hindsight, the problem with OCU was that Coach O'Keefe was not a tennis coach. He was more of an administrator of the team. He did not have playing experience, nor did he have coaching experience in the sense that he could improve strokes or provide strategy. Clearly, Emmett Paré had made it to the highest levels of the professional ranks. It is likely that he could have helped my game more. I also expect that I would have played higher on the Tulane team. Maybe I just reached my zenith in college and it just wasn't quite high enough, but I think other factors were about to come into play.

Despite the scholarship offers, the coach of De Anza Junior College, Bob Potthast, wanted me on his team badly. I would play #1, if I went there. California JCs at that time offered free tuition for all eligible Californians. Going to De Anza would mean bypassing my first two years of NCAA Division I tennis in favor of JC matches and tournaments. It felt like that would be a step back. Usually, players went to the JCs to continue to build their games and then get a scholarship for their Junior and Senior years of college.

My dad told Bob that we couldn't give up the scholarships to play tennis at De Anza and have me live at home. Bob was angry. He must have been counting on me coming to play for him. Looking back on everything, it makes me wonder if we should have accepted Bob's offer. I might have learned a lot from him. Still, my folks didn't have much money and it meant that I would be at home for another two years. Besides, I was eager to be out of my folks' home and off on my own. I would also get to play at the NCAA Division I collegiate level starting as a freshman.

While I was away at OCU, Bob was diagnosed with pancreatic cancer. I heard that in a matter of months he was down to 138 lbs. shortly before he died. He was only in his 30s and much too young to die. It was a very sad situation.

In late June of 1969, I played in the California State Junior Championships at the San Jose Swim and Racquet Club. I won four matches to make the round of 32 by defeating players from various parts of the country.

In the main draw, I ended up facing Roscoe Tanner of Lookout Mountain, Tennessee, who was seeded #5. Tanner had a huge serve, likely the biggest on the junior circuit and superior to most of the top US Men's players. He won 6–2, 6–2. Roscoe had won the United States Lawn Tennis Association (USLTA) National Boys 18 Hardcourt Championships the week before. In the California State Championships, he went to the finals and defeated Jimmy Connors. At the end of the 1969 season, he was ranked as the #1 junior in the country with Connors at #2.

Tennis had started as a lawn game in 1874 and Wimbledon is still played on grass. USLTA was the name of the national tennis organization starting in 1920 that, in 1973, was to become the United States Tennis Association (USTA).

Mike Prineas and I played in the doubles at the 1969 California State Championships tournament. Mike was a rising young player out of Seattle. He was a year younger than I was. In the first round we ran into the #1 seeds, Roscoe Tanner and Brian Gottfried from Fort Lauderdale, Florida. Mike and I did OK, but we lost 6–3, 6–3.

Tanner went on to win 17 pro singles titles including the 1977 Australian Open, was a finalist at Wimbledon in 1979, losing to Bjorn Borg in five sets, and reached a career high ranking of World #4. His serve was clocked at 153 mph at a tournament in Palm Springs, California, which was the highest speed recorded for many years.

Gottfried went on to win 25 singles titles and 54 doubles titles on the professional tour. He was a finalist at the French Open, and won two French Open doubles titles along with one Wimbledon doubles title. He reached a high ranking of World #3 in singles and World #2 in doubles.

The summer of 1969, I headed up to the Pacific Northwest circuit for the second consecutive year. Great things were expected of me because of the success that I had had the year before. I was seeded #1 in some of the early tournaments, but I was getting beat, which was very frustrating. I was again playing doubles with Mike Prineas. We played pretty good doubles together. We reached the finals of the Oregon State Championships, where we lost to Bob Pierce and Tom McArdle 6–4, 7–5. Mike went on to win the singles.

The culminating event was the 1969 Canadian National Junior Championships, which was being played at the Jericho Tennis Club in Vancouver, British Columbia, Canada. My understanding was that every few years, they would move the tournament from the eastern Canadian locales such as Toronto out to the West Coast. Vancouver is the largest city on Canada's West Coast and not too far over the U.S. border.

In the 1960s, countries that held their own tennis events would often provide two separate seeding lists. There were the Canadian seedings and the Foreign seedings. In this case, there were eight seeds for each. I was the 5th foreign seed in singles. Exactly how they interspersed these into a single tournament draw, I don't remember. This tournament was not only drawing the top junior players from throughout Canada, but it was also drawing the players from the Pacific Northwest Circuit. That year, we had players from Washington, Oregon, Northern California, Southern California, and Arizona. Also showing up were two very highly touted Australians, Ross Case and Adi Kourim.

As I recall, Case was seeded #1 in the Foreign singles and with Kourim, #1 in overall doubles. My reputation from the previous year's success seemed to have bolstered my seeding. The one concern that I had was that this tournament was on clay. Attacking the net, which was my forte, was dangerous on clay. The slower bounce allowed the backcourt player to get set up on the balls, resulting in better passing shots and lobs against net players.

On the clay courts that we were playing on, I thought that I needed to rely on my ground strokes, although these were the weakest part of my game. In the tournament, I ran into my doubles partner, Mike Prineas. Mike took a different approach in his match with me. He served and volleyed. He deftly angled volleys off to the sides, or hit outright drop shot winners, which would not bounce forward toward me. For my side, I was not hitting enough passing shots to overcome his volleys, and he won 8–6, 6–1. This was one more loss that I was not supposed to have. In doubles, Mike and I ended up playing Case and Kourim. I don't remember the scores, but we did lose. This was all very frustrating. On the Pacific Northwest Circuit, I had lost matches in several tournaments to players that I should beat. Lastly, in the mixed doubles championship, I teamed up with a young woman from Southern California. We were seeded #1 overall. There was only one seedings group in the mixed. We lost in the quarterfinals to a team that had the #1 junior girl from Mexico.

In Vancouver, Bob Pierce and I started to pal around together. Bob was a Southern Californian, who was a year younger than I was. One day, we didn't have any matches to play and it was the late afternoon. The Jericho club is located on Burrard Inlet, which is a primary waterway for Vancouver. The Inlet is part of what is known as English Bay. Bob and I, along with another player named Grant Smith, went to the beach behind the club. Grant was another Southern California junior, who I think was a year younger than Bob, and two years younger than I was. On the beach we discovered what I can only describe as a very large paddleboard. This was roughly 12 feet long and maybe 4 feet across in the middle. The board gradually came to a point on both ends. There were no sides and there was no rudder, so it was somewhat like a raft. We decided to borrow this paddleboard and two oars that were with it. We started to paddle away from the club. The paddleboard was sitting pretty well above the waterline even with three of us on it. However, we could not coordinate the paddling to go in a straight direction. I figured out that if the person in the back would put the paddle side of their oar in the water, it could act like a rudder. Then one of us could paddle with the other oar. The paddler would sit in the front and paddle on either or both sides of the paddleboat. The third person would sit in the middle of the paddleboard and rest. We now had propulsion and steering. We could see the far distant shore. It was about 6:00 PM, so off we went. We would alternate so that everyone would get a rest. As we were crossing this expanse of water, we saw that we were sharing the seas with huge ocean-going freighters. We realized this could be a bit dangerous, but we were never close to any of those ships. Over two hours later, we reached the other side.

We had drifted toward downtown Vancouver where there was bridge in the distance. I would estimate that the current may have forced us about a half mile from our intended landing spot, so we paddled back along the shore and against the current until we were well past our originally intended landing spot. We figured that the current would once again push us and by going well past our intended landing spot, we should end up back at the club. We were proud of ourselves. We parked the boat and found a pay phone. In those days, there were no cell phones. We called the Jericho Club and told them that we had taken a paddleboard to the opposite shore and we were heading back. We didn't want them to try to stop us, so after giving them the message, we hung up and began our journey back to the club. I would estimate that it was about 8:30 PM, and there was still plenty of light because it was the middle of summer. After making our way across most of the Inlet, it was getting pretty dark. We were trying to judge which lights were likely to be the club. We finally spotted it.

As we approached the club around 11:00 PM, we were singing, as we had triumphantly accomplished our mission! I don't remember what we were singing, but we were singing in cadence with our rowing. Looking up we saw that there were all sorts of people on the 2nd story balcony and they were cheering as we made our way to shore. We parked our paddleboard where we had found it. The tournament director met us on the beach and told us to get into the men's locker room where we could take warm showers. He followed us in and told us that he had called the Canadian Air and Sea Rescue Patrol. He told us that people had died in small boats because the Burrard Inlet narrows from about four and a half miles across from where the club is to a bridge that is a mile or less across and this narrowing happens in only a mile or two. All of that water squeezing through the narrowing shores created dangerous whirlpools. After he finished recounting the dangers to us, though, he told us, "Tell your housing that I gave you supreme shit, but that was one of greatest things I have ever seen!" So he wasn't mad at us at all, particularly since we were unharmed, and we now had a great story to tell.

Bob Pierce ended up going to the University of Tennessee, where he was to play #1 for them. Sometime after that Bob won money on a TV game show. He used the money on acting lessons and began a career in Hollywood as an actor. He landed a recurring role on the 1982–83 television show *Joanie Loves Chachi* as Bingo Pierce, the spaced-out drummer. This sitcom was a spinoff from Happy Days and started off strong, but was then dropped after the second season. Bob continues in the entertainment business to this day. He also continued to play tennis, and I saw him years later at the Men's 40 and over National Grass Court Championships in Santa Barbara, California. We have kept in touch since reconnecting.

Later that summer I played in the Nevada State Championships, which were being held in Reno. I remember the housing where I stayed. The people lived out west of Reno on a hill overlooking the city. When we pulled up to their house, the first thing that I was greeted with was the huge head of a Great Dane at my car window barking. I was just amazed at the size of that dog. I think their place had a swimming pool, but I don't remember swimming. I was thinking that I would sure like to live like that someday. I made it to the finals before losing 6–3, 10–8 to Bob Reynolds of Sacramento, California. Bob had been ranked ahead of me in the previous year and was a very good player.

At the end of the year, I ended up ranked #5 in the 1969 Boys 18 and Under Singles for the Northern California Section. I hadn't played enough national junior tennis tournaments to end up with a national ranking in the

Boys 18 and Under, primarily because that involved further travel and further expense for my folks, which they could not afford.

WAITING AT O'HARE

I continued through the afternoon checking the status of flights to Madison, Wisconsin, where my folks were living. The news had not changed. The airport was still shut down and there were no takeoffs or landings, due to the heavy fog. They didn't know when the airport might resume normal operations. It would depend upon when the fog would lift. The fog had been very heavy for most of our road travel through Missouri and Illinois. Based on what I had seen, there was no reason to expect the fog to lift any time soon, but it couldn't last forever.

So I was in a waiting mode. Air travel in those days was a lot more casual than it is today. There was no TSA or security screening equipment used before boarding your designated flight. There had been hijackings, which were, at that time, a major threat to airplanes. I would periodically go to the ticket windows and check to see if any planes would be leaving for Madison soon. My plan was to buy a stand-by ticket, and if there was room on the flight, I could simply board. The airport was crowded as there were many stranded passengers and we were getting close to the Christmas holidays. Not much I could do but bide my time.

OKLAHOMA CITY UNIVERSITY

In the fall of 1969, I was off on yet another major adventure. I was going to be living on my own and going to Oklahoma City University. My folks had always been strict, and I couldn't wait to get out from under their control. I had been pretty independent, having traveled to Oregon, Washington, Colorado, and Canada on my own. I was ready for this great adventure.

I had already picked out my college major. OCU was a small university with about 1,500 total students in 1969. That was about a thousand less than I had in high school. My folks had always favored a small school, perhaps believing that the student gets more attention in such an environment. That might be true, but I was ambivalent as to whether my university should be small or very large. When I received the list of possible majors in the OCU curriculum, I needed to decide. I started by picking those majors that I did not want. I kept discarding majors until there was just one left: economics. Why economics? I had been interested in politics in high school and earlier, being spurred on by the presidential campaign of Barry Goldwater. Economics would deal both with financial issues and political systems.

I was assigned to a dorm room. My roommate was one of my teammates, Arturo Rojas. Arturo was from Costa

Rica and was one of the top tennis players there. I soon met my coach, Ray O'Keefe, and the school's Athletic Director, Abe Lemons. Abe was a rather famous basketball coach. I also met my other teammates.

There was Australian Lindsay Straney, who was a sophomore. He would play #1 on our team for the upcoming 1970 season. Lindsay had a lot of international experience. He ended his tennis career having played the Wimbledon qualifier event three times, and the French Open qualifier event once. At 26, he was eight years older than I was. He played from the backcourt and used a heavily sliced backhand, but he didn't miss much and was a very tough match for opponents.

There was Jim Hill, who was a junior. Jim was a Texan, over six feet tall, with a very solid game. Jim relied on his big serve. He played #2 for us my freshman year. There was another Texan on our team who was also a junior, named John Burkman. John played below me in my first year of tennis, 1970.

Tony Dawson, another Australian, came to OCU as a freshman at the same time that I did. He was one year older than I was. I was unaware at the time that he had played in the 1968 Australian Open in the Men's Division. I knew that he was one of Australia's best juniors. Tony ended up playing one spot ahead of me on our team until our senior year. In 1972, Tony played in the Wimbledon and French Open Qualifying events. In 1975, he would go on to play in the Australian Open again, beat Tom Gorman in the Houston Open, and garner a world ranking of #234. Gorman had a world ranking of #30 at the time that Tony beat him and in 1974 was ranked in the top ten in the world. Tony and I played a lot of doubles together over the years for OCU.

In college tennis in the early 1970s, the teams typically had about nine players on scholarship. The top six would play singles and often would also play in the three doubles matches. That meant that there was a total of nine possible matches and it was the first team to reach five wins that would take the team contest. Often, particularly against weaker teams, we would play the singles and if we could win at least five out of six, we would simply not need to play the doubles. This allowed us to leave matches earlier than we might otherwise, which helped when we were traveling a lot.

We would travel with a school-owned station wagon. Quite often, we would only take seven players and the coach. It was a tight squeeze with two in the front seat, three in a middle seat, and three in a third set of seats. We would put our eight bags of tennis equipment and clothes into the back of the station wagon, and we were off. We traveled by car north through Kansas, Missouri, and into Illinois. To the west, we would travel up into Colorado to play schools there like Air Force and the University of Colorado. We didn't go very far east at all, but we did travel throughout Texas. It was a lot of driving, but Texas had long straight open roads with minimal traffic outside of the cities.

As a freshman, I was the butt of one team joke. I'm not sure how or why this occurred. There had never been anyone singled out before or after, so I guess it was just me. The team decided to go into downtown Houston to explore a bit. We went into Foley's Department store in the late afternoon. This department store had many floors and we went up them by escalator. At one point, I got on the escalator going up to the next floor and the player behind me started to get on, but then stepped off and spoke to another player nearby. Once I reached the top, I waited for the rest of the team to come up. No one followed me. I went back down one floor, but nobody was there. I searched the department store, but I couldn't locate them. Here I was, an 18-year-old, in a large metropolitan downtown area, that I didn't know, and without any transportation. Remember, there were no cell phones in those days. I had to start walking the streets looking for a pay telephone. It was getting dark and the downtown section looked a bit sketchy and not particularly safe. I called the hotel where the team was staying which was on the outskirts of Houston, maybe a half hour away. Jim Hill answered the phone, and after a good laugh, he said they'd come to pick me up. I never really did understand this, because they had to drive a half hour back to the hotel after leaving me at Foley's, and then another hour to come get me and drive back to the hotel. But apparently, they found it humorous enough to be worth it.

On one trip, we went to Reynosa, Mexico. I had never been before. We walked the streets, stopped in a few of the bars, and turned down the hookers who lined the streets. At the end of our travels was Pan American University in Edinburg at the southern tip of Texas. The distance to OCU from there was just short of 700 miles. We drove straight through what would normally take us about ten and a half hours to get home. We left after our matches in the evening. Tony was driving as dawn broke and I was in front next to him. We were the only two that were awake. I watched Tony increase the speed to 105 mph and hold it there for an hour and a half. It really wasn't dangerous. There were hardly any cars on the road and we could see far out in front of us. I appreciated the fact that we had saved time by covering over about 160 miles so quickly.

The curriculum at OCU was challenging. To my surprise, I loved economics and the professors loved me. I bought into the economic argument that the government borrows now to spur the economy and pays it back as the economy improves. As the years after college went by, I realized that government simply borrows more, never pays it back, and the debt grows. The government that would try to manage the economy was also the same government that I hated when it came to conscription for the Vietnam War. These days I believe in limited government leading to social and economic freedom. Back then, it was good to believe what my professors believed.

As a freshman, our tennis team's record was 16 wins against 11 losses. I played #4 most of that year behind Lindsay Straney, Jim Hill, and Tony Dawson. Arturo Rojas and John Burkman played the final two positions behind me. This was not the powerful team that had Colin Robertson, Karl Coombes, and Brian Wilkinson playing the top positions for them the year before. Brian had gone on the be a tennis pro in Kansas, while Colin had been asked by the President of OCU, at the behest of the Mayor of Oklahoma City, if he would take over the brand-new Oklahoma City Tennis Center. This was a very large public tennis center, with 18 courts available to residents of Oklahoma City. Colin's scholarship was left intact long enough for him to complete his degree.

Over the next three years, our team would become very strong as more powerful players were added. Karl Coombes, who had played for OCU previously, came back the following year. Karl was an Australian who had won the 1966 Australian Open Juniors Championship. He had wins over top players. As with most of the Australians on our team, Karl was a very personable guy. He and I got along well and often practiced together. He played #1 for the 1971 and 1972 OCU teams. Karl had played in the 1967 Australian Open, the 1968 U.S. Open, and the 1970 Australian Open. He would go on to get a high ranking of #162 in the world after leaving college and going back out on the tour.

Dale Power was a Canadian who came to OCU having been a top Canadian junior tennis player. He had won the Canadian National Junior Championships in 1967. He was also drafted by the Montreal Canadians of the National Hockey League (NHL) out of high school. He played one year of minor league hockey before coming to OCU. After OCU, he returned to the Fort Wayne (Indiana) Komets for the 1974–75 hockey season and led the team with 29 goals and a total of 78 points. He tried out for the Buffalo Sabres and another NHL team, but did not make their rosters. Shortly thereafter, he injured his knee and was told by doctors that it could not take more hits, so Dale returned to tennis. He was ranked #1 in Canadian tennis in 1979 and ranked in the top five a total of eight times. He was ranked in the top ten of Canadian Men's rankings 13 times between 1968 and 1983. He also has the best singles Davis Cup winning percentage for Canada of any Canadian player in history having won six of his eight matches. Dale went on to an ATP high singles ranking of #210 in the world. Dale and I also got along very well and we practiced together quite often.

Epaminondas Argyriou, known to us as "Nondas", was a player from Greece who joined our team for a couple of years when I was a sophomore. He was older and had played on the international circuit. He had also played on two Greek Davis Cup teams playing in singles and doubles in 1969 and just singles in 1970.

Brian Mitchell came to OCU from Canada. He had been a Canadian junior tennis player. Alan Dabney was a top junior from Oklahoma City. Both of them always played behind me.

During my senior year at OCU, we were joined by two top-notch Australian juniors. The first was Dennis Maddern from Melbourne. Along with Dennis came Steve Wedderburn from Sydney. Both Dennis and Steve were very strong tennis players.

Colin Robertson, Karl Coombes, Dale Power, and Steve Wedderburn would all end up inducted into the Oklahoma City University Athletics Hall of Fame. Dale was also inducted into the Canadian Tennis Hall of Fame.

In the spring of 1970, I started making plans to travel to Europe to play circuits over there including the Wimbledon and French Open Qualifying. Apparently, I had started too late. I was told that accommodations at the tournaments probably wouldn't be available. I decided to go back on the Pacific Northwest Circuit for the third consecutive year, this time to play strictly in the adult tournaments since I was no longer eligible for the Juniors.

CHAPTER 17
1970

BACK ON THE PACIFIC NORTHWEST CIRCUIT

My results on the Pacific Northwest circuit were mediocre at best. I never advanced as far as the quarterfinals in any of these tournaments. The men were extremely competitive and a variety of players from around the country would travel to play the Pacific Northwest tournament circuit since they were used for national rankings. I had a couple of good wins, but that was about it. I had beaten Ron Zielinski, who was ranked #6 in the Pacific Northwest Men's rankings in 1969. I also had a win over Earl O'Neill, who had just won the 1970 NCAA Division II Men's Singles Championships.

I made some friends and hitting partners on this 1970 Pacific Northwest circuit. One was John Fort, an Arizona State Player who had also played for Brigham Young University and Santa Monica Junior College. John was playing exceptionally well and went on to win the Oregon State Championships that year. John won the singles again and the doubles in 1971.

Another player who was drawn to our little group was Dean Paul Martin. Dean, sometimes known as "Dino" and later Dean Paul, was the son of Dean Martin, the popular singer who was part of the "Rat Pack" with Frank Sinatra, Sammy Davis, Jr., Joey Bishop, and Peter Lawford. Dino was actually quite shy. He and I practiced a lot together during those weeks on the tour. He was never able to win a set against me. There were some parties thrown at the various tennis locations for the players. John, Dean, and I would go. This was good for us because Dean would attract quite a few girls, so we would get a chance to talk to them. For me, nothing ever resulted from these interactions, but it made the parties more fun to go to.

When he was in his early teens, Dean Paul was part of a band called Dino, Desi, and Billy made up of Dean Paul, Desi Arnez Jr., and Billy Hinsche. Desi was the son of Desi Arnez and Lucille Ball. Their first audition was for Frank Sinatra, who owned Reprise Records, the label for Dean Martin. They had a few U.S. Billboard Hot 100 hits making it to #17 and #25 on the charts in 1965. This success was all before any member of the group had reached 15 years of age. Also, in 1965, they played on "The Dean Martin Show." They appeared in the Dean Martin film "Murderer's Row" performing a song. They toured as the opening act for the Beach Boys. They also opened for such popular bands and musical personalities as Paul Revere and the Raiders, Tommy Roe, Sam the Sham, the Loving Spoonful, and The Mamas and the Papas. The band broke up in 1969, when Desi joined his mother's show "Here's Lucy" and Billy wanted to start university studies.

So he was famous and popular. However, the reason that Dean Paul was not interested in the girls at these parties was because he was in love with the actress Olivia Hussey. He went on to marry her the following year. She was coming off of great cinematic success from playing Juliet in the movie Romeo and Juliet. Dean Paul had been a pilot and was a Captain in the California Air National Guard. In 1987 his F-4 Phantom jet fighter crashed in the San Bernardino

Mountains during a snowstorm. Both he and his weapons systems officer were killed. He was only 35 years old at the time. It was just tragic.

OKLAHOMA CITY UNIVERSITY

When I got back to college for my sophomore year in the late summer of 1970, our tennis team was hearing a rumor. It was hard for us to believe this rumor, but it turned out to be true. Dr. Ray O'Keefe, our OCU tennis coach, was head of the two-man philosophy department at OCU with Dr. Leo Werneke. What we heard and had later confirmed was that Ray and Leo had gone to Alaska to hunt bear. They were in a cabin about 25 miles from civilization when Ray was accidentally shot. Ray O'Keefe was dead. This was simply unbelievable. The tennis season wasn't until spring, so there was time to wait for the University to decide what to do about the team leadership.

What they did was to hire an athlete who had played basketball, baseball, and tennis for OCU in the early 1950s. Arnold Short was hired as the tennis coach. Arnold was smart, athletically talented, and very kind. He also was an exceptionally good tennis player. I never worried that he could beat the better players on our team including myself, but he wasn't that far behind us. He was raised and went to high school in Weatherford, Oklahoma which is about 70 miles directly west of Oklahoma City on Interstate 40. Arnold was one of the top basketball players in the country during his three years of playing varsity ball. Back in those days, freshmen were not allowed to compete at the collegiate varsity level. Arnold was a 6'3" guard who became the University's first of eight NCAA Division I All-American basketball players. In his senior year, 1953–1954, he averaged 27.8 points per game and finished 4th in the national scoring race. He was drafted 13th by the NBA, but opted to play in the Amateur Athletic Union (AAU) instead. He made the 1956 Olympic basketball team but became injured and his roster spot had to be replaced. He was allowed to travel to Melbourne, Victoria, Australia with the team.

I have seen film of Arnold in action, and boy, could he shoot the basketball. Before I knew how well he could shoot, I saw him demonstrate his prowess in an unexpected way. We had a tennis match against Oral Roberts University at their Tulsa, Oklahoma campus. It had started to rain and they moved our tennis matches indoors. The Oral Roberts basketball team, which was among the top 20 Division I teams in the country at the time, was finishing up their practice as we came in. One of the basketballs came over to us and Arnold picked it up. He was standing on the sideline, just out of bounds, when he put the ball behind his head and launched it. Swish! I could see that the Oral Roberts players who saw him shoot it were looking incredulous. I could just imagine them saying "Yeah, right…very lucky!." The player who caught the ball coming through the basket passed it back to Arnold as if to say "show us that again." Arnold caught the ball, positioned it behind his head and shot it again with the same "swish" result! Now the player catching the ball as it came through the basket looked irritated as if saying "you can't be that lucky." He passed the ball to Arnold one more time, and for the 3rd time in a row, Arnold demonstrated his great shooting ability with his 3rd straight swish. This time, the player catching the ball under the hoop kept the ball, and walked off. These Oral Roberts basketball players were really good and you could tell that they were truly amazed that Arnold could do what most of them could not. Of course, they had no idea who he was, or why he was able to make those shots.

Another interesting situation occurred when the Virginia Slims Tennis Circuit came to Oklahoma City in 1971 and 1972. This was the precursor to the Women's Tennis Association (WTA). There was a group of nine women who went on tour led by American Billie Jean King, who is one of the all-time greats in women's tennis. She won 39 grand slam titles, including 12 in singles, 16 in doubles, and 11 in mixed doubles. On this tour with her were Americans Rosie Casals, Nancy Richey, Peaches Bartkowicz, Kristy Pigeon, Valerie Ziegenfuss, Julie Heldman, Australians Kerry Melville Reid and Judy Tegart-Dalton.

The players on our team often spoke about the ability of the women tennis players compared to the men. One of the players had had a conversation with the #3 British Men's Singles player who happened to be married to the #3 US Women's Singles player. This British player had apparently told of practicing with his wife. He had said that when they would play five sets, she could not get one game. To those who don't know tennis this may seem far-fetched, but let me assure you that it is not. Tennis is a game of consistency, but it is also a game of power and foot speed. The differences were more pronounced in the era of wood racquets because it was harder to hit ground stokes with power.

This point was further reinforced by Tony Dawson, the Australian who had joined OCU at the same time that I did. During these discussions, I asked Tony if he thought I could beat the top women players. He told me that I would easily beat the top women in tennis. He told me the story of playing in Australia when he was growing up. He was playing a girl about 1 year younger than Tony when both were juniors. This particular woman went on to win seven women's grand slam championships. Tony told me that he would play her almost every day on grass. They would play one set and Tony said that she never got more than two games off of him in any one set.

One day I was practicing indoors on wood at OCU's Fredrickson Field House. I think I was hitting with Nondas, our Greek Davis Cupper. Two people approached our court and asked me if they could share the court with Nondas and I, so that they could practice. I said "Sure," and Nondas and I moved over to hit on half a court. The player who came onto my side of the court was the great Billie Jean King. She was hitting with her husband at the time, Larry King. As we hit the ball, I was struck by how much harder we were hitting the ball than the Kings were. I could visually see that the differences between Men's and Women's tennis were indeed substantial.

Years later, my sister Jayne told me that she knew Larry King, who had settled in the same city that Jayne lives in.

The tennis team was also recruited to call lines in a mixed doubles exhibition during the Virginia Slims of Oklahoma City tournament. I believe that Billie Jean and Rosie paired individually with Colin Robertson and Jim Hill. I was calling one of the service lines. I don't remember who won, but it was fun and entertaining.

Another fascinating encounter showing skill differences was brought out in a discussion between Lindsay Straney, one of my Australian teammates, and a student named Harvey. Harvey had been a pretty good high school player in New Jersey, which is where he was from. Lindsay was incredibly steady meaning that he didn't miss shots often. Harvey was telling Lindsay that he could get at least one game off of him. Lindsay argued that there was no way Harvey could win a game. Lindsay was quite the gambler and typically won when he bet. He told Harvey that he would bet that Harvey could not win a match consisting of a single set. To make it more interesting, he would start with Harvey given a 5–0 and 40–0 lead and serving. So for the first three points Harvey would have match points and only need a single point to win. I thought that might be a little risky for Lindsay because one lucky shot and Harvey would win. The match began and Lindsay won the first 3 points. There were some good rallies during those points as well. At three points all, the score was deuce and it would take a two-point advantage to win that game. Harvey got to his advantage twice more in that first game, but Lindsay wouldn't let him win. Once Lindsay won that first game, everyone watching knew it was over. Lindsay only lost a few more points and Harvey was never close to winning a game after that. Lindsay proved his point with this 7–5 victory.

Dale Power told me another story about Harvey and Lindsay. In another bet, Harvey and a friend of his were to play Lindsay and Dale to a doubles match. I assume that Harvey's friend was probably about the same caliber of tennis player as he was. I know that Harvey didn't understand the huge divide that there was between good players and circuit players. I am sure that Lindsay may have instigated the bet when Harvey may have challenged the assertion as to how much better we were. Dale told me that Harvey and his partner would use normal equipment. Dale and Lindsay used a frying pan and a racquet with no strings. Dale said that the net player would use the wooden racquet and try to strike the ball on the edge of the racquet. If the net player missed, the player with the frying pan would play from the backcourt, lobbing the ball into the air and deep into the opponent's court. They would trade the frying pan back and forth to receive and serve. If you don't know tennis well, you might not guess this, but Harvey and his partner could not get a game.

For these kinds of challenges, you have to keep in mind that Lindsay had beaten Wimbledon champions, and Dale was to become the number one Men's player in Canada. To be that good, you had to play all the time and become extraordinarily adept at the use of the racquet. We can bounce balls on the edge of the racquet. We can hit balls behind our backs and between our legs. We could place the ball within a foot of almost any target that we aimed at. Harvey didn't want to believe in the great disparity in ability when these bets were being made, but I'll bet he did afterwards.

THE TWISTERS HIT

Oklahoma City is at the center of "Tornado Alley." Storms passing through Oklahoma City on April 30th, 1970 spawned three tornadoes. The first tornado appeared just after midnight, crossing over mostly open territory a couple of miles northwest of the city. Two other tornadoes made their appearance about an hour later. These latter two tornadoes were identified as the Mustang tornado and the Camelot tornado.

The Mustang tornado passed within two miles of Oklahoma City University to the west while causing severe damage along the path where it touched down. All students in my dorm, and I am sure in the other dorms, were awakened and told to go to the basement. As a Californian, I had never seen a tornado. We were told that it was close, so instead of going immediately to the basement, I headed outside to see it. Well, it was night time and raining hard, so sighting the tornado was not possible. What was unusual was watching the rain swirling and falling with a strong circularly spinning wind. But that was all I was able to see and I don't think I was out there for more than 30 seconds before heading back into the basement.

The Mustang tornado damage began at a farm a little over 30 miles to the southeast of OCU. Then, in Mustang, the City Hall and a shopping center were damaged.

Mustang is a little over 17 miles southeast OCU. As the tornado continued to move to the northwest, it crossed Highway I-40 damaging two semis which were blown off of the highway and onto their sides. It appears that this was roughly four miles from campus. As the Mustang tornado entered Oklahoma City, it continued on its path from southwest to northeast through the city as it left over a half mile width of destruction.

In Oklahoma City, there were damages estimated at $6.3 million in 1970. In 2019, that would be over $40 million. Damage in Oklahoma City included 215 poles down according to electric utility officials, 293 businesses, 8 schools, 12 churches, 300 signs, and 1473 homes. The damage included roofs rotated on houses. The storm went on to cause a bit more damage after leaving Oklahoma City. During the 100-block area where the tornado touched down, some of the most extensive damage occurred just three miles from OCU. Here a roof from a small grocery store landed in the front yard of a residence nearly a block away. Roofs were also torn off of two sections of an apartment complex. Homes and businesses in the area took a beating.

As the tornado came closer, a couple of automobile dealerships suffered extensive damage. A restaurant had a wall collapse and another was completely destroyed leaving only its sign. The tornado was now passing 1.4 miles from where I was sheltered. As the storm continued to the northwest and away from me, it continued to cause more damage. An automobile was picked up and deposited in the living room of one home several houses away. Another home had a steel beam thrust through it while it was moved off of its foundation with the walls bowed out and the roof thrown in the yard of a nearby home. Tornadoes often behave oddly. In one area to the north of OCU, houses on one side of a street were hit hard by the twister and homes across the street were not touched.

The Camelot tornado followed a path to the west of the Mustang tornado tearing another path of destruction through Oklahoma City. This was further away from OCU, which was to the east of the Mustang tornado's path. The next day, some of my friends and I drove around the nearby neighborhoods and saw the damage. I still marvel to this day at how only two persons received minor injuries and nobody died.

This wasn't the only wild weather that I saw in Oklahoma City. In the summer, I saw a dashboard that was warped by sitting in the humid heat of summer. It was wavy, rising and falling. I also saw a hailstorm where the sizable falling hailstones were so bad that it left every exposed car damaged. It was as if the cars took hundreds of strikes each from ballpeen hammers. But when the tornadoes came to town, another amazing experience in my life had taken place!

RACISM IN OKLAHOMA

I had never really seen racism in the upper Midwest or in California. The 1960s had been a time of great racial upheaval throughout the country. It is not that we lived without other races nearby. In Wisconsin, our cities and towns often contained Native Americans. It seemed as though everyone lived in relative harmony.

In California in the 1960s, if you lived in the suburbs, as we did in Sunnyvale, you were a bit isolated from other races. We only had a handful of students from different races at Homestead. I never saw any of the strife that was displayed on our television sets with the race riots that occurred in the 1965 Watts section of Los Angeles or in 1967 in Detroit.

I had several situations, incidents, and observations about race while I was in Oklahoma. One observation was that African Americans on campus that had come from the New York City area or the Chicago area seemed to have a chip on their shoulder. They tended to stay together in small groups and some of them were a bit surly. The African Americans on campus that were from Oklahoma were friendlier. I had great sympathy for the plight of black people, particularly in the South. The University in general was liberal and had students from around the world.

One situation was that Dale Power, the Canadian player on our tennis team, had a black roommate who was a very nice guy. The odd thing was that Dale's roommate wanted to join one of the four fraternities that were on campus. The one that he wanted to join was all white and seemed to me opposed to having black members. He was friendly with many of the members of the fraternity and tried very hard to become a member. I don't believe that this particular fraternity had ever had a black man as one of their brothers. He couldn't get in and there was no reason that I could see except that he was black and they weren't ready to accept blacks.

I met and dated a beautiful African American girl at OCU. She looked to me to be an ebony goddess. I think she was a year younger than me, so this was probably in the fall of 1970. I saw nothing out of the ordinary with this relationship. I remember going out with her a few times. After a few dates she sat me down to talk. She said that we were going to have to stop dating. She said her family had told her she needed to stop seeing me because I was white. She said that "you may not agree with this," but she felt that she owed it to her family to listen to them and do what they asked. I was not happy about this. I thought it was a new era, and if we wanted, we should be able to see each other. I realize now that her family was most likely concerned for her safety. At the time, I just saw it as more racism from her family. The summer after we dated, I was at a laundromat just off of campus. I had not seen this girl since she had said that we should stop dating. I ran into a friend of hers and I asked how she was doing. I was told that she had died from a brain aneurism very suddenly and unexpectedly. This seemed so unusual that I felt it must be true. Very sad to lose your life at such a young age.

The most vivid example of racism on campus came one evening when quite a few hooligans drove up to the campus, parked on a city street, and, as a group, began to look for OCU African American students, apparently to beat them up. I would guess that there were seven to ten of them and they appeared to be older high school students. The OCU school grounds were not that big. Parking on the surrounding streets, one could walk to the center of campus in about a minute. I remember that most of the African American students flooded out of the dorms. The attacks must have started and the yelling, both from the attackers and from those being attacked, had quite a few of us venturing outside to see what was going on. I watched as these hoodlums went after every African American that they saw. OCU didn't have that many African Americans, but they made up half of the basketball team. As you might expect, the basketball players were quite large. I remember the average-sized attackers getting their clocks cleaned as they went right after these big ball players. Our basketball center at the time was a powerfully built 6'9" player named Willie. He grabbed the front of the shirts of two attackers and with one shirt in each hand he lifted them both into the air and brought them together very quickly. It appeared that their heads collided. He let them go and they both collapsed. This attack ended as fast as it had started. The beaten attackers made a hasty retreat to their cars. I don't think any of the campus African Americans were hurt. I had hoped that the attackers had learned a lesson, but probably not the right one. This situation brought it home to me that racism was definitely alive in Oklahoma despite the move toward civil rights in the 1960s.

The last example that I recall was when Coach Short had the tennis team do some community relations by going into the northeast section of Oklahoma City. I had not been to that area, but I was shocked. Going into that section of Oklahoma City, I found out what true segregation looked like. We went from white suburbs into the black section of the city. Once we had crossed over into that area, I never saw another white face other than my teammates and my coach. The event was to provide some tennis instruction at a local high school in that section. I think the community was invited. We had a pretty large turnout and taught tennis lessons to all. I haven't been back to Oklahoma City in many years, but I suspect that it has changed voluntarily so that different races could live together throughout the city in harmony.

These situations and events left me knowing that Oklahoma was more racist than either Wisconsin or California had been in the early 1970s. I was never taught to be racist and did not understand racism. My dad's good friend, Dr. Larry, whom he had met at the Fairbrae Swim and Tennis Club in Sunnyvale, was an African American medical doctor. He became my doctor and he operated on me while I was in high school. I really liked him and appreciated his professionalism. Whenever I lived in the South Bay, I went to either him or his son, who was also a physician. I was with them for about 40 years until an insurance change forced me to look elsewhere.

Segregation was something that I thought should not be legislated out of existence, but was something that people should choose to dissolve. Every individual should be free to choose where he or she wants to live, even if that results in segregation. I would hope their choices would lead them to a multi-racial inclusiveness.

CHAPTER 21
1971

WINE, WOMEN, AND SEEKING LOVE

In high school, my best friend, Steve Sharp, took me to the beach with a number of people, including his girlfriend at the time. This was to be a nighttime firepit drinking party. This must have been during my junior year of high school, or perhaps the summer just after my junior year. I was not a drinker and had never had more than a sip previously. So this was a first, and what did I do? I established that I was an alcoholic, but I didn't recognize it until many, many years later. At this party, I had something like one beer and about half a gallon of red wine. I don't know anybody who does that on their first drinking excursion, unless they have a proclivity to alcohol. Steve got me home, but not before I had puked. There was no hiding this from my parents when Steve got me home. It took me at least two days to recover and I had a junior tennis tournament, which I played with a hangover, and did not play well. I also couldn't think about drinking red wine ever again.

As I stated earlier, I was also very shy around girls in high school. I hardly dated at all. I remember only one date, and that was a bit of a disaster, because the girl that I asked out lived across the street from us. I didn't want my parents to know, but I needed to borrow their car for the date. I somehow managed to borrow the car and not let them see me pick her up. I think we went to a drive-in

117

movie, but I don't remember clearly. When I dropped her off, I may have gotten a quick peck of a kiss or I may have just said good night and that was it.

I also never went to a prom. I can't say why. Maybe I was just disappointed that girls that I may have liked didn't like me in the same way. I had tried during 7th and 8th grades to ask a couple of girls if they would like to get together, but the answer was no. So I focused on my sports activities.

When I got to college as a normal red-blooded male, I was interested in girls, but I was terribly inexperienced when it came to sex and dating. I went to parties to meet new people, but I was in a new and unfamiliar city. I had started drinking beer, when I could get it. I went to one party at Colin Robertson's apartment. This was in high rise where Colin and his wife Phyllis lived. I may have brought my bottle, or maybe it was part of the party alcohol, but I had access to a quart bottle of vodka. I started drinking, and in two hours I had finished that quart bottle. It doesn't take much imagination to know that this is a recipe for disaster. I ended up out on their balcony some 20 plus stories high, throwing up over the railing. Oklahoma City is always very windy. And I am pretty sure that as I threw up, the wind was blowing the contents onto other balconies below. Not good! I should have figured out right then and there that I should not drink, ever, but I didn't.

The drinking age in Oklahoma was 21. Pubs near campus often just let college students in to drink. I remember that I convinced a good friend of mine, David N., to give me his old expired driving license. Driving licenses in those days had the person's information typed directly on to a card that served as the license and there was no picture. I went about changing the expiration date so that I could use that fake license to get into bars. I would often drink a couple of pitchers, which was about 60 ounces of beer each. One of my favorite places to drink was The Brass Keg, which was owned by a soccer-playing fellow from Peru named Chico. We had a lot of fun at his bar, but I became too consistent of a customer.

Speaking of soccer, OCU put together a formidable soccer team as a club. They were recruiting a lot of the foreign players who grew up playing soccer. Chico played and an Englishman named Tom played goalie. OCU students from many different countries joined the team and some non-students who were friends with Chico. Many of our tennis team members joined and I played as well. We played in the State of Oklahoma "B" or second level league. We didn't really know how good we were. It turned out that we were really good. We quite easily beat all of the teams in the "B" league. I am pretty sure that we didn't lose a match. We were declared the "B" league champions. A match between us and the "A" league champions had been set up. This would determine who was really the best soccer team in Oklahoma. We played the match in Tulsa. We just had too much speed and skill. We won four goals to one.

I didn't date much during my first two years at OCU. I didn't really have a relationship until I met Pam in the spring of 1971. She was a dark-haired beauty with a very nice figure. I don't remember how we met or where our first date was. I do remember that we went back to her place after our first date. It was an apartment where she was living with her mother. It was late and her mother had gone to bed. Pam told me that her mother was sleeping upstairs and wouldn't come down at this hour. We started kissing and one thing led to another. I lost my virginity that night on the living room floor, somewhat concerned that her mother would catch us in the act.

This all happened in April, less than a month before my 20th birthday. At least I could say that I was still a teenager when I lost my virginity although I was almost through with two years of college. This was the 1970s. The AIDS epidemic was not recognized or even known by most Americans until 1981. Avoidance of pregnancy occurred primarily through the female's use of birth control pills. During my single days prior to 1981, I went under the assumption that it was the woman's responsibility to be taking birth control pills, if she was ready to have sex and wished to avoid pregnancy. These things were not thought out in my relationship with Pam.

Pam and I started a very heated relationship over the next few months. After maybe a month, Pam informed me that she was pregnant. I was very surprised. She thought it would be best that she should go to Kansas and have an abortion. Abortions were not legal in Oklahoma, but they were legal in Kansas. Instead, I asked her to marry me. My dad was down in Oklahoma City shortly after this and he did get to meet her. I suspect he was very worried about this situation, but I don't remember any of our conversations on the matter. After all, I didn't have a job, and my college scholarship and future tennis career could be at stake.

Not too long after that, Pam's best friend pulled me aside. She started telling me that I was just such a good guy that she couldn't let Pam continue with her story. Her friend told me, as she started to cry, that Pam didn't know who the father was. I could tell that she was telling me the truth. I think the other relationship happened just before I met her, but Pam had not been completely honest with me. I confronted her and although I do not remember that particular conversation, I broke up with her. Pam came to my summer workplace at the Oklahoma City Tennis Center and asked me for the money to pay for an abortion. I told her no. She said that she would take care of it and left. I never saw nor heard from her again. I like to believe that I didn't want an abortion on my conscience. I still, to this day, ask myself if I allowed this woman to abort my child, without at least trying to intervene. I will never know the truth.

After that first summer of 1970 playing on the Pacific Northwest tennis circuit, I had decided to stay in Oklahoma City and work for Colin Robertson at the OKC Tennis Center. I would teach classes, string racquets, and monitor the desk. The desk monitoring was a city job consisting of assigning the courts and collecting whatever small fee the city charged. We were paid the minimum wage of $1.75 per hour for that job. $1.75 doesn't seem like a lot in today's economy, but it does demonstrate the effects of inflation. I had bought a used Toyota sedan from my folks for $1,000. I remember filling up my car's gas tank in Oklahoma City, which was about ten gallons, for $2.20 on one occasion. That is the entire tank, not the price per gallon. The price per gallon was in the low 20 cent range.

The teaching and stringing jobs were paid by Colin. Those of us given that work would earn much more than minimum wage. I also remember that Colin set up initial group tennis lessons and he would recruit members of the tennis team and others who knew how to teach. At the time there were 18 courts at the newly constructed center.

For Colin's group introductory classes, he would put up to 20 people on a court. It was a challenge to keep 20 people busy and learning. It was too many people, but the turnout was huge. I know most of the courts were in use and if each court had 20 people on it, then we would have had close to 300 people taking introductory lessons.

One day while I was working the desk monitoring job, I received a telephone call. I was very surprised when the caller announced himself as David Hall, the governor of Oklahoma at the time. He asked my name and whether or not I could help to arrange a tennis match for him. He wanted to play some doubles. I told him that I was pretty sure that I could. I had gotten to know a lot of the regulars who attended the center and made some telephone calls. It did not take long for three of our regulars to accept the offer to play with the governor. I called him back and he came out to tennis center where the doubles match was played. Randomly receiving a telephone call from a sitting governor was just one more unusual incident in my life.

Upon following David Hall's career, I found out that he served as the governor of Oklahoma from January 11, 1971 to January 13, 1975. He was unsuccessful in his bid for re-election in 1974. Three days after Hall left office, he was indicted on federal racketeering and extortion charges. He was convicted of bribery and extortion. After failing to overturn the verdicts through appeals, he served 19 months of a 3-year sentence at the Federal Correctional Institution, Safford, a prison for male inmates in Arizona. After completing this sentence, he was disbarred by the Oklahoma Bar Association, which prevented him from practicing law in Oklahoma. He moved to La Jolla, California, where he worked in real estate and other ventures.

He went on to publish an autobiography in 2012 entitled "Twisted Justice: A Memoir of Conspiracies and Personal Politics." David Hall died in a San Diego, California hospital on May 6, 2016 at the age of 85.

Typically, the tennis players on our team were short of money and looking for ways to earn some. We received the NCAA authorized stipend of $15 per month which was intended to be used for laundry. We did receive free books, room, board, and of course an education. We had the extra advantage of being able to work at the Oklahoma City Tennis Center, but we also worked other jobs. One of those jobs that I worked while at OCU was waiting on tables for conventions. The company that hired us would feed attendees in very large rooms with as many as eight people at a round table. We would deliver the set menu. As with many of these encounters, the company was trying to minimize expenses by keeping the number of waiters to a minimum. At one such convention, I received the assignment to handle five tables of eight people each. Waiting on 40 people was a bit too much.

Another interesting adventure was working as a concert "barker." I was placed in the lobby of the concert hall to sell trinkets and artifacts. It was an exciting job because the performer was Elvis Presley. Even in the early 1970s, he was still a huge deal. I was placed behind a mobile counter where opera glasses and other Presley memorabilia were to be sold. I was fairly busy, but on at least one occasion during the performance, there was no one in the lobby. I was able to go to the entrance, open the door, and watch a minute or so of his performance. It was a commission job and I sold enough to earn $21, but a couple of items were missing and I was docked $6. Still, I made $15, or $5 an hour, which was pretty good at the time, and gained another very interesting experience.

As the summer of 1971 progressed, I had a couple of other encounters with women. My roommate that year was David T. David was a very conservative guy who was also a youth minister at one of the Methodist churches in the area. I had come with David to his church to help him out. I don't know what he thought he was doing by bringing me, but maybe he thought he could eventually recruit me in as a member of the church. Possibly, he just wanted my company. He and I had acted as youth counselors for teens on a camping trip over one weekend and I think David appreciated the help. Some of the teenage girls were interested in me. Although I wasn't much older than they were, I had no intention of getting involved with girls who were not at least 18.

It was at the church's youth center that I met a different group of teenagers who were hanging out there. One of them was Kathy. Kathy was a beautiful brunette with long hair. She had just graduated from a local high school and was going to be headed to college in the fall. She had a boyfriend named Tim, from high school, who was also at the youth center during that first visit. She and Tim weren't exclusive, at least at the time that I met her, and so I knew she was not tied up in a relationship. I asked her out, she accepted, and we hit it off.

That summer the romance blossomed, with our love growing as time progressed. We were definitely looking forward to a future together. She had chosen to go to college at Oklahoma State University (OSU) in Stillwater, which was 75 miles northwest of Oklahoma City. Starting in the fall of 1971, we were seeing each other primarily on the weekends and holidays. We wrote letters, which is what was often done back then, to stay in touch. Two or three letters per week were often sent. Kathy's letters always professed her love for me and that nothing in the world could ever change that. Kathy didn't like Oklahoma State. Kathy and her roommate had decided to transfer to Oklahoma University (OU) which was about 15 miles south of Oklahoma City.

Kathy's mom didn't want me dating her. They were church-going Christians and they didn't want their daughter dating a non-believer. I believed in God, but had never joined any formal religion. Kathy and I had begun to discuss eventual marriage. She had even suggested that during the summer of 1972, we should live together in an apartment in Norman. I also know that my roommate David had stopped by Kathy's home on one occasion. During his conversation with Kathy's mother, he asked her "When are Todd and Kathy getting married?." David may have been asking a serious question, but the topic was not something that Kathy's mother would have appreciated.

CHAPTER 22
1971

MY FAMILY RETURNS TO WISCONSIN

My folks, who had been living in Sunnyvale, moved to the Madison, Wisconsin, area at the end of October of 1971 and arrived in early November. Since they were born and raised in Wisconsin, I think they just felt more comfortable there, plus my Dad got a book-selling job opportunity in the upper Midwest. Mom had only been working as a substitute teacher in California, which was a situation brought about by the union's control of the California teachers and their employment. By going back to Wisconsin, Mom could get a full-time teaching job, and that would help out the family finances greatly.

I always joked that my folks had moved in the dead of night, and had not told me about it or where they were going, in an effort to lose me, but I found them. I know when I found out that the family had moved, I was very surprised. Being in Wisconsin made the travel to see my family shorter and a little easier than when they were in California. At least that's what I thought at the time.

My sister Nancy told me about my family's trip to Wisconsin. In 1971, Jayne was 13 and Nancy was 11. On Saturday, October 23rd, Nancy had stayed overnight at her friend Heather's house. The next morning, which was a Sunday, Heather's family took her to either an early brunch or late breakfast. She let Heather's father know that Dad had wanted her home by 9:00 AM. Heather's father had one of his older children call Mom and Dad and let them know that Nancy would be late. Nancy was a bit relieved, but still thought that she would be in big trouble when she got home. To her relief, when she got home she was not in trouble. The folks were working on the house for the move because the packers were coming the next day.

My family most likely left Sunnyvale on Wednesday, October 27th. The route would be to head north along the east side of the San Francisco Bay or head out to the central valley from Danville. Both routes lead to Highway 80 and passed through Sacramento, California, and then on to Reno, Nevada. The next major stop would be Salt Lake City, Utah. They probably arrived there on the evening of the 28th. There, Nancy thinks she remembers seeing the Mormon Tabernacle. From Salt Lake City, my family would continue on Highway 80 which heads up into Wyoming. They were in for an adventure.

As they approached Evanston, Wyoming, Nancy remembers that they saw semi after semi pulled off of the road. Mom and Dad kept commenting on it wondering if there was a semi convention in town. Nancy thinks that Dad must have stopped at a gas station or a motel and found out that there was an early season blizzard that was to hit Evanston that day. The Friday, October 29th, 1971 blizzard was severe enough to have stranded about 1,000 motorists. There were not enough motels or hotels, so churches and private homes opened their doors. Also, the local National Guard Armory was opened. The mystery of the semis was solved. Back then, the truckers driving semis used Citizen Band (CB) radios to communicate. It was a short distance radio that was often used to communicate locations of highway patrol, or freeway slowdowns, such as accidents. In this case, the impending storm had been broadcast and the semis were pulled off of the roads to wait until conditions were better.

The weather was bad enough that Mom and Dad did not want to drive any farther. They went to the National Guard Armory, which was all that was available to wait out the storm. Nancy remembers that Mom and Jayne slept that night like logs. Jayne always seemed to sleep well, but Mom seldom did. Mom sleeping soundly was a surprise. Dad and Nancy, on the other hand, could not get to sleep. They walked around the inside of the Armory. There were lots of occupied sleeping bags which were probably supplied by the Armory. Nancy said "There was the quietest poker game going on. You could only hear the clinking of the poker chips. Several guys had their sleeping bags in a circle with the poker game going on in the center of their circle where the heads of their sleeping bags were. They were on their stomachs and forearms playing poker."

The next day, Nancy did not feel well. Mom and Dad took her to a doctor and found out that she had strep throat. Those in charge of the emergency shelters were now able to find a hotel room for my family because they did not want to infect others at the Armory. Who knew that having strep throat could be a good thing? Nancy remembers looking out of the window of the hotel and seeing snow falling. She also remembers how happy Dad was to be in a hotel room. The next day, October 31st, they were able to drive to Rock Springs, Wyoming, which was just over 100 miles from Evanston, but they had to stay there. The roads were still very bad. After that, they were able to drive through Nebraska and Iowa before arriving at their new home in Madison, Wisconsin.

CHAPTER 23
1972

OKLAHOMA CITY UNIVERSITY

My roommate during my junior year was a Japanese student named Yoshi. Yoshi told me that he had earned a martial arts black belt in Japan. He told me that he did not like the U.S. system of martial arts where there were many belts leading to a black belt and then advancing degrees of black belt. He said that in Japan, there were only two belts, white or black. I think he said that it took about six years to achieve his black belt in Japan.

Yoshi had some issues. He often drank too much and he liked to demonstrate his skills. He once asked me to watch him do a kick. He stood in our dorm room, jumped up and kicked the ceiling which was about eight feet high. It was impressive, to say the least. At one point in the spring of 1972, Yoshi got a job as a bouncer. Now Yoshi was only about 5'7" and maybe 135 lbs. I did not think this was a good idea. Bouncers are usually very big guys who can stop fights before they start because their size will intimidate even drunks. Yoshi did not have this advantage. He did tell me that he had to take out a few guys and he liked to hit them just hard enough that they wouldn't fall so that he could hit them again if they still wanted to continue to fight.

One day, he told me that he was coming back to OCU and he was attacked by five guys. He said that he put the first two or three down and that was enough for the other guys to run away.

Yoshi also became a martial arts trainer of sorts to my teammate Dennis Maddern. Dennis had come to OCU at the start of the 1972 year. OCU had a full contingent of scholarships, so Dennis was red-shirted which means that he was given a scholarship to cover that first semester, but he wouldn't play and would retain four full years of college playing eligibility. I had a different roommate named Zach in my senior year. Yoshi was a time bomb and I didn't want him going off near me. Dennis continued working with him and the following year, I noticed that Dennis could really stretch to get down low for his volleys. I knew this was a result of working on his flexibility with Yoshi.

In January of 1972, Kathy and I went to the Great White North of Wisconsin. There, she would meet my parents and sisters. I don't remember much about that trip, but I do remember going from Madison, where my folks lived, and later on to Reedsburg, Wisconsin, where my cousin Randy, was the point guard for his high school basketball team. I believe that we drove first to my Aunt Dido's home in La Valle, Wisconsin, to meet my aunt, who was Randy's mom and my dad's sister along with her husband, Jordan. After that, we went to the basketball game. Reedsburg is a small town, and Randy was not only the starting point guard on the basketball team, but he had been the starting quarterback on their football team.

As to the trip as a whole, I have a foggy memory that Kathy was shocked. Wisconsin is quite a bit different from Oklahoma and my folks were different from her parents. I don't know if anything came out of all that which might have affected her attitude toward our relationship. I doubt it, but I am not certain.

Another interesting thing about Oklahoma City was that big-name bands would often pass through the city on concert tours and the tickets were remarkably low-priced. I was able to see some of the all-time great acts of the 1970s, such as Chicago, the Moody Blues, and Cat Stevens. There was also a concert in the OCU Fredrickson Field House, where our basketball games were held. This was a relatively small venue of only a little over 3,000 seats. The band was Santana, led by the fabulous guitarist Carlos Santana. Here though, the tickets were more expensive for some reason, and I opted not to go.

The Field House was close to our dorms and I wandered over there near the end of the concert. To my surprise, the doors were wide open and no one was preventing entry, so I went in. I immediately knew why they had been left open. The small venue must not have had its air conditioning available. It had to be over 100°F. inside. Nonetheless, I got in just in time for them to finish up the concert with a few of their hit songs. In particular, I got to hear them play "Evil Ways" and "Black Magic Woman." I missed most of the concert, but hearing those two songs was great!

Kathy and I continued with our relationship through the winter and into the spring of 1972. Easter was on April 2, 1972 and spring break was around that time. We would have about a week off from school. I think she had wanted to spend it on Padre Island, a barrier island off of the south coast of Texas. Kathy had a friend whose parents lived in Galveston. Galveston is located on Galveston Island and Pelican Island, which are also just off of the south Texas coast. Kathy and I drove down to Galveston to her friend's house. I think we may have stayed there one night, but then we drove along the island. I don't know exactly where we stopped, but it was likely on South Padre Island. We swam in the Gulf of Mexico and at night we pitched a tent on the beach. This trip did not go well. While swimming in the Gulf, Kathy was surrounded by a large number of jelly fish, that were floating where the waters would take them. She noticed them too late and she was stung. She exited the waters as quickly as she could. The stings were quite painful. Also, on this trip, my car, which I had not had all that long, broke down. I had very little money and I did not want to ask my parents for money since I saw it as a reduction of my independence. In the end, I called my folks to send the money to repair the car. In any case, the car was repaired and we made the roughly 500-mile drive back to Oklahoma City.

On Sunday evening, April 23rd, Kathy came to see me at OCU. We went to one of our cars and she told me that her old boyfriend Tim was back in Oklahoma City and she was leaving me for him. I believe that she said she had already slept with him. I had heard that Tim had joined the Army, but he must have been home on leave. This struck me like a lightning bolt out of the blue. I was expecting that Kathy and I would continue to head toward marriage. Here she was suddenly dumping me. I didn't know how she could do this to me or how she had been able to hide her true feelings so well. It was her loss, or at least that was what I told myself at the time. I was shocked, devastated, and angry, which was a strange combination. I know that I was using the anger to shield myself from as much of the pain as I could.

Two days later on Tuesday, April 25th, our tennis team had to play Oklahoma University on the OCU courts. We only had four courts, so two of the six singles matches went on the courts after the first two singles matches finished. Although we were among the top 15 teams in the country, OU was a very tough team. Matches were contests of six singles and then three doubles with five wins out of the nine matches determining the winner. OU won four of the singles matches that day, but Tony won his match and that brought the score to OU 4–OCU 1. I was still playing my singles match against Dale Quigley, whom I had beaten the previous year, 6–0, 6–0' at OU. Today, I dropped the first set against him, but I came back to win the next two sets. The score was then 4–2 in favor of OU. Tony and I played together in the #3 doubles match against Dale Quigley and I think it was Rick Lashley. Rick was to play 3rd doubles for OU with Dale in the Big Eight championships the following month and win it, so it was likely Rick. In the meantime, OCU's 1st and 2nd doubles teams finished with victories. Now the score was 4–4, and our match would determine which University would win the team match. We pulled out the win in three hard-fought sets. This meant that I had won two matches including the decider in our 5–4 come-from-behind victory over OU. This, for me, was a redemption for what Kathy had done to me. I was very proud of this achievement.

I loved playing against OU. They were a very good team and had been in the top ten in the country the year before I joined OCU. We played them at home and away every year except in 1972, when we only played them once. This was a total of seven matches. OCU won all of those matches, and I won all seven of my individual singles matches, as well. I do not remember ever losing a doubles match to them, either. This was another achievement that I take great pride in. Of course, it helped that I was playing #4 singles and below.

Oklahoma was the Team Big Eight Conference Tennis Champion from 1965 through 1974 which meant all four years that we played them. From 1970–1973, the Oklahoma tennis team won 28 of 36 possible Big Eight Singles and Doubles titles. They were no pushover. Oklahoma City University was an independent school not tied to any one conference. The Big Eight Conference in those days was made up of Iowa State University, the University of Nebraska, Kansas State University, the University of Kansas, Oklahoma State University, the University of Oklahoma, the University of Colorado, and the University of Texas. The Big Eight Conference was one of the premier conferences in the country for major athletic programs.

OCU matches with OU during my years of 1970–1973:

1970–April 10th at OCU = OCU 4–OU 3 and May 5th at OU = OCU 5–OU 4.

1971–April 28th at OU = OCU 7–OU 2 and May 4th at OCU = OCU 7–OU 2.

1972–April 25th at OCU = OCU 5–OU 4.

1973–at OU = OCU 6–OU 3 and at OCU = OCU 5–OU 3. No dates were found for these 1973 matches, but the timing was most likely early April and early May respectively.

On Saturday, April 29, 1972, I went out to the bars to celebrate my 21st birthday. I was now able to drink legally in Oklahoma. At the end of the night, I ran into a woman who was from Shawnee, Oklahoma. We hit it off, and although she was a bit reluctant at first, I talked her into letting me follow her in my car as she went back to her house. Shawnee was about 40 miles southwest of Oklahoma City. I believe it was past midnight when we arrived, but our night's activities were a nice birthday present for me. When morning came, I told her that I needed to get back to Oklahoma City. It was Sunday, so she may have been expecting me to stick around, but I thought it was best that I leave. As I said my good byes, she tried to talk me into staying. I was getting the idea that she wanted a full-blown relationship, which wasn't something I was interested in, particularly since I was less than a week past my break up with Kathy. I started to leave and she hugged me as if to prevent me from leaving. As I moved toward the door, she slid down my body and now had her arms wrapped around one of my legs. I quite literally dragged her across her living room floor to the front door where she finally let go. I was shocked by her reaction. I had no idea why she would be so insistent. No promises had been made, but in any case, that situation was too crazy for me, and now I was glad that my dorm was 40 miles away.

Tennis at OCU went very well except for my playing at #5 for most of the last 2 years that I was there. As a team, we went 16–11 for 1970, 22–3 for 1971, 21–3 for 1972 and 21–3 for 1973. Tennis West magazine preseason issue ranked the top 20 Collegiate Tennis teams in the nation listing all 6 singles players for each team. For 1972, they ranked us 11th in the United States. For 1973, they ranked us 13th in the country. Almost all of our losses in my last three years came to teams ranked in the top 10 in the NCAA Division 1 Rankings.

In 1972, we played the #1 team in the country, Trinity University of San Antonio, Texas. They traveled to

Oklahoma City to play us. We played at one of the local clubs so that there would be enough courts to be able to play all six singles matches at the same time. Trinity University had Richard Stockton, Brian Gottfried, Bob McKinley, Paul Gerken, Pancho Walthall, and John Burrman. In 1972, Stockton ended up #4 in the U.S. Men's Singles Rankings with Gottfried at #10, McKinley at #15, Gerken at #19, and Walthall at #34. The U.S. Men's Doubles Rankings had Gerken/Gottfried at #4 and McKinley/Stockton at #5. I don't remember if Burrman played #6 that day, but he was ranked 8th in the U.S. in Boys 18 and Unders in 1971.

Not only was Trinity #1 in the rankings, they finished the season winning the NCAA Team Championship. The NCAA Singles Championship allows four players per team for singles and all four Trinity players made it to the quarter-finals or beyond with Stockton defeating Gottfried in the finals of the 256-player format. The two doubles teams made the semi-finals of the NCAA Doubles Championships with Gerken/Gottfried losing in the finals.

OCU, as strong as we were, was able to win just one set against this very powerful opponent, and I won that set. I played Pancho Walthall and lost in three sets. Walthall was a top player, having played in the 1971 and 1972 US Opens. In 1973, he reached the third round, which is the last 32, at Wimbledon. The Grand Slam tournaments only allow 128 players into the main draw. Here was another example where I played a close match, but couldn't get consistent wins against players of that caliber. Nonetheless, I was proud to be the only player from Oklahoma City who took a set against the extremely powerful 1972 Trinity University National Champions.

There was a tournament called the Mid-Continent Tennis Championships, which was played in Wichita, Kansas. I was staying with local housing, which is where a family allows a tennis player to stay at their house during the tournament. I do not remember what happened in the singles, but this was a big tournament with quite a few top players from throughout the Missouri Valley Section playing in it. Arnold Short, the OCU coach, and I somehow ended up playing doubles together. Arnold was old in tennis terms, being just over 40 years of age. Doubles is easier at that age because there is less court to cover. We reached the finals of that tournament and were set to play the top seeds, Colin Robertson and Mervyn Webster.

The night before the finals, I met up with a couple of tennis-playing friends. We decided to go out for a drink. I didn't know Wichita drinking establishments at all, so I suspect that one of my friends suggested the location. We ended up at a strip club where we had some drinks and were being served by a bartender/cocktail waitress who was quite good-looking in her own right. After a few drinks, both of my companions were ready to leave. Teasing me, they said "We can go home to our wives while all you can do is go back to your housing alone." They were married and I was just the lonely single guy. They had a good laugh, and left. I don't remember the specifics, but I ended up making a date with our server after she got off of work. I went back to my housing and told them that I had a date and they arranged for me to reenter the house after my date.

Well, my date went very well. The woman, Sandy, had two or three kids and was working at that club to support them. She was not a stripper. I don't remember if we went for coffee or exactly what we did, but we ended up back at her place. Upon waking up the next morning, I knew I had a problem. What I had done was very rude to the people providing my housing and I decided to tell them that we went back to her place where I fell asleep. It was true as far as it went. Also, I got the last laugh on my two married friends. My housing folks were not very happy with me, but there wasn't a lot that I could do about it after the fact. Thankfully, that was my last night to stay with them since the tournament ended that day.

I still had a doubles final match in front of me, and I was playing with my coach against one of the top teams in the Missouri Valley Section. The Missouri Valley Section included the states of Oklahoma, Kansas, Missouri, Nebraska, and Iowa. As I mentioned earlier, Colin Robertson was playing with Mervyn Webster. Mervyn was a South African who had played #1 for Wichita State University, where he was later inducted into their Hall of Fame. He was a head tennis professional in Wichita at the time. Mervyn played in the 1967 Wimbledon Qualifying, reaching the 3rd round, and the 1967 French Open Qualifying, reaching the 2nd round. Colin had played in the 1967 US Open.

Just before the match started, the son of the people that I had been staying with showed up to watch the match. I thought he was going to talk to me about the match, but instead, he congratulated me on my previous evening's adventure. I think the doubles final was a three setter, but in any case, we won. Considering the caliber of the two players we were up against, that was a very good tournament win. It also showed that Arnold could play top flight tennis doubles, even at his age.

I continued to see Sandy a few more times. Wichita was only a two-hour drive from Oklahoma City. She was a very nice woman, but it just didn't seem like this relationship was going anywhere.

Another interesting situation occurred in a summertime tennis tournament in Dallas, Texas. A number of my teammates were entered into the tournament, which was played outdoors. On this particular day, the temperature in Dallas was at 110°F and humid. The humidity was the real killer. That and the fact that the asphalt courts that we were playing on were a dark green, with out of bounds being a lighter green. It is not an exaggeration to say that the temperature on the courts had to be around 140°F. I played a fellow named Ronnie Fisher. He had very good groundstrokes and was undoubtedly used to high heat and humidity. The courts were slow, meaning that they would grip the ball and slow it down, allowing a player to run down balls that they would not get to on a faster court. This was an advantage for Fisher.

Fisher had been ranked as #1 in the 1968 and again in the 1970 Men's Singles rankings in the Texas Section. I knew this match was going to be difficult. I was a quintessential serve and volley player. My serve was very big, particularly for my 5'9" frame. My volleys were another strength for me. I was also very fast, which helped me get to the net quickly and to cover the court.

In the early stages of the match, I served and volleyed well. I also broke Fisher. I was leading 4–1 when "WHAM!", I felt the energy just leave me. In an instant, I could not move very fast. The heat had gotten to me after just 5 games. Fisher started climbing back into the match, I realized that I could not get to the net quickly enough any longer to hold my serve, plus it took extra energy. I started to serve and stay back, but against a groundstroker of Fisher's caliber, that did not play out well. He simply moved me around until he could win the point. He won the match 6–4, 6–1. It was very frustrating. When I got back to the tournament desk, I found out that there had been seven first round defaults for heat exhaustion. That is a very high number. Tennis players in Texas and Oklahoma are used to playing in high temperatures, but this was above and beyond. I had also suffered from heat exhaustion, except that I had elected to continue to try to play rather than just default. I was beat the minute that my energy left me. I don't ever remember losing another match due to the heat, and I was to go on to play in high heat on a number of occasions.

During the summer of 1972, I partied and chased women. A friend of mine came to Oklahoma City once or twice and we would go out drinking together. During one of our outings, I met Debbie, the beautiful blond that I was with on the night before I left for O'Hare. Debbie was in a nursing school, or so she said. We began to date on and off until right after the 1972 Christmas break.

I think it was during my senior year that I was asked by the OCU administration to be on a committee to select the next Dean of the Business School. There may have been another undergraduate on the committee, but it was primarily comprised of professors. I was very honored to be asked to participate.

My studies were going well, particularly in Economics. I ended up with nearly straight "A"s in the 10 Economics classes that I took. I got a "B" in one class. I was selected as one of 39 students at OCU to be named to the annual "Who's Who Among Students in American Universities & Colleges." OCU had more selections than either OU or

OSU. Both of those other schools had 38 selections. Both also boasted tens of thousands of students whereas we only had about 1,500. I didn't know it at the time, but there were more academic honors to come.

My involvement with alcohol and partying did not serve me well. Although I was always sober and ready for my tennis matches, the partying life style was not conducive to climbing to the top of the US national tennis rankings. I was to realize only later that I was an alcoholic as my consumption would gradually increase with time. This was probably one of the primary reasons that my tennis skills did not increase greatly while I was in college. I was also a little frustrated at having difficulty beating my teammates. These players were not top 100 ATP players. That is not to say that they weren't really, really good, because they were. And a number of them had wins over players who were in the top 100 in the world. To go on to a pro career, I would have needed to raise the level of my play to consistently beat them. Maybe I wouldn't have made it anyway, but the alcohol, drugs, and partying did not help.

During my years at OCU, I also played Intramurals. I was in the top five when we ran long-distance cross-country races. Another intramural sport was flag football. The tennis team members put together a flag football team that won the intramural championships. How does a team with a lot of foreigners play successful American football? We put Americans at key positions and recruited some very large Americans to play the line and block for us. Our speed was the true key and I played wide receiver. One funny incident occurred when I was trying to block Bud Koper in our flag football game.

Bud was a former United States Basketball Writers Association (USBWA) 1964 1st Team All-American basketball player for OCU. He was drafted by the then San Francisco Warriors and played one year. He was back on campus teaching or assisting athletics. Now Bud was a big guy from Rocky, Oklahoma.

He was about 6'4" and 240 lbs. I took my 5'9" 155 lbs. frame and went to block him. He was maybe ten yards downfield. I hit him with everything I had. It was like hitting a brick wall. With my arms against my chest, I drove into him and came to a screeching halt. Then I slid down to the grass having made very little impact on him at all. I had been expecting to knock him back a few yards, but that clearly failed.

There was also intramural basketball, and in my senior year I led a team of friends, some of whom were just adequate at basketball. I do remember that I scored a lot for our team. Our toughest competition, though, was against a faculty team. This team had the Athletic Director and Head Basketball coach Abe Lemons. Abe was a renowned coach of the highly regarded OCU Chiefs basketball team. Paul Hansen was another player who was the Assistant Basketball coach. Arnold Short, the tennis coach and former basketball All American along with Bud Koper, another basketball All American, and an instructor at OCU. The first four at this team had all played collegiate basketball at OCU and all four are in the OCU Athletics Hall of Fame.

As I said, we were not very big. I played center, the position usually reserved for the tallest player, because I could outjump everyone else on our team. At that point, I could almost, but not quite, dunk a basketball into the 10-foot standard basket. Without a ball, I could jump and hit my wrist on the rim which is not bad for my height. I remember playing the "faculty" team and we got blown out something like 71–29. The opposing center was Bud Koper. At 6'4", he was the tallest player on the faculty team. I felt I owed Bud for stopping me from blocking him on the football field. Early on in the game, Bud got the ball in the lane, maybe 10 feet from the basket. He went up to shoot and I went up to block it. I got my hand on top of the ball and completely stuffed him. That was the first and last time that I ever stuffed someone who had played in the NBA. Even though we lost the game, I had my sweet revenge.

CHAPTER 24
Wednesday, December 20, 1972

RUNNING TO THE GATE

As I waited through the afternoon, I was not sure when I would get home. I was days ahead of Christmas and had a whole month off from school, so I was not in danger of missing Christmas, but the waiting was tedious. I had been periodically checking to see if any flights were available yet. It was shortly after 5:30 PM and I was talking to a ticketing agent who said there was a flight leaving for Madison. She gave me the gate number, but said that I would have to run because they were going to close the airplane doors soon. There was no security to pass through that I remember and my bag had been checked already, so it would go out on the first flight to Madison. I was not burdened with a carry-on bag, so I was able to run easily through the airport. When I arrived at the gate, I found that I was just in time to board the plane. I felt very lucky to have gotten to the plane before they closed the doors. This was North Central Airlines Flight 575. It was headed to Madison, Wisconsin, and then on to Duluth, Minnesota. Little did I know that the aircraft was never going to arrive at either place!

I boarded the plane. The other passengers were already seated, but there were plenty of seats as the plane appeared to only be about half full. I found a seat in the seventh row against the window, which was on the right side of the

144

aircraft when facing forward. The plane was about 20 rows deep with two seats on the left side of the plane and three on the right side, separated by the aisle. There was a woman in the aisle seat, but no one in the middle seat. I took off my letterman's jacket and put it in the overhead bin before moving next to the window. I had on tennis shoes, jeans, and a thin brown T-shirt. I sat down and buckled myself in. I was very thankful that I was on the first flight out of O'Hare to Madison that day. Since I was going standby, I would not have been able to board if the plane was full. I must have been the last person to board the plane.

The letter jacket that I had with me was my pride and joy. It had beige leather arms with "OCU" in white lettering across a light blue vest. The light blue and white were the school colors.

In 1972, passengers were allowed to smoke on airplanes. They were not allowed to do so on takeoffs or landings, but once cruising altitude had been reached, people could smoke. However, those who wished to smoke had to be sitting in the smoking section, which was in the back portion of the plane. I was glad that I was not a smoker and was seated toward the front of the aircraft far enough away from the smoking section that I didn't have to smell or directly breathe anyone's smoke. I didn't know how important my dislike of smoking was to become.

CHAPTER 25

THE CRASH

We taxied from the gate for a couple of minutes and stopped on a runway in position for takeoff. I figured that the wait shouldn't be long as I understood that we were first in line to depart from O'Hare that day. Then we started to roll, picking up speed as we headed toward takeoff. As we neared takeoff speed, suddenly the plane pitched up rather steeply. This was the steepest pitch during a takeoff of any plane that I have ever been on, before or since. It must have been about a 45-degree angle to the ground as we were lifting off. Then there was a sudden jolt which jerked my head, thereby straining my neck. Just that one jolt and we were up in the air. I had no idea what had just happened. I wondered if the pilot slammed the landing gear up at that very moment, but I knew that didn't make sense.

We continued upward for a few more seconds and then leveled off. I don't know how high we were, but I am guessing between 50 and 100 feet off of the runway. I could see the terminal off to my right through my window. Crap! I knew we were in trouble. We were rocking a bit side to side. The lights in the cabin flickered and then went out. Then we were descending and I waited for that terrible crash that I just knew was coming. I was expecting that we would hit the ground extremely hard and potentially begin tumbling if a wing were to catch the ground. We were plunging into hell.

I was sitting bolt upright as I stared at the terminal for a few seconds. Oh, how I wished I were in there instead of seated where I was. I suspect many of the passengers were bracing for impact, but I wanted to see what was happening.

When we hit the ground, it was much smoother than the smashing and possible tumbling that I had anticipated. We were skidding along the runway. I was worried we would go right off the end of it. After maybe 30 seconds of sliding, we came to a stop.

CHAPTER 26

THE FIRE

I relaxed for a second, thinking that we could now simply disembark. I was just getting ready to spring out of my seat when all of a sudden all of the windows turned yellow with flames. The flames covering the outside of the windows must have occurred within a second or two after the plane came to a stop. The entire plane was immediately encased in bright yellow flames. I sat back. I knew it was over for me. I was surely dead! Strangely, I felt no fear. A great calm came over me. This was definitely an unexpected feeling. I knew my fate was sealed and oddly enough, I had accepted it. The flames over the windows lasted for maybe five seconds and then they receded. I realized that maybe I still had a chance to make it out of there!

My memory is not clear as to what happened over the next two or three seconds. I am pretty sure that I had my hand on my seat belt's buckle release mechanism. This would have allowed me to release my seat belt very quickly. I do remember looking toward the back of the plane where I saw flames. This was a huge floor-to-ceiling fireball. I presume that it was coming up through the cabin floor. I was thinking that it was so big and hot that you couldn't run through it without dying. In fact, it must have come up right where people were sitting because five people in the back never left their seats. This fireball was toward the back third of the plane and my seat was toward the front third.

As the flames that were surrounding the plane receded from outside of the windows, the great calm and serenity that I had felt was replaced with panic. This juxtaposition of feelings must have been spurred by the realization that I was no longer certain to die. My need to escape, fueled by the flames that were so close, filled me with sheer terror! I must have slid past the woman in the aisle seat before she got up. At that point, I was laser-focused on escaping this death tube!

Since I was located in front of the wings, my closest exit was the front door that I had entered from just minutes ago. I moved up a couple of rows quickly before other passengers filled the single aisleway blocking my forward progress. I knew those flames were not far behind. I needed to get off of this plane fast! It was pitch black both outside and inside the plane at this point. I was not breathing smoke…at least I was not choking yet. I heard a male voice shout, "Don't panic!" That voice shook me out of my panic mode. I couldn't go forward any more with people pouring into the aisle. Now I could only hope that this line of people would be able to move quickly as the growing fire behind me was coming!

To my relief, the line did move pretty quickly, as everyone realized that death was close and they urgently needed to move. When I got near the front and turned left to the exit, there was enough light from outside to see that there was an object on its side curved across the exit pathway. For years, I thought that it was the exit door, but that's not possible since the door swings outward and is on hinges. Besides, the door is at least three feet wide by six feet high which was bigger than the object in question. Most likely the object was the casing that enclosed the slide. This object was roughly two feet wide by four feet long and resting on its approximately two or three-inch side. I stepped over it, but when I got to the exit itself, there was no slide, only a six to eight-foot drop to the runway below. With the flames behind me and a fear that the plane might explode, I did not hesitate in jumping to the tarmac.

I landed without injury and ran about 100 feet away from the plane. There was a young blond woman about my age standing there. She said with great anxiety "I hope everyone made it off the plane ." We were both watching the DC-9. The flames were now five times as high as the burning wreckage of the fuselage. I told her "There is no way!" I was convinced that the fireball that I saw inside would have cut off the people in the back of the plane. There was an exit door directly behind the tail, but I never saw it open. I figured that those people were dead or going to be. I estimated that I was out of the plane in about 30 seconds from the time the plane stopped. This was faster than most of the other passengers and before there was a lot of smoke. From my perspective, there were at most 60 seconds from the time the plane skidded to a stop to the time when leaving was no longer possible. After watching the plane burn for a short while, we saw the arrival of the fire trucks that were stationed at O'Hare Airport. Reportedly, the tower controllers could not see the fire through the fog. It took them two minutes to determine that there had been an accident and to contact the fire department. The fire trucks arrived by 6:03 PM, which means within a minute of when they were contacted. I could see the firefighters begin spraying water and fire suppressant on the plane. The fire was not put out until 6:17 PM. In that short 17-minute window, the plane burned so profusely that it was turned into rubble. Only burned out sections of the cockpit, tail, and wings remained as recognizable parts of an airplane.

The range of feelings while I was on the plane throughout the crash and fire varied greatly from trepidation of the impending crash to the ground, to relief upon crashing without tumbling, to serenity upon seeing flames surrounding the entire plane, to sheer terror at the proximity of the flames in the plane during my escape. I know other plane crash survivors have experienced the calm of events being out of their control, and the terror of the crash and/or fire. I don't believe that these wildly different emotions are unusual. The feelings of terror explain why plane crashes are such feared events, and why most survivors have to deal with the repercussions of Post-Traumatic Stress Disorder.

My memory is not clear on this, but reports from other passengers were that we stood on the runway for about a half hour while rescue personnel dealt with the injured passengers first. A bus was sent for the surviving passengers who were not being treated for injuries. We would end up sitting for another half hour on that bus. The cold weather and no jacket made this uncomfortable. I am sure that the bigger problem was that most of us were in shock.

CHAPTER 27

THE BUS

We were told to get on the bus that had been sent to the scene for the uninjured survivors. I got on and went to the back-left side and took a window seat. I could see the plane through the window. I was pretty cold. After all, this was December 20th in the upper Midwest and nighttime had fallen. I was wearing my skintight thin brown short sleeved T-shirt, which was not much of a barrier against the cool weather. I'd had no choice but to leave my prized letter jacket behind in the plane. Between standing on the runway and sitting on the bus, about an hour must have passed.

To make matters worse, after sitting on the bus for a short while, a survivor came aboard covered in jet fuel. I don't know how he had gotten jet fuel on him, but immediately the interior of the bus had the suffocating, toxic smell of jet fuel. We opened every window on the bus in order to get fresh air. There was a wind, which was good, in that it cleared the smell, and bad, in that sitting on that bus got colder still. We had to leave those windows open as long as that fuel-drenched survivor was on the bus. After an hour in 35°F temperatures, waiting to find out what would happen next, the bus headed for the terminal.

I was to find out later what had happened. We had rolled down the runway reaching our takeoff speed of just over 160 miles of hour when our pilot spotted another plane on the runway. Our North Central Airlines (NCA) DC9-31 had a capacity of about 100 passengers. We only had 41 passengers with a crew of four on board. Our crew was comprised of the pilot, copilot, and two flight attendants, known as stewardesses at the time. The plane that our pilot spotted was a Delta Convair 880 which was at full capacity with 86 passengers and a crew of seven. This plane had just landed after having come from Tampa, Florida, and it had taxied to a point just before reaching our runway. Through a miscommunication with the air traffic control (ATC) tower, they proceeded to cross our runway, not aware that it was being used for takeoffs.

The fog was still heavy at O'Hare, which was a contributing factor to the accident. The NTSB report on the accident indicates that visibility was only one quarter mile. In all probability it was significantly less than that. Suffice it to say that the ability to see through the fog was extremely limited. The First Officer, Gerald Adamson, was flying the North Central airplane with Captain Ordell Nordseth monitoring. By the time Captain Nordseth saw the other plane on our runway, it was too late. He ordered his co-pilot to help him pull up on the yoke, creating a very high pitch attitude, hoping to climb over the Delta plane. Our plane began its abrupt takeoff angle, but we didn't make it. We hit the Delta plane, breaking off their stabilizer (tail), part of their left wing, and putting three huge gouges in their fuselage. These gouges were at the top of their fuselage, which meant that the Delta plane's occupants were extremely lucky, because they ended up with only two minor injuries. These were a couple of bumped heads resulting from the impact rocking their plane. I imagine that it had to be very frightening to look out the left window and suddenly see a plane come out of the fog headed right at those passengers!

Our NCA DC9 was not as lucky. The collision had torn off the right main landing gear, the right leading-edge flap, and had broken our fuselage. We were in serious trouble, and the plane would not stay airborne. Captain Nordseth did a remarkable job of landing our damaged airplane back on the runway, where our remaining landing gear collapsed and we started the long skid. I did not realize until later that we skidded off of our takeoff runway, went across a grassy infield where we continued our skid, and finally ended up back on an adjacent runway, where we came to a stop. I imagine that skidding on our broken fuselage created sparks which ignited spilling fuel. The flames must have been burning and trailing off the back of the plane as we skidded to a stop. At that point, the flames caught up to the plane, which resulted in every window going yellow. The flames found better material to burn through the broken fuselage and into the cargo bay, hence their retreat from the windows.

Looking back on the fireball that I saw, I began to question how could the fireball could have come through the floor of the plane and burned all the way to the ceiling so fast. After all, that was only about five to ten seconds after the plane had come to a stop. I think that I have figured out the likely reason.

First, the DC-9 that I was in has two engines, both of which are located at the back of the plane, attached to the fuselage under the tail on each side of the plane. Fuel lines run through the bottom of the fuselage. There is at least one center fuel tank in the fuselage. Some versions of the DC-9 have two. There may also have been fuel tanks in the wings. These fuel tanks held 22,000 pounds of Jet A aviation kerosene which is about 3,300 U.S. gallons of fuel. When the North Central plane struck the Delta plane, the fuselage was broken. When the plane came back down onto the runway, the fuselage was likely broken further with the collapse of the remaining landing gear upon impact with the ground. Fuel would have been spilling and with metal scraping on the runway, sparks were generated setting off this massive fire. I suspect at this point that the fire was also in the cargo hold where the baggage was. As the plane carved a large semi-circle while it skidded from runway 27L, across a grassy infield, and then onto runway 32L where it came to rest, that cargo bay would have been fully burning. I suspect that this skidding would have opened the fuselage breaks even further. Any cracks or separations in the passenger flooring were also likely toward the rear of the plane where the initial and largest ruptures took place. This would have allowed the flames to expand upward into the passenger area. This explains why I would have seen fire in the back part of the cabin as I was leaving.

Eventually, the bus that we were sitting on drove us to a terminal. We had no idea where we were or exactly what had happened to us. I am sure we were all in shock. To this day, there is a lot of emotion with the fact that something this monumental had actually happened to me. It is just very hard to fathom. As we got off of the bus and headed into the terminal, airport personnel tried to keep us together and moving. One passenger broke away and they tried hard to get him back in line but he effectively told them to leave him alone and he disappeared into the terminal. The rest of us assumed that the people leading us knew what they were doing.

CHAPTER 28

THE VIP LOUNGE

Upon entering the terminal, we were led up to a second-floor VIP lounge. There were about 15 of us from the North Central plane. I arrived at this estimate because we were to find out that nine people didn't make it off of the plane and 16 others were taken to local hospitals. All four crew members survived, but were taken to a local hospital. We had 41 passengers minus nine dead, 16 injured, and the man who broke away. That left 15 of us. We were to learn later that one of the injured, a 68-year-old man, died five days later from smoke inhalation.[1]

There we were in this lounge. We were offered all of the free drinks that we wanted and after that experience, quite a few of us took the drinks. We wanted to leave to go make telephone calls, but we were not allowed to leave. It turned out that the Chicago FBI had taken control of the passengers in the lounge. We could not even go to the restroom without being accompanied by an FBI agent. In 1972, the only phones were landline phones, and if you didn't have one nearby, you would need to use a pay phone. For most passengers, pay phones were the only option. We were informed that arrangements for a number of telephones to be installed for our use had been made, but this would take a while. This was very frustrating and seemed like a really dumb thing to do. Why weren't they letting us go to the nearest phones to call our loved ones? They refused to tell us. None of us understood this, but in the aftermath of the catastrophe, I don't think that we were thinking straight or ready to defy the orders of the FBI.

We sat in the lounge, which had a bank of TVs on. The primary and only channels available at the time were the big three: ABC, CBS, and NBC. There were no other channels. It was quite surreal to look up and see that our crash was on all of the channels and dominating the national news of the evening. These shows once again illustrated the enormity of the tragedy and just how unbelievable it was that all of us had been sitting on the inside of a massively burning airplane with our lives hanging in the balance. I imagine my fellow survivors were all thanking their lucky stars to have lived through this devastating experience. I certainly was. I don't remember talking to the other passengers, which is odd, because I am sure that I did. It has been a lot of years since that night. Maybe there wasn't anything particularly notable in any of the conversations that I might have had, but I am betting that my lack of memory was due to shock and Post-Traumatic Stress Disorder.

On a trip to the restroom, I remember looking out from the second-floor railing and down on the very crowded terminal, one floor below. I realized it was nearing Christmas and the airport had been shut down all day. Now it was shut down due to our accident. Everyone at O'Hare had been affected in one way or another. I was to learn that it was not just affecting O'Hare. Due to the North Central wreckage still sitting on the runway, incoming flights were delayed by up to a couple of hours. The whole country was now being impacted by the crash.

Finally, around 9:00 PM, a full three hours after our crash, the phone installation was completed and we were allowed to line up and call our loved ones. When I called home, Dad answered the phone. I told him that I was pretty shook up. He said, "Don't worry about that crash. Just get on the next plane to Madison.." I suddenly realized that he was assuming from the fact that I was calling him hours after the crash, that I was not involved in the crash. I raised my voice in an anguished cry and said "I WAS ON THAT PLANE!!!" Now he understood. I told him that arrangements were being made to provide transportation for survivors that wanted to go to Madison.

We stayed in that VIP lounge for about five hours. It was now six hours after the crash. We were still being detained. I have since surmised that the Chicago FBI was concerned that there might have been an aircraft hijacking or someone deliberately bringing our plane down. Hijacking of an airliner was often referred to as skyjacking. It should not have taken much investigation to realize that this was not a conspiracy or a hijacking. I am still very unhappy with the FBI not making it a priority to allow us to make calls to our loved ones. In hindsight, I am sure that they were taping our conversations which would explain why they installed new phones. They should have known before we got off of the tarmac that this was not an airplane crash caused by the North Central passengers. This was very, very exasperating!

The FBI had their reasons and it may be helpful to understand that it was a very different world in the 1970s. In 1972 alone, there were 13 airplane hijackings around the world. We just don't see that situation much these days, particularly with the restrictions after 9/11. In 2017, there were no skyjackings in the United States but, in 1972, skyjackings were a priority for law enforcement. Nevertheless, the FBI greatly overstepped their legal authority in the immediate aftermath of my crash.

By my estimates, about midnight, those of us wishing to go to Madison were led through the terminal to a very large bus. I remember that only seven of us boarded that bus.

A small "Delayed" sign served as a grim reminder that North Central's flight 575 out of Chicago would not be arriving Wednesday night in Madison. The DC-9 jet crashed on takeoff from Chicago's O'Hare International Airport, killing nine and injuring 15 of the passengers on board. The plane hit a Delta Airlines Jet which had landed moments earlier and was taxiing across a runway. (Staff photo by Dave Sandell)

North Central Flight 575 "Delayed" Arrival status in the Madison Airport. The Capital Times, Thursday December 21, 1972, Page 31. Photo by Dave Sandell.[2]

The burned-out hulk of a North Central Airlines DC-9 lies on the tarmac at Chicago's O'Hare Airport on Thursday morning, December 21, 1972, where it came to rest after colliding with a Delta Airlines Convair 880 on the evening before. (AP Photo/Larry Stoddard)

The burned-out shell of the North Central Airlines DC-9 nose section lies on the Chicago's O'Hare Airport tarmac where it came to rest after the collision. (AP Photo/ET)

The nose section of the North Central Airlines DC-9 lies on the ground at Chicago's O'Hare International Airport, December 20, 1972, following the collision with a Delta Airlines CV-880 during the DC-9's takeoff. (AP Photo/ ET)

The fuselage of a North Central Airlines DC-9, which crashed on takeoff from Chicago's O'Hare International Airport Wednesday night, December 20, 1972, smolders in fog as firemen and rescue workers search the wreckage. (AP Photo/DLD)

The burned-out fuselage of a North Central Airlines DC-9 lies on the ground at Chicago's O'Hare International Airport, December 20, 1972, following a collision with a Delta Airlines plane. (AP Photo/ET)

North Central Plane Wreckage on Day after the Crash. Illustrated by William Lum.

Police and Fire Rescue Workers Near the Smoldering Remains of the North Central DC-9. Illustrated by William Lum.

Tail Section of North Central Airlines Plane. Illustrated by William Lum.

Delta Convair 880 on the tarmac after having its stabilizer ripped off. Illustrated by William Lum.

North Central Airlines DC-9 Tail Section Resting on Tarmac. Illustrated by William Lum.

CHAPTER 29
Thursday, December 21, 1972

MADISON, WISCONSIN

We arrived at the Park Motor Inn in Madison, which was a predesignated drop-off point, at about 2:30 AM on December 21st. I am not sure if only Dad showed up or both Mom and Dad, but I was picked up there and then taken to my parent's home in west Madison. I don't remember how much we discussed that night. I am pretty sure that I went to bed shortly after arriving home, because I had been awake for much of the previous night driving through the fog. I was exhausted. There had been very little sleep during the previous 43 hours and the great trauma of the horrific crash had left me drained.

I slept until noon and upon rising, Dad told me that he had contacted a local TV station to provide them with an on-air interview of me. I think it was the local CBS television station. I went there in the midafternoon and did the interview. I wish that I had access to the video, but through current searches of the internet I have not been able to locate it.

My sister Nancy was 12 years old at the time of the crash. She remembers that our folks were very worried because they thought that I would have taken the first flight out to Madison and they knew that I would be traveling standby. They also had heard about the crash on TV. She said they were very anxious! Dad had been on the phone trying to find me. This brings me back to the Chicago FBI and their high-handed and unconstitutional tactics which totally lacked compassion for the survivors by not allowing us to immediately contact our loved ones. Dad was probably calling the airlines trying to find out about my status. He was not getting much information. Nancy said that she was calm because she firmly believed that I was both on the plane that crashed and alive. She felt that if I had died, she would have intuitively known it. The feeling she had that I was alive was very strong and she had no doubt whatsoever. However, she was only 12, and had no way to convey this to our parents that would make sense to them.

Once I had called, both Mom and Dad were very relieved. Apparently, Dad had had a dream the night before the crash. He saw coffins in a room, as many as 13. He always shared strange dreams when he had them with Mom. Nancy also remembers that I had a rash or hives, which my folks had attributed to the stress of the plane crash. While I have no reason to doubt this, I do not remember it.

I remember very little of that holiday season. Certainly, some of this is due to the fact that it occurred over 46 years ago, but I wonder how much of it might be due to post-traumatic stress. I am reminded that Dad could remember very little of what happened during the Battle of Iwo Jima in World War II.

What I do remember is that I had to get back on an airplane to return to Oklahoma City about a month after the incident. Typically, I would have to fly Madison to Chicago O'Hare to Oklahoma City, but I only remember sitting on the plane going from O'Hare to Oklahoma City while waiting for takeoff. I do remember being on the plane and gripping the seat handles very tightly, as I was very wary of flying again. I was telling the person sitting next to me that I was quite fearful after having survived that crash. He told me that he had been in a plane on the O'Hare taxiway that same night. It is a small world.

A tired and happy Hiroshi Aoki, of Japan, squeezes his eyes as he was met at the Park Motor Inn here Wednesday night by Howard Voegeli, of Monticello. Aoki was one of 36 persons to survive the crash of a North Central Airlines jet at O'Hare International Airport in Chicago Wednesday night. He is staying with the Voegeli family on a two-year government sponsored program to aid Japanese students in the study of dairy farming. (Staff photo by Dave Sandell)

Hiroshi Aoki—Survivor Arriving in Madison at 2:30 am on December 21st, The Capital Times (Madison), Thursday, December 21, 1972—Photo by Dave Sandell[3]

CHAPTER 30

NORTH CENTRAL PASSENGER STORIES

Immediately after the accident, I began collecting newspaper articles and stories about the crash. This has become my treasure trove of photos and other passenger stories that are used for many of the pictures and quotes in this book.

I have recounted my story. I can add that I was listed in the Wisconsin State Journal, Thursday, December 21, 1972 among those not hospitalized as *"a Mr. Overgaard."*[4] There was a more extensive write-up in the Wisconsin State Journal on Saturday, December 23, 1972, where the intermediary headline to an article declared "3ʳᵈ City Person Survives Crash." My dad may have called the paper, which would not surprise me. He probably considered my home to be in Madison, even if I did not. The article went as follows:

"A third Madison resident was among the survivors of a collision of a North Central DC-9 with a Delta Airlines Jet at O'Hare International Airport in Chicago Wednesday night.

Todd Overgard, 21, son of Mr. and Mrs. E. Ted Overgard, 5402 Flad Ave., was returning to Madison for the holidays from Oklahoma City University where he is a student.

Overgard was seated in the seventh row of the North Central plane and escaped injury by jumping from the front exit of the plane. Overgard's name was inadvertently left off of an earlier list of Madison Survivors."[5]

Other stories of harrowing escapes were told to the newspapers. O'Hare reported that the North Central DC-9 was taking off when it hit the Delta Convair 880. Immediately after impact, flames and smoke came from the North Central plane. The inside of the plane was destroyed by fire within minutes, leaving only part of the burned-out fuselage, wings, tail, and cockpit. The fuselage was broken in a number of places.

Richard Ojakangas, 40, and his son Greg Ojakangas, 13, were both hospitalized for smoke inhalation. It was reported in the Capital Times on Thursday, December 21, 1972 that Richard Ojakangas (incorrectly identified as Raymond) said *"We came to a stop...the plane filled with smoke and somebody said go for the exits. We headed for the front, crawling on our hands and knees to try and get a breath of air and a voice said 'keep coming forward and keep low.'" He said the plane burst into flames as he and his son ran from the jet."*[3]

I would point out that they probably hadn't noticed the extent of the fire as they were running from the plane. I would guess that I was out of the plane less than 30 seconds before they were, but the flames were absolutely huge when I jumped from the plane, ran, then looked back.

There were several articles on that day's Wisconsin State Journal's front page, including *"To Some, A Nightmare Ends After Long Vigil at Airport."* It is a story about 22-year-old Jackie Hesse who was waiting with her 18-year-old sister, Jeanne, at Madison Municipal Airport for word on the status of their father, Francis Turner. They were not sure if he was on the North Central plane. Word finally came down at about 9:00 PM that their father had missed the flight when he was five minutes late. *"'I think God was on our side,' Jackie told reporters, letting loose the tears which had been building up for two hours."*[6]

"*Mrs. Melvin Volbrecht of Montello, whose son Roger was injured in the crash, went around the lobby displaying a piece of paper confirming that he had survived. 'I'm going to frame it.' she said"*[6]

Dawn Harbort, 17, was on the North Central plane and survived the crash. She was not hospitalized. Her mother and father were frantic as they went back and forth from the airport until word came that Dawn had called the airport and was finally connected with her father. She told him that she had lost her baggage on the flight. He said *"You lost everything, huh? Well, that's all right."*[6] Dawn was reported in one newspaper as telling her parents that "everything was on fire." Her comments were further explained in Madison's The Capital Times: *"I was sitting in the fifth row back from the front and suddenly the plane sort of rocked and we landed on the wheels, I think, then sort of belly-flopped on the ground." She went on to say that the plane was filled with 'really thick black smoke after the crash'. 'I couldn't see anything, but I could hear people yelling to get on the floor. I grabbed the guy ahead of me and followed him out the door.' Miss Harbort said when the plane suddenly quit climbing and started rocking, 'I realized we were crashing, but I didn't really think about dying or anything. There was fire outside of every window and the guy behind me stood there and watched a window melt. She said there was little panic among the passengers and said people urged each other to stay calm. It was amazing how calm most of the people were. And the stewardesses did a really good job. A man was pushing on a door trying to get it open. A stewardess ran up shouting 'Open that door' and threw herself against it. Miss Harbort said as far as she knew 'everyone sitting in front of me got out, all of them that I'm aware of anyway. 'One of the stewardesses shouted out that there was a lady in the back that couldn't walk and to get her out, but I don't think she made it.' Miss Harbort lost all of her personal belongings which she had on board including her luggage, a purse and coat.*

She was critical of the handling of the survivors by North Central officials and the FBI, who had men on the scene. 'They wouldn't let us make any phone calls for quite a while —a couple of hours—but they didn't give us any reason for it,' she said. While that was going on in Chicago, Miss Harbort's parents, along with friends and relatives of others on board were frantically waiting at the Madison Municipal Airport for some word on survivors. 'Lots of people were really upset and felt like telling North Central where to go,' she added. 'The FBI agents stood by the door,' she said, 'and wouldn't let anybody out of the room. If you wanted to go to the ladies' room you had to give them your name, age, address, and then they would escort you there and wait until you came out,' she said. 'They all had badges which said 'U.S. FBI' and they just sort of stood there and didn't answer any questions. They never gave us a reason for not letting us call and let people know we were all right,' she added. When asked if she would fly again Miss Harbort replied: 'I think I could get back on, but I'm scared that if there was a little bump taking off I would go into shock.' Her mother, after talking to her on the phone said 'She seemed a little hysterical but I guess that's understandable isn't it.'"[2]

Clearly, I was not the only one upset with the FBI that night. It was an appalling lack of empathy to ignore the emotional pain of both the survivors, who had already gone through enough that night, and the survivors' loved ones. It was clearly an illegal detention, although no one pushed it far enough to see if they would actually arrest us. Their ill-treatment of us was second only to the shock of the night's events and our ability to cope with them.

One unnamed passenger was purported to have said, *"The North Central people were great. Without them a lot more people might have died."*[3]This may be true, but the stewardess located in the front of the plane was nowhere to be seen as I came to the exit door. I realize now that she had been pushed out of the front door exit, but I do not remember seeing her at all. My understanding is that the captain climbed back into the front door to try to help passengers out, but I don't remember seeing that either. North Central came under criticism from the National Transportation Safety Board in their report of this crash.

For many years, I believed that the main problem with North Central was that they had not positioned a stewardess in the rear of the plane to aid in exiting from the rear. Instead, there was one flight attendant located in the front of the airplane and the second flight attendant was located in seat 13B which was an aisle seat next to the rear left over-wing exit or possibly one row behind that exit. Upon studying the accident more thoroughly, I have come to the conclusion that exiting from the rear of the plane was probably impossible. There was an engine located under the tail on each side of the DC-9. As a result, the exit is located in the center, a little further back from two lavatories. The lavatories were one on each side of the plane and behind the passenger seats. Complicating the scenario was that the rear exit expanded into fold-out stairs. "Well", you might be saying, "what's wrong with using that exit?"

Remember that during our initial impact with the Delta plane, we lost our right landing gear and upon crashing, the left landing gear collapsed along with the front landing gear. This put the plane directly on its fuselage. There is a slight incline where the rear exit would unfold, but I don't think that it was large enough to allow for opening that exit door with its stairs. I now believe that if a stewardess had been stationed in the rear of the plane, she would have perished along with the other passengers in that section. The stewardesses were where North Central had wanted them positioned.

Among the injured was Jo Carol Hatcher. Miss Hatcher was hospitalized for smoke inhalation. Miss Hatcher was a sophomore at Kilgore College in Texas and was a member of the Kilgore Rangerettes. She had planned to be back at Kilgore on the 26th in order to prepare for the Rangerettes' half time show at the Cotton Bowl, but she didn't think she would make it now, because she had no intention of flying again soon. She explained that as we were taking off, there was a loud noise and a jolt. After a few moments, there was another jolt, followed by some screaming. All she could think of was running to the front exit. She had been sitting next to a window and had a little difficulty with the seat belt. In a move similar to mine, she jumped past the person sitting next to her and moved toward the front. She thought the woman that she scooted past got out also. Miss Hatcher said there was a man sitting across the aisle from her, and she wished that she knew his name, because he took care of her. When she got to the exit, she jumped out and ran as fast as she could away from plane, fearing that it would explode. Miss Hatcher was one of 13 injured persons that had been taken to Resurrection Hospital in Chicago.

Pat Helgesen suffered foot and knee injuries, along with smoke inhalation. She was also taken to Resurrection Hospital where she shared a room with Jo Carol Hatcher. Miss Helgesen, 21, was headed to her home in Evansville, Wisconsin, where she was on vacation from St. Mary's College in South Bend, Indiana. She told the Wisconsin State Journal that she felt lucky to get a seat on the plane. *"I'm just glad that I don't smoke,"* she said. *"That's why I sat up front in the no-smoking section. I don't think I would have made it if I had been farther back."* She said *"The plane just didn't seem to take off. A guy sitting in front of me in the front of the plane said, 'Take my hand and let's get out of here'...There were no flames in the plane before we jumped,"* she said. But *seconds later, as she looked back, it burst into flame.*[8]

This was her experience. I could no longer see flames inside the plane as I approached the front exit. I believe that the smoke was so heavy near the flames in the back part of the plane that they completely blocked any light. However, I know that there was fire because I saw the flames on the inside of the plane before anyone could have exited. The darkness was deceiving.

Miss Helgesen later sent a letter to the Wisconsin State Journal which was printed in their Saturday, January 6, 1973 paper in an article entitled "God Guided Me from Crash." Her letter follows: *"In a time of dehumanized mechanization, deemphasized materialism, and self-centered egotism, one is fortunate to find that people do care!*

"It isn't often one is fortunate enough to have experienced the survival of an ordeal which approaches fatalism and is allowed the privilege of the prayers and sincere best wishes at seeing one 'alive' and well. These expressions have come to me from all over the United States in the form of phone

calls, prayers, cards, and letters. The most amazing thing is that many of these people I have never met and probably never will.

"I feel myself more than lucky, as I did that night. I know it was God who guided me from that plane. His helper, as yet unknown to me, took my hand. I feel also as I did that night as I stood watching the plane I'd just been sitting on burst into flame—amazed that I got off so easily and in disbelief that I had actually been aboard it.

"Then as I lay on a stretcher in the recovery room, I felt helpless among those hurt so much more than I. I was embarrassed and disgusted at being kept for my insignificant bruises while I watched those around me singed and coughing. I wished I could help them instead of lying there witnessing their discomfort.

"I had never realized how bad the accident was until reading and seeing pictures after my return home. I remain, now, grateful at the experience and hopeful that it will be remembered and appreciated. My thanks is to God and everyone who has been so kind and generous with their thoughts, prayers and time to make these expressions. People do care. Although it is not always so openly displayed, it is there, and it will be shown. Thank you everyone."[7]

Roger Volbrecht, 20, of Montello, Wisconsin, was also in the hospital with flash burns and smoke inhalation. He recounted his tale. He was seated in the 11th row on the left side above the wing. He stated that the very steep takeoff was followed by the collision, and then the plane bounced back down to the runway and erupted into flames. As we have seen from other survivors, Roger said that the man next to him went right over him. Roger followed that man as they crawled toward the front. He said that he choked a bit before reaching the clear air as he jumped from the plane. He said that there was a girl behind him and he thinks she also got out. Roger said that he intended to "go home and live it up."

University of Wisconsin—Madison Professor Carl Loper Jr., 40, of Madison was returning home from a business trip to Chicago. He was sitting toward the front of the plane. *"We were generally proceeding in normal fashion and the front of the plane lifted up as though we were going to take off. Then the rear of the plane hit something. There was no warning, but we knew we had hit something,' he said. 'After the initial collision the plane waved rather violently from side to side. There was no sudden stop just a mild stop with little impact.' From then on, according to Loper, everything happened so fast 'there wasn't time to be surprised. Apparently flames started coming out of the back and outside of the plane. The lights went out and everything went black. We just sort of felt our way out of the plane.' Loper said that the only injury he suffered was a slightly sore back from the eight-foot jump from the exit in the front of the plane. 'The captain was at the door when we jumped out, there was lots of smoke but everyone proceeded as rapidly as we could, there was no panic.' After almost an hour's wait on the airport runway, Loper relayed a message to his wife and family in Madison that he was all right."[8]* By 2:30 AM, about eight and a half hours after the collision, he was back in Madison.

Raymond Higgins, 53, a former state senator from Minnesota, was also a North Central passenger. *He said the takeoff seemed smooth until it became airborne when "the landing gear hit the tail of the second plane and knocked us out of the air." He said the plane pancaked to the ground and he jumped four feet to the ground from an exit door.*[3]

Hiroshi Aoki, 20, of Japan, was another passenger on the ill-fated North Central DC-9. He was flying to Madison and would be staying with the Howard Voegeli family of Monticello, Wisconsin. He was in Wisconsin while on a two-year dairy study program. He escaped injuries.

Adrienne Trangle, of Boston, Massachusetts, was yet another passenger on the North Central jet who was able to escape injuries.

Robert Seim, 20, of Superior, Wisconsin, was hospitalized in serious condition from smoke inhalation and flash burns to the hands and face. Seim's mother, Bernice, his wife, Rose, and his two-year old son Michael, were all at the Duluth Airport awaiting his arrival when they found out about the crash. I have exchanged emails with Michael after he had seen a first-hand account of the accident that I had written on www.catastrophecast.com. He suggested that they ought to make a movie about this crash.

Steve Kuhlman, 20, of Stoughton, Wisconsin, was hospitalized in intensive care for smoke inhalation, lung and throat injuries, and interior burns. Mr. Kuhlman was a private in the National Guard and was stationed at Ft. Polk, Louisiana. He was on a two-week leave when the accident occurred, and was to be given an extension so that his two weeks would start upon his release from the hospital to make up for his time there. He stated, "I was sitting in the fifth row next to the window. All I saw was flames, then black smoke. Someone told us to 'hit low' and leave to the front."[9]

I find Steve Kuhlman's story very interesting. Remember that the left side of the DC-9 had two seats and the right side had three seats. I was in the window seat on the right side, the three-seat side of the seventh row. That is the

worst seat in the seventh row to make an escape from. Mr.
Kuhlman was also in a window seat in the fifth row. He
doesn't say whether it was the left or right side, but he was
two full rows closer to the front exit door than I was. He
may have had passengers in both the middle and aisle seats
blocking him from moving quickly, but I must have been
very fast in exiting the plane before he did. I am sure that
I did get out before him, based on his injuries. He theo-
retically had the better seat and I was closer to the flames
initially, but it didn't turn out that way in the end.

North Central Airlines Captain Ordell Nordseth testified during the second day of the National Transportation
Safety Board hearings on Thursday, January 18, 1973. He
described his efforts on the night of the crash. He stated
that he remained in the cockpit "just a bit" pulling handles that discharged fire extinguishing substances into an
engine after noting that his instruments indicated that an
engine was on fire. He then exited the cockpit and went to
the front exit door where he began helping passengers who
were afraid to jump from the burning plane. He said, "We
pulled some of them out," and he stated that he let others,
"jump on me or fall on me." The plane was filled with thick
smoke, but Captain Nordseth asked his stewardess to help
lift him back into the plane so that he could continue to
help passengers get out until the heavy smoke forced him
to leave.

Nordseth testified that the fire equipment stationed at
the airport had not arrived by the time he made his second
exit. Testimony on the prior day, Wednesday, January 17,
1973, at the hearings indicated that notification of O'Hare
Fire Department units was delayed nearly two minutes
and that firemen had trouble locating the accident scene

in the heavy fog and darkness. Nevertheless, the fire fighters arrived at 6:03 PM. So Captain Nordseth was probably back in the plane for less than a minute before the smoke and flames became too much and he had to leave.

As to the accident, Nordseth testified that as his DC-9 was taking off normally and its nose had just left the runway when he spotted the Delta Convair 880 crossing his runway. "It was too late for us to stop the plane," Nordseth said. "The only thing for us to do was to try to go over the top of the other plane. When the planes collided, I knew from the size of the impact that we were in a crash situation. There was nothing we could do, because we were strictly out of control."

Nordseth was also asked about how he would have handled the miscommunication that the Delta pilots had encountered. "I might have done the same thing as the Delta crew," Nordseth said. But later he amended his statement, "I am sure I would ask for clarification of clearance" if the tower gave him no taxi route. He testified that he could not remember any circumstance where he did not receive specific taxi route information.

Stoughton Man Hurt Seriously

(FROM PAGE 1)

swar, 66, Chicago; and Mrs. Margaret Jordan, 70, Wheaton, Ill.

NOT HOSPITALIZED —R. Betz, L. Keshishian; two persons with the last name of Yasuhara; Dr. C. Loder; James Gehrmann, North F r e e d o m; Miss J. Yavitz; A. Trangle; a Mr. Overgaard; a Mr. Aoki; Dawn Harbort, 17, daughter of Mr. and Mrs. Robert Harbort, 4120 Elinor St., Madison, all Madison destination; and Ray Higgins, C. Dryer, P. Bennett, Charles Diamon, G. Caspars, a Mr. Lasserd, C. Appleby, and a Mr. G a l l o p, destinations not given.

THE CREW of four, all safe were Capt. Ordell N o r s e t h; First Officer Gerald Adamson; and Stewardesses M a r l y s Bertsch and DeAnn Sutley. All are based in Minneapolis.

Hospitalized with minor injuries from the Delta plane were Robert Miller, East Naperville, Ill., and T h o m a s Stoll, 31, Holmes Beach, Fla.

3rd City Person Survives Crash

A third Madison resident was among the survivors of a collision of a North Central DC-9 with a Delta Airlines jet at O'Hare International Airport in Chicago Wednesday night.

Todd Overgard, 21, son of Mr. and Mrs. E. Ted Overgard, 5402 Flad Ave., was returning to Madison for the holidays from O k l a h o m a City University, where he is a student.

One of the survivors, Steven K u h l m a n, 20, Stoughton, remained in fair condition Friday in the Resurrection Hospital intensive care unit.

Hospital officials said he was s u f f e r i n g smoke inhalation. They said they did not know when he would be released from intensive care or from the hospital.

Overgard was seated in the seventh row of the North Central plane and escaped injury by jumping from the front exit of the plane. Overgard's name was inadvertantly left off an earlier list of Madison survivors.

The other two Madison survivors were Prof. Carl Loper Jr., 40, of 4730 LaFayette Dr., and Dawn Harbort, 17, of 421 Elinor St.

Killed in the crash were two electronic research technicians at the University of Wisconsin-Madison, Charles D. Blair, 31, of 4714 Martha Lane, and John Kruse, 33, Sun Prairie.

Todd Overgard (name misspelled), *Wisconsin State Journal,* Thursday, December 21, 1972[4]

Todd Overgard, *Wisconsin State Journal,* Saturday, December 23, 1972[5]

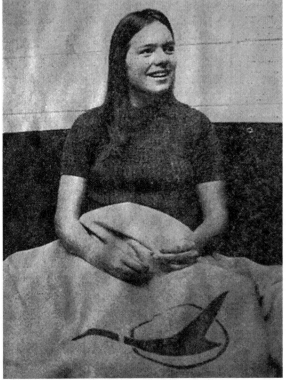

Dawn Harbort (Survivor), *The Capital Times* (Madison), Thursday, December 21, 1972. Photo by Bruce M. Fritz[2]

Dr. Carl Loper (Survivor), *Wisconsin State Journal,* Friday, December 22, 1972[8]

CHAPTER 31

DELTA PASSENGER STORY

Many of the Delta passengers said that they felt a jolt when the collision occurred. Roy Ritter, 60, of Rockford, Illinois, was in an airplane for the first time, riding in the taxiing Delta Flight 954. In describing the accident from his perspective, he said, *"After we slid down the emergency chute we saw the tail section of our plane 200 feet from the rest of it.*[3] He went on to say that the people in the back really felt the jolt, but he didn't feel it too much. If the North Central pilot had been two seconds earlier, our plane would have been done for.

The two injuries aboard the Delta Flight 954 occurred to Robert Dillon, East Naperville, Illinois, and Thomas Stoll, 31, Holmes Beach, Florida. These were bumped-head injuries, presumably from the Delta plane's rocking after the collision with the NCA plane occurred. Both men were treated at a local hospital and released.

CHAPTER 32

THE DEAD

The local Madison newspapers had extensive coverage of two of those that died in the North Central Flight 575 crash since they were Madison-area residents and worked for the University of Wisconsin—Madison (UW—Madison). Charles D. Blair of Madison and John Kruse of Sun Prairie, Wisconsin, were killed in the crash and subsequent fire. Both worked as electronics research technicians at the UW-Madison Space Science and Engineering Center.

Charles was 31 and married. His wife Nancy first heard of the crash shortly after the collision on a radio news bulletin. Confirmation of his death from the airlines did not come until after midnight. They had no children. Charles did not have a college education. His electronics expertise was self-taught.

John was 33 and also married. He and his wife Marilyn had three young children aged seven, five, and one. John had two bachelor's degrees from UW-Madison. One was in electrical engineering and one was in business administration. He also had a master's degree in electrical engineering from Iowa State University.

Charles and John were returning from Texas, where they had conducted successful tests on a large-scale weather monitoring system that they and two other members of their UW-Madison team were working on. The chancellor of UW-Madison, Edwin Young, described them "as a vital part of the scientific staff of the University of Wisconsin-Madison Space Science and Engineering Center."[10]

One of those killed in the North Central crash was Darlene Darby, 20. Miss Darby was the daughter of a Seventh Day Adventist pastor. She was on her way to visit the Reverend Lester Merklin, who was an intern pastor at the Madison Seventh Day Adventist church. He was also her fiancé. She was a theology student at Walla Walla College in Washington. Miss Darby's parents were in Sedalia, Missouri at the time of the crash. She had left her parents to come to Madison to visit her fiancé. Darlene and Lester had met when they were students at Walla Walla College. After the holidays, they were planning on driving back to Sedalia. It was during these holidays that the two were going to plan when they would get married. Alas, they would never get that chance.

Lester had spoken to Darlene earlier on the day of the crash. She had told him that her flight from Chicago to Madison was delayed until 3:30 PM. He had gone to the Madison Airport to pick her up and had been waiting since just after 3 PM. Initially he heard that all North Central flights would be arriving a half hour later than scheduled. He waited in the busy terminal for more than three hours. Then there was an announcement over the public address system that due to mechanical difficulty, North Central's flight from Chicago had been delayed. Lester decided that he should leave to go get something to eat and then come back to the airport. He went to his car and, upon starting it, he heard a radio announcement that a North Central airlines plane headed for Madison had crashed on take-off from Chicago's O'Hare Field just a few minutes ago. The number of people killed or injured was not yet known.

First descriptions said that the North Central plane was consumed by flames after the crash.

On Thursday morning, Merklin traveled to the Cook County Morgue in Chicago. He was accompanied by his pastor and a church elder. After arriving, he was taken down to the morgue where he was shown the badly burned body. It appeared to be of a similar size. He was also shown a wrist watch and contact lenses. Darlene had worn contacts and the watch looked much like hers. Lester couldn't tell if it was Darlene. About all that Lester could say was that the body looked similar.

Mr. and Mrs. Edward W. Wolf, along with Mrs. Beverly Long, were on their way to the Schumacher Funeral Home in LaCrosse, Wisconsin. All three had traveled from the Edgewater, Florida/New Smyrna Beach, Florida area. Mrs. Wolf and Mrs. Long were sisters who were traveling to the funeral of their mother, Mrs. Hazel G. Wisler, 72, which had been scheduled for Friday at 11 AM. All three were former Wisconsin residents who died on the North Central plane.[3]

Additional persons who died on the North Central plane were Mrs. Helma Aalto, 79, of Aurora/Omega, Minnesota, Mrs. Beverly Dempsey, 23, of Rantoul, Illinois, and Mrs. E. Tonder of Hasle, Norway. Mrs. Dempsey was on her way to visit her sister. All three were headed separately to Duluth, presumably for the upcoming holidays.[3]

The tenth person to die was Serge Pakswer, 68, of Elmhurst, Illinois. There are conflicting reports, but suffice it to say that he died on either Sunday or Monday, December 24th or 25th at Resurrection Hospital in Chicago, where a number of the injured were taken after the crash. Mr. Pakswer was suffering from smoke inhalation. I saw him being escorted from the plane after his exit. He was the last person to get out of the burning plane that I saw. His widow filed suit for $1 million about a month after his death.

In another interesting aspect of this accident, it was reported that materials, and particularly plastics, which burned inside the plane produced a cyanide gas which can be deadly. This is particularly true when the cyanide gas is combined with carbon monoxide. The Cook County coroner, Dr. Andrew J. Toman, said there was a sufficient amount of cyanide in the blood of the victims to cause death. This is true for at least some of the victims. However, he continued, the victims died of a combination of smoke inhalation and cyanide. There was another crash at Midway Airport in Chicago just 12 days earlier in which 45 people died. Of the 55 to die in both of these Chicago area crashes, ten of them had lethal levels of cyanide in their systems. It means that a burning airplane is also a deadly plastic-filled gas chamber.

Airplane manufacturers have been questioned and even encouraged to consider changing out the materials in their planes to prevent the deadly gas from being discharged during a fire. The FAA had not yet required this to be done, and manufacturers had not yet made the determination to start the retrofitting process on their own.

Charles Blair and John Kruse – Both Died in the North Central Crash, Wisconsin State Journal, *Friday, December 22, 1972*[10]

CHARLES BLAIR   JOHN KRUSE

CHAPTER 33

PASSENGERS & CREW STATUS LISTS

There is a discrepancy between my count of the injured based on newspaper articles and the NTSB report which states ten dead and 17 injured. On the night of the crash, nine died and 17 were reported as injured. Serge Pakswar was counted among the injured and not the dead. When he died, five days later, the numbers changed to ten dead and 16 injured. The NTSB report lists two crew members as injured, one of the flight attendants and the captain, who received minor injuries upon reentering the plane. However, both flight attendants were listed as hospitalized/injured in newspaper accounts and therefore three crew members are listed below among the injured resulting in a total of 10 dead and 17 injured.

Died – Total/Passengers/Crew (10/10/0) Aboard the NCA Flight 575:[10]

- Mrs. Helma Aalto, 79, Ogema/Aurora, Minnesota
- Charles D. Blair, 31, Madison, Wisconsin
- Miss Darlene Darby, 20, Baker, Oregon
- Mrs. Beverly Dempsey, 23, Rantoul, Illinois
- Mrs. Beverly Long, Edgewater, Florida
- John Kruse, 33, Sun Prairie, Wisconsin
- Serge Pakswar, 68, Chicago, Illinois (Initially hospital ized, but died five days later)
- Mrs. E. Tonder, Hasle, Norway

- Mr. Edward Wolf, Edgewater/New Smyrna Beach, Florida
- Mrs. Edward Wolf, Edgewater/New Smyrna Beach, Florida

Injured – Total/Passengers/Crew (15-12-3) NCA Flight 575:[3/4/10]

- Laura Biglow, 52, Chicago, Illinois – Smoke Inhalation - Intensive Care – Serious
- Marlys Bertsch, 27, Bloomington, Minnesota, Crew – Stewardess – Observation.
- Sally Dangelo, 28, Waukegan, Wisconsin - Smoke Inhalation – Intensive Care – Serious Condition.
- Elsie DeLang, 60, Villa Park, Illinois – Smoke Inhalation, Burns, & Cuts - Intensive Care – Serious Condition.
- Jo Carol Hatcher, 19, Laird Hill, Texas – Smoke Inhalation – Fair Condition.
- Patricia Helgesen, 21, Evansville, Wisconsin – Foot and Knee Injuries, Smoke Inhalation – Fair Condition.
- Julie Holmlund, 34, Duluth, Wisconsin – Intensive Care – Serious Condition.
- Mrs. Margaret Jordan, 70, Wheaton, Illinois – Smoke Inhalation and Back Pains - Fair Condition.
- Steven Kuhlman, 20, Stoughton, Wisconsin – Smoke Inhalation - Intensive Care – Serious Condition (returning to his parents' home in Stoughton, Wisconsin after National Guard training in Louisiana).
- Captain Ordell Nordseth, 49, Crew - Flight Captain – Good Condition.

- Richard Ojakangas, 40, Duluth, Minnesota - Smoke Inhalation - Fair Condition.
- Gregory Ojakangas, 13, Duluth, Minnesota – Smoke Inhalation - Intensive Care – Serious Condition.
- Robert Seim, 20, Superior, Wisconsin – Flash Burns to the Face and Hands and Smoke Inhalation – Intensive Care - Serious Condition.
- DeAnn Sutley, 26, Pierre, South Dakota, Crew – Stewardess – Observation.
- Roger Volbrecht, 20, Montello, Wisconsin – Flash Burns and Smoke Inhalation - Fair Condition.

Injured – Total/Passengers/Crew (2/2/0) for Delta Airlines Flight 954:[3/4/10]

- Robert Dillon, 29, East Naperville, Illinois, minor injuries, treated and released.
- Thomas Stoll, 31, Holmes Beach, Florida, minor injuries, treated and released.

Not Hospitalized – Total/Passengers/Crew (20-19-1) NCA Flight 575:[4]

- Gerald Adamson, 32, Crew - First Officer.
- Mr. Aoki.
- C. Appleby.
- P. Bennett.
- R. Betz.
- G. Caspars.
- Charles Diamon.
- C. Dryer.
- Mr. Gallop.
- James Gehrmann, North Freedom, Wisconsin.

· Dawn Harbort, 17, returning home to Madison, Wisconsin from school in North Carolina.
· Ray Higgens.
· L. Keshishian.
· Mr. Lasserd.
· Dr. C. Loder, Madison, Wisconsin.
· Todd Overgard, 21, Oklahoma City, Oklahoma.
· A. Trangle.
· Yasuhara.
· Yasuhara.
· Miss J. Yavitz.

CHAPTER 34

THE NATIONAL TRANSPORTATION SAFETY BOARD REPORT

The National Transportation Safety Board organized and sent eight teams of investigators, totaling 60 people, from Washington D.C, to arrive on Thursday, December 21st. When they left, they had planned to land in Milwaukee, Wisconsin, due to the poor weather conditions at O'Hare. The teams would begin their task of going through the wreckage, and listening to tapes of the exchanges between the control tower and the two airplane crews. They would also interview the flight crews of both airplanes. Rudolph Kapustim led the NTSB's investigation. They used the Sheraton-O'Hare Motor Inn, which was close to O'Hare, as their base of operations.

O'Hare was closed immediately following the airplane crash after having been shut down prior to the accident. This heavy fog also closed down Chicago's other airports as well. O'Hare was packed with travelers who were apparently unaware of the drama playing out on the runways. Christmas carols were on the public address system playing throughout the huge terminal. It had been very hard for anyone, other than those of us involved, to know that an airplane crash had taken place due to the visually impenetrable fog. The control tower saw the North Central plane disappear from their radar screens. Then they relayed this account from the control tower: "We saw it explode. All we saw was a big fire."

The two planes involved in the collision were a North Central Airlines DC9-31 with 45 aboard and a Delta Air Lines Convair-880 (CV880) with 93 on board. There were 138 people involved directly in the accident. The casualties from my plane crash and subsequent fire were ten dead and 15 injured. That means that 25 of the 45 people on board were either killed or injured. But that's not quite right. I never made a medical injury claim, but my neck was hurt from the jolt of our plane colliding with the Delta plane. I feel it to this day, although it is only a minor annoyance. I was also to discover that this accident was to become one of the more important crashes in aviation history. Now that sounds like an overly bold claim, but it's true.

Visibility at the time of the crash was officially declared to be a quarter of a mile by the National Weather Service. Air traffic controllers are authorized to make decisions regarding visibility at O'Hare. Lloyd Eastburn was working the south side of the O'Hare tower on the night of the crash. He told the NTSB at its hearings that he estimated the visibility on Runway 27L, where the North Central airplane was to takeoff, at one-eighth mile. He was overruled by his superior, the tower supervisor, Russell Lawson. This is important because takeoffs with less than a quarter mile of visibility are not allowed on runways like Runway 27 Left because it was not equipped with Runway Visual Range (RVR) equipment. The air traffic controller working the north side of the O'Hare tower, William Gratzke, also testified that he estimated visibility at one-eighth mile. Eastburn testified that he "still felt it [visibility] was one-eighth mile" even though reports from the Weather Service at the time said one-quarter mile. The air traffic controllers use visibility markers to determine visibility in bad weather, so I believe that they were correct in their assessment.

I got a chance to speak with Lloyd Eastburn, who contacted me after hearing about my first-hand account on the internet. Lloyd was the controller who authorized the North Central plane's takeoff. The takeoff was delayed a short while when the disagreement over the visibility distance was being discussed before Lloyd was ordered to authorize the takeoff. Lloyd said that after the accident, he went through nightmares for about a year, and had to deal with feelings of guilt. Of course, Lloyd didn't know that the Delta plane was heading toward our take-off runway. He did say that the Delta pilots continued taxiing while they called their company to find out their gate location rather than immediately contacting O'Hare ground control upon landing, which, he told me, they were supposed to do. The Delta plane had a gate delay and needed a place to park their aircraft while they waited for a gate to clear. This added to the confusion. If they had called immediately upon landing, then they might have ended up parked at the intended 32R pad.

Lloyd went on to be laid off in the air traffic controllers' strike in 1981, and he was one of only 700 to be rehired later. In the interim, he became a deacon in the Catholic church. He also told me that he was in the O'Hare control tower on 9/11 when all planes were told to land and O'Hare had planes stacked up around the airport. That was his busiest day ever.

Picture of Lloyd Eastburn in the old O'Hare tower in 1961. He was in the new tower on the night of December 20, 1972, when the crash occurred.

The cause of the accident, as determined by the National Transportation Safety Board (NTSB) in Report Number NTSB-AAR-73-15[1], was poor communication between the Chicago O'Hare ground controller, Patrick O'Brien, and the Delta Airlines Flight 954 flight crew, which consisted of Captain Robert McDowell, First Officer Harry Greenberg, and Second Officer Claude Fletcher. The Delta plane was a Convair 880 which had just come in from Tampa, Florida. Some of the confusion started when the Delta flight crew heard an Automatic Terminal Information Service (ATIS) broadcast stating that runways 14L and 14R were being used for departures. When the O'Hare operation was subsequently changed to use Runways 14L and 14R for approaches, the flight crew was not informed that departures had started on Runway 27L. Runway 27L was the runway assigned to North Central Airlines Flight 575 for takeoff.

The Delta plane had been cleared for landing on runway 14L at 5:52:30 PM. At 5:55:05 PM, the O'Hare local controller requested that Delta Flight 954 report when it had cleared runway 14L. The Delta plane reported clear of the runway 14L at 5:56:18 PM. After this, the flight was turned over to Chicago O'Hare ground control. At this same time, O'Brien attempted to contact Delta Flight 954 without success. At 5:57:29 PM the first officer on the Delta plane established radio contact with O'Brien stating "Delta nine-fifty-four is with you inside the Bridge and we gotta go to the box." The bridge is a taxiway bridge over an airport access road which is well past the Runway 32R runup pad.

The bridge runs between the Runway 32R runup pad and the North-South taxiway. O'Brien replied, "Ok, if you can just pull over to (the) thirty-two pad." The Delta first officer replied, "Okay, we'll do it." There were no further communications between the Delta plane and ATC. The "box" is a holding area officially designated as the Penalty Box.

O'Brien had made a note on a scratch pad which he later stated was to remind him that he had sent CV-880 to the 32R pad to hold awaiting a gate assignment. The report goes on to state that the captain of Delta Flight 954 taxied the plane via the Bridge, the Outer Circular, and the North-South taxiways en route to the Runway 32L runup pad.

It came to my attention that Patrick O'Brien may have suffered a great personal tragedy one week before the crash. Assuming this to be true, how would this have affected his ability to focus on the demanding job of an air traffic controller? I suspect that it would have been very difficult to maintain one's concentration. Was this situation at the root of the mistake that O'Brien made? I would venture to guess that even O'Brien can't say for sure one way or the

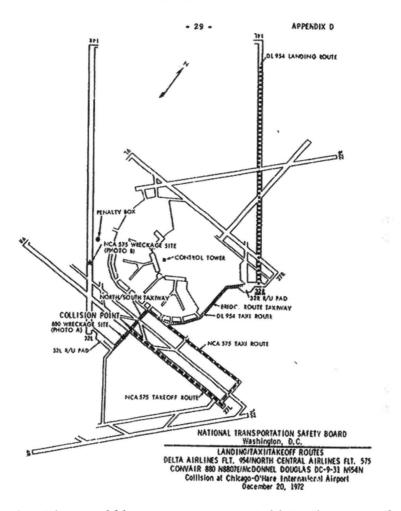

- 29 -   APPENDIX D

NATIONAL TRANSPORTATION SAFETY BOARD
Washington, D.C.
LANDING/TAXI/TAKEOFF ROUTES
DELTA AIRLINES FLT. 954/NORTH CENTRAL AIRLINES FLT. 575
CONVAIR 880 N8807E/McDONNEL DOUGLAS DC-9-31 N954N
Collision at Chicago-O'Hare International Airport
December 20, 1972

other. This would be just one more wrinkle in the series of events that led to the disaster.

O'Brien later stated that he had not heard the words "inside the bridge" from the Delta First Officer's initial transmission. The ground controller had thought that Delta Flight 954 was just taxiing clear of the landing runway (14L) when he was contacted. In replying to that initial transmission, it was his intention to determine whether the flight could hold on the Runway 32R runup pad.

The NTSB report goes on to state that the captain and first officer of the Delta plane both thought that ATC was telling them to proceed to the Runway 32L runup pad. So the stage was set through these misunderstandings and miscommunication.

Concurrently, North Central Airlines Flight 575, which was a DC-9, was in communication with the local controller, Lloyd Eastburn. At 5:50 PM, the North Central was cleared to taxi to Runway 27L for departure. At 5:58:52 PM, the Lloyd cleared the North Central plane into the takeoff position on Runway 27L and advised the crew the visibility was one-fourth mile. At 5:59:24 PM the local controller cleared North Central Flight 575 for takeoff. The captain reported that he was beginning his takeoff roll.

The first officer of the North Central plane made the takeoff and all was initially normal. The plane was gathering speed and approaching its 160 mile per hour takeoff speed with its nose gear just leaving the tarmac when the captain saw the Delta plane directly ahead on his runway. He immediately called "Rotate" and assisted the first officer in applying additional control pressure to gain altitude in an attempt to clear the other aircraft. The attempt was unsuccessful. The collision occurred at 6:00:08.7 PM. The North Central plane was no longer flightworthy after the collision. The pilot took control and brought the aircraft back onto the runway.

At 6:00:7.6 PM, the flight recorder for the Delta Convair 880 Flight 954 showed that in response to a crewmember's statement concerning passenger inquiries about connecting flights, the captain said, "Ah, we can't even ooh!" Impact sounds were heard 1.1 seconds after the start of that statement. At 6:00:13.7 PM, the first officer exclaimed, "That guy crashed!" This exclamation was followed by

statements about a fire and "Shut 'em down." The voice re-
cording ended at 6:00:26.8 PM.

The North Central Airlines crew was criticized for not
being well enough trained to evacuate people as swiftly as
possible. The NTSB report faulted North Central for not
training their personnel under more realistic simulated
conditions so that the crew would be more familiar with
what to expect in a real emergency. The report stated that
"None of the training they received was conducted under
conditions of real or simulated cabin emergency lighting
or a smoke-filled environment."

Although the training may not have been up to par, I felt
that I was off the plane very quickly considering the darkness, smoke, and the number of people ahead of me. There
were six rows of five seats each in front of me. There were
also the four seats on my seventh row that had better access
to the aisle than I did. That is a total of 34 seats that were positioned better than mine for a quick exit. Most likely there
were three or four passengers per row since the plane was
not full. Also, I scrambled up a couple of rows before my way
forward was blocked by other passengers in the aisle. So it
is likely that between 12 and 16 people got out ahead of me.
Considering the numbers of people who were uninjured, the
fire and smoke must have been pretty close behind me. I am
thankful that I was able to leave the plane as quickly as I did.

On the diagram (Appendix D) you can see that the collision took place on Runway 27L just after the Delta Flight
954 had left the North-South taxiway heading toward the
32L runup pad, which was on the other side of Runway 27L.
The NTSB report goes on to identify a reference point as
the centerlines of Runway 27L and the North-South taxiway. This is where the collision took place. The following

are a list of evidentiary items and their distances from the reference point found upon investigation.

There was a gouge in the runway 394 feet east of the reference point. The North Central plane was traveling east to west on runway 27L, so this is before the collision. The gouge *"was attributed to the impact of the DC-9 tailskid with the runway."* This means that the plane was over-rotated to the extent that the tailskid struck the runway upon takeoff. The tailskid is a metal or rubber item on the underside of the tail area to protect the plane should the tail strike the asphalt. This explains why this was the steepest angle of takeoff that I had ever experienced.

"Dark, rubberlike scrub marks lined part of the surface of Runway 27L, beginning 547 feet west and 25 feet north of the reference point. The marks continued 15 feet farther west. Gouge marks on the runways and adjacent sodded areas indicated that the DC-9 had left Runway 27L and had scribed a curved path to the point where it stopped on Runway 32L" My plane was traveling at approximately 160 mph upon takeoff. It would have been slowed by the tailskid strike above, by the collision with the Delta plane's wing tip and stabilizer, both of which were torn off, and by the North Central plane's landing gear contact with the top of the Delta plane's fuselage, where large indentations were found. All of this would have slowed the North Central plane down. I figure that my plane would have slowed from 160 mph to 120 mph, and maybe less. At 120 mph, my plane would have been in the air for just over three seconds before crashing back down onto the tarmac. At the time, it seemed a bit longer than that, but maybe time was not moving as fast for me between the collision and the crash.

"The DC-9 came to a stop on Runway 32L on a mag-netic heading of 352°, approximately 800 feet north of the centerline of Runway 27L and 3,200 feet from the reference point. (See Appendix D.)" After crashing on the runway, the plane skidded off of runway 27L almost immediately, then traveled across a grassy infield until ending up on runway 32L. The plane crashed after flying 547 feet and skidded another 2,653 feet before stopping. This means that the skid lasted for 30 seconds if the average speed was 60 mph during the skid. I estimated 60 mph because if we were crashing at 120 mph, then a consistent slow down to a stop would average 60 mph. These calculations work out quite well, since my recollection was that we skidded for about 30 seconds.

"The right main landing gear lay 1,583 feet west and 114 feet north of the reference point. One of two sections of the right leading-edge flap was found 259 feet west and 140 feet north, and the other, 1,248 feet west and 140 feet north, of the reference point." As can be seen from this, pieces of the DC-9 were strewn quite a distance from the crash site.

There are a couple of other interesting notations con-cerning the damage to both planes. The North Central DC-9 had damage to its right engine (Engine No. 2) in the form of an 18-inch piece of a horizontal rib from the Con-vair-880's vertical stabilizer lodged against the inlet guide vanes of the engine.

A large portion of the Delta Convair 880's vertical stabi-lizer was found approximately 17 feet west of the reference point. *"A narrow strip of tire rubber was imbedded in the lower part of the rear spar of the stabilizer. The left wingtip was found 82 feet east and 84 feet south of the reference point. The top of the fuselage was substantially damaged in three areas. The first area was centered at Fuselage Station (FS) 1192 where the damage consisted of two 22-inch depressions into the top of the fuselage. The combined width of the depressed surfaces was 31 inches. A rubber-like substance was deposited on the depressed surfaces. The second area was at the point where the vertical stabilizer fairs into the fuselage. A large 20-inch V-shaped depression was located 10 feet aft of the first area. The depression was streaked with green-blue paint. The third area was centered 16 feet, 8 inches aft of the first area. The top of the fuselage between the center and aft spar attachment stations of the vertical stabilizer contained a 28-inch depression. A 6-by-6-inch piece of a tire was found in the fuselage below this area. The piece matched the torn remains of one of the tires on the right main landing gear from the DC-9. The interior ceiling in the aft cabin was compressed to 38 inches above the cabin floor.*[1] That is a lot of damage, with parts flying off of both planes and both fuselages heavily damaged.

Questions arose as to why ground radar was not used by the O'Hare ground controller. O'Hare had an Airport Surface Detection Equipment (ASDE) radar system installed at the tower facility. This was a high resolution, ground surveillance, dual-channel pulse type of radar. It was primarily used to detect land vehicles and aircraft on airport runways, taxiways, and aircraft parking areas. FAA maintenance personnel examined the ASDE radar system shortly after the accident occurred. The system was operating within prescribed tolerances. O'Hare tower controller personnel testified that during periods of low visibility, the ASDE radar is used almost exclusively by the local controllers to determine whether approaching aircraft have landed or executed a missed approach, when and where landing aircraft are clear of the runway, and when departing aircraft begin and complete the takeoff. The ASDE is adjusted and centered by the local controllers for these functions. The tower controllers also testified that they considered the ASDE equipment unreliable for the identification of airport traffic movements because of blind spots, the inability of the equipment to distinguish aircraft from other vehicles, and the inability to identify targets during periods of moderate to heavy precipitation. Tower personnel stated that ground controllers rarely used the ASDE equipment because of these limitations.

So there was ground control radar, but it was inadequate for tracking airplanes on the ground and therefore not used. In bad visibility, the knowledge of location of airplanes was limited to the verbal communications between pilots and ground control personnel. The ground controller on duty at the time of the accident was not required to be qualified, nor was he fully qualified, in the operation and use of the ASDE. He said that he did use the radar to assist another flight in locating the Penalty Box, but not to identify the position of the CV-880.

"While evacuating the main entry door of the plane, there was no visible evacuation slide. It turns out that a discrepancy was found in the maintenance of the evacuation slide. Examination showed that the slide would not have inflated when the inflation lanyard was pulled because the lanyard was wrapped around the neck of the inflation bottle. An evaluation of the effect of not inflating the slide indicates that the escape of those persons who used the main entry door might have been expedited. Had the slide been inflated, it would have extended at a shallow angle because of the attitude of the airplane. Therefore, the evacuees would

not have been able to slide out of the aircraft, but rather, they would have had to walk or run out on an unstable slide. This would have increased the possibility of a fall and subsequent injury. On the other hand, had the slide been in-flated, it would have been easier for crewmembers to return to the cabin when the flow of passengers slowed or stopped."

I question this last statement from the report. By the time the flow of passengers had slowed, the smoke and fire would have made it too dangerous to reenter the aircraft. I know the pilot did reenter the aircraft, but he couldn't have stayed there very long. The smoke and fire had quickly become too intense.

CHAPTER 35

THE NTSB REPORT CONCLUSIONS

THE FINDINGS:

The NTST identified eight findings in this crash.

1. *The visibility at O'Hare at the time of the accident was one-fourth mile in fog.*
2. Airport traffic beyond the confines of the main terminal area could not be observed visually from the control tower.
3. The ASDE "BRITE" equipment at the O'Hare tower provided indistinct displays of airport ground traffic.
4. The ground controller's transmission to the CV-880 was ambiguous because he did not specify which of two similarly numbered runup pads was to be used as a holding point.
5. The flight crew of the CV-880 did not request clarification of the ground controller's ambiguous transmission.
6. Flight crews and controllers in the Chicago terminal area both deviated from the prescribed ATC communication procedures.
7. The captain of the DC-9 was operating under a valid clearance.
8. Neither the local controller nor the flight crew of the DC-9 was aware of the proximity of the CV-880 to Runway 27L.

THE PROBABLE CAUSE:

The National Transportation Safety Board determines that the probable cause of this accident was the failure of the traffic control system to insure separation of aircraft during a period of restricted visibility. This failure included the following: (1) the controller omitted a critical word which made his transmission to the flight crew of the Delta CV-880 ambiguous; (2) the controller did not use all the available information to determine the location of the CV-880; and (3) the CV-880 flight crew did not request clarification of the controller's communications.

THE RECOMMENDATIONS:

The NTSB has submitted six recommendations (A-73-21 through 26) to the FAA concerning air traffic control procedures. These are identified in Appendix E of the NTSB report. The first four recommendations pertain to a technical issue as to efficacy of the Bright Radar Indicator Tower Equipment (BRITE) display system for radar. This BRITE system was, in 1972, used in only three of eight ASDE user facilities. The three facilities using that BRITE display with the ASDE radar system were Chicago O'Hare International Airport, New York's John Fitzgerald Kennedy (JFK) International Airport, and San Francisco International Airport. This display system was discouraging the use of the ASDE system by air traffic controllers even though it was specifically designed to locate air traffic movement in low visibility. Today's airports have overcome these issues, so I will not repeat the recommendations here. These radar systems were passive, meaning that planes were not using transponders. In today's large airports, planes taxi with their transponders on in order to provide an exact location of each plane on the ground radar system. It is a massive improvement over the now-antiquated systems used in 1972.

The fifth recommendation to the FAA, A-73-25, reads as follows: Establish and publish taxi routes for arriving and departing aircraft to be used during periods of restricted visibility on the order of ½ mile.

The sixth recommendation to the FAA, A-73-26, reads: Require pilots to obtain the controllers' approval before crossing a lighted runway during periods of restricted visibility on the order of ½ mile.

Five additional recommendations (A-73-39 through 43) concerning the crash survival aspects of this accident were sent to the FAA. These survivability recommendations were a combined response from three December 1972 crashes. These were the December 8th Chicago Midway crash, the December 20th Chicago O'Hare collision and runway crash, and the December 29th Miami crash of an Eastern Air Lines plane into the Everglades.

The first two survivability recommendations were for pilots to be using their shoulder harnesses and for cabin attendants to be provided with shoulder harnesses. The third recommendation had to do with providing stowed and portable high-intensity lights at cabin attendant stations. The fourth recommendation pertains to emergency lighting.

The report says, "*Emergency Lighting. Evidence obtained during the investigation of the North Central DC-9 accident and the United B-737 accident in Chicago, indicated that many passengers had difficulties in escaping from the wreckage. These difficulties were a result of inadequate illumination, combined with a heavy smoke condition in one of these accidents. In the United accident, survivors specifically mention the absence of any light in the cabin. In the North Central accident, passengers experienced great difficulty in locating the exits, reportedly because of the darkness and heavy smoke in the cabin. Yet, the crew testified that the emergency lighting system was armed, and the investigation indicated that they should have been operational. However, four of the nine fatally injured passengers apparently died while they were attempting to find an exit. One passenger was found in the cockpit, one near the cockpit door, and two others were found near the aft end of the cabin. The five remaining fatalities apparently had not left their seats.*

"Numerous recommendations and proposals to improve occupant escape capabilities in survivable accidents have been made over the years by various Government and industry organizations; and, indeed, significant improvements have occurred. Unfortunately, however, experience indicates that the existing escape potential from aircraft in which post-crash fire is involved is still marginal. These accidents illustrate the vital role that adequate illumination can play in contributing to such post-crash survivability.

"A review of 14 CFR 25.811 and 25.812 indicates that paragraph 811(c) requires means to assist occupants in locating exits in conditions of <u>dense smoke.</u> Yet, information from the Civil Aeromedical Institute in Oklahoma City indicates that the illumination levels specified in paragraph 812 are not predicated on a smoky environment, and therefore may be ineffective under conditions of dense smoke. In order to eliminate this inconsistency, the Board believes that illumination levels should be specified in paragraph 812, which are consistent with the requirements of 14 CFR 25.811(c). Moreover, these and other accident experiences have shown that for various reasons aircraft emergency lighting systems often do not work or are proved ineffective in survivable accidents. Therefore, the Safety Board recommends that the Federal Aviation Administration:

4. Amend 14 CFR 25.812 to require exit sign brightness and general illumination levels in the passenger cabin that are consistent with those necessary to provide adequate visibility in conditions of dense smoke.

5. Amend 14 CFR 25.812 to provide an additional means for activating the main emergency lighting system to provide redundancy and thereby improve its reliability."

As to the final conclusions, the NTSB recommendations listed in the NTSB report on this crash are as follows:

"2. Require flight crews to report their aircraft position on the airport when establishing radio communications with controllers and require the controllers to read back the reported aircraft position when it cannot be verified either visually or by means of radar. (Recommendation A-73-54)

"3. Require flight crews to read back taxi clearances when operating in visibilities of less than one-half mile. (Recommendation A-73-55)"

Note that I have left the first recommendation for last. I had initially thought that all nine people who died on my flight got trapped in the back section of the plane behind the area where I had seen the fireball. This did not turn out to be the case. Of the nine people who died, five people were found in their seats. This fits with my understanding that the flames were so intense that those people died before they could even leave their seats. One of those individuals was an invalid who could not walk, so she would not have been able to exit on her own. Four other people made it out of their seats based upon where their bodies were found. Two people were found in the back end of the cabin. I presume that they were trying to open the rear exit door located toward the tail section. I had stated earlier that I do not believe this exit door would open, or at least open far enough to allow for escaping, due to the fuselage lying directly on the tarmac. Another passenger died near the cockpit door and one died in the cockpit. Here is where the crash has an impact on all flights today. It is apparent to me that these last two must have been in front of the area that was burning. As passengers were evacuating, the smoke inhalation and burning issues were becoming more intense, and many of the later evacuees ended up hospitalized. I can only presume that these two individuals came from the back portion of the aircraft, maybe the last two with a chance to exit. The fact is that the main entry door was wide-open. Apparently disoriented by the smoke and unable to see in the darkness, these two men wandered directly past that open door and toward the cockpit where they collapsed and died.

The NTSB report stated, *"an additional survival aspect, a need for improved emergency evacuation capability in darkness and smoke conditions, was illustrated by this accident. In the darkness and smoke, the passengers had extreme difficulty in finding their way to the main exit and in locating exits. Four passengers left their seats and apparently attempted to find an exit but were unable to do so under the conditions that existed."*

The survivors, myself included, when interviewed by the NTSB, reported that there was no exit guidance, pathway lighting, or exit location lighting visible. Supposedly, it was working, but to no avail. This brings me to the first of the three recommendations of NTSB-AAR-73-15:

"1. Amend the existing certification and operating rules for air carrier and air taxi aircraft to include provisions requiring tactile guidance and improved visual guidance to emergency exits, as well as more efficient methods of indicating the location of emergency exits in a dark or smoke environment. (Recommendation AA-73-53)"

The emergency lighting recommendations led to emergency exit pathway lighting that can be seen despite the presence of dark or smoky conditions. All aircraft today carry this lighting as a direct result of this accident and is a tribute to those who lost their lives, for they shall not have died in vain. That is not much consolation for the friends and families of the dead, but it is a better result than most airline crashes provide. This is why my crash is considered to be one of the more important crashes in aviation history.

CHAPTER 36

MY CRASH—THE UNKNOWN CRASH

In the years after my Chicago O'Hare accident, I found that most people had never heard of my crash. Gloria, a high school classmate of mine, was aware of my crash when I contacted her years later. She had been a flight attendant on United based out of Chicago's O'Hare for many years, so this crash was one of just a few at the world's busiest airport. Very few other people that I have met over the years knew about it or its significance.

That is why I was very surprised when, while I was doing a routine internet search one day, I discovered a podcast of my crash on a website called Catastrophecast.com. The website is run by Walter Hopgood. His podcast of my crash was quite detailed and went on for over 17 minutes. His written introduction to the podcast blew me away, since it placed the relative importance of this crash much higher than was generally understood. Walter introduced the podcast with the following:

"Today's podcast is on a catastrophe that's relatively un-known in the realm of airline crashes and catastrophes, but the effects as a result of the investigation into the crash is something that we can see, and live with to this day. As a matter of fact, you basically pay honor or tribute to all those involved in the crash of Delta Airlines flight 954 and

North Central Airlines flight 575 every single time you get on an airplane!"[11]

When I contacted Walter and told him that I was a survivor of that crash, he asked me to write a first-hand account for his website. I agreed to write it. Although it was only a few pages long, I thought it was important to give people a sense of what it was like to be inside an airplane that was on fire. One of the commenters to my article was a Michael Seim, whose father, Robert Seim, had survived the crash also. He had suggested that they ought to make a movie about this crash. Well, I had contemplated writing this book for years, and now that I was retired, I thought it was time.

An interesting point noted by Walter was that the Tenerife crash of 1977 had similarities to this O'Hare crash. One of the similarities was that the Tenerife crash was the collision of two aircraft on a runway due to miscommunications or misunderstandings between air traffic control and the pilots of one of the airplanes. A second similarity was that there was heavy fog, creating visibility problems for both of the pilots. A third similarity was that airport personnel did not initially understand that there were two aircraft involved in the Tenerife crash. These similarities to my crash are a bit eerie. In my crash, the Delta plane was not recognized as involved in the accident until 28 minutes after the collision. Luckily, the Delta plane was not on fire and had minimal injuries that did not require immediate attention. This was not the case with the Tenerife disaster. One of the differences is that the Tenerife crash involved much larger airplanes. Both the Pan Am Flight 1736 and

KLM Flight 4805 were Boeing 747 passenger jets. The KLM jet was taking off, and struck the Pan Am plane almost full on. Both planes burst into flames, resulting in all 248 people on the KLM flight dying and 335 dying on the Pan Am plane, while 61 people on the Pan Am flight survived with injuries. The resulting totals of 583 dead and 61 injured made this the deadliest crash in aviation history.

So why isn't my O'Hare crash well known to the general public? One reason is that it happened almost half a century ago. Another is that, even though every life is very important, ten dead is a relatively low number compared with those that died in most other airplane crashes of 1972. Still another reason that my crash is not well known was that there were many more crashes around the time of my crash, which means that a lot of publicity went to those other crashes. A number of these were very spectacular and are among the most well-known crashes in history. I will explore some of these crashes in the following pages.

Before I do that, let me bring to your attention to the fact that 1972 was truly a year in which being killed due to an air crash was at its zenith. More people were killed in commercial plane crashes in 1972 than in any other year in history. There were 72 air crashes around the world that year. In 1948, there were 99 planes crashed, but due to the larger seating capacity of the planes of 1972, more people would die.

The following is a listing of the five deadliest years in aviation history:

Year	Number of Deaths
1972	2,370
1973	2,023
1985	2,010

Year	Number of Deaths
1974	1,989
1996	1,845

The following is a listing of the six deadliest decades in aviation history:

Decade	Number of Deaths
1970s	16,766
1960s	13,692
1990s	12,241
1980s	11,558
1950s	8,702
2000s	8,318

Remember also that there are many more flights and passengers flying today than there were in the 1970s. Safety methodologies and technologies have greatly improved air safety. These include safety factors such as crew resource management (CRM) programs. These were begun by airlines in an effort to ensure that distractions didn't cause unseen issues. CRM required flight officers to speak up early about potential crash risks despite a captain's superior rank. CRM began to break down the authoritarian nature of a flight captain's position. Distraction was a key factor in a number of crashes, and safety was to become every flight crew member's responsibility.

Most of the crashes in 1972 were controlled flight into terrain (CFIT). Common technologies have since been instituted to more effectively recognize and avoid this type of accident, such as ground proximity warning systems (GPWS). GPWS was made mandatory for airliners in December of 1975. Another common technology now used is traffic collision avoidance systems (TCAS) which has largely eliminated mid-air collisions since it was implemented in the U.S. in the late 1980s.

Dan Jacobson, a commercial aircraft pilot, told me in 2019 that *"TCAS is only required on large aircraft. Small airplanes are not equipped with it, even when sharing the same airspace. But TCAS systems can see non-TCAS equipped aircraft. In 2020, there will be a requirement for all aircraft to be ADS-B (Automatic Dependent Surveillance-Broadcast) equipped, which for most airplanes means that they will have the ability to accurately see the location of other airplanes around them, but it is still not as robust as TCAS. TCAS also provides Resolution Advisories, which are directive commands from the system to the pilot to maneuver the airplane to avoid a collision with another aircraft. If both aircraft are equipped with TCAS, the two TCAS systems coordinate with each other and give opposite commands to each cockpit, i.e., one plane is told to climb while the other is told to descend. It is SOP (Standard Operating Procedure) that we immediately follow the TCAS RA (Resolution Advisory) guidance, and we trust that the other crew is doing the same. It is a great system."*

In 1972, pilots were under larger workloads, and today, automation has made a big difference in helping pilots avoid dangerous situations. Still, 1972 was a safer year than a decade earlier, based on passenger miles traveled. For instance, between 1959 and the late 1960s, the death rate was to drop from 40 deaths to just two deaths for every million scheduled passenger miles. To look at it another way, in 1959, a passenger had a 1 in 25,000 chance of being involved in a fatal air crash. This means involved in, but not necessarily killed. By the late 1960s, that number had dropped to 1 in 500,000 of being involved in a fatal crash. By 2015, the chances of being involved in a fatal plane crash had fallen to 1 in 29 million scheduled passenger miles, while air travel had increased nearly ten times. In 1972, approximately 360 million people flew on scheduled flights, whereas in 2015, the number had risen to about 3.4 billion people. A third of that increase had taken place in just the five years that had preceded 2015. In 2015, only about 1/4 of the number of people died in plane crashes as had died from them in 1972, and the growth in the number of travelers makes these figures all the more astounding. In 1972, there were 185 people killed in six commercial jet crashes in the United States. By contrast, in 2017 there were no commercial airplane deaths or crashes in the U.S.

My crash was lost in most people's memories due to the publicity sparked by some of the world's most famous crashes. The Chicago Midway crash occurred at Chicago's second largest airport, Midway International Airport, on December 8, 1972. This time, a Boeing 737-222, United Airlines Flight 553, was coming from Washington National Airport in Washington D.C., stopping at Chicago Midway International Airport, and then was to proceed on to Omaha, Nebraska. The airport was overcast with visibility only good when airplanes were under 500 feet above ground level (AGL). As the United Airlines plane approached the airport, they were told by the Midway control tower to execute a "missed approach."

They performed the missed approach procedure, but while maneuvering for a second approach, they ended up at 2,200 feet above mean sea level (MSL) when they should have been at 1,500 feet above MSL. The captain recognized this as being far too high, so he increased his descent rate to get back to the proper altitude. To descend faster, the captain deployed the aircraft spoilers, which are also known as speed brakes. The spoilers are the flight controls that can be extended upward and seen above trailing edge of the wings. These were designed to "spoil the airflow" going over the wings and reduce lift in a controlled manner. The plane descended quickly and upon reaching 1,040 feet above MSL, the captain leveled the plane. Due to Midway being 611 feet above MSL, the plane was only 429 feet above the ground. The plane continued to descend as the pilots apparently did not notice that the throttles were not fully advanced and the spoilers were still extended. In six to seven seconds, the stall warning device known as the "stick shaker" activated meaning the plane was now in an aerodynamic stall. At 2:28 in the afternoon, United Airlines Flight 553 began clipping trees, then roofs on W. 71st Street before plowing into a house at 3722 W. 70th Place. They were 1.89 miles short of the runway.

Five houses were completely destroyed and three houses were damaged. *"There were 55 passengers and 6 crewmembers aboard the aircraft. Forty passengers and three crewmembers were killed. Two persons on the ground also received fatal injuries."*

In the official finding, *"The National Transportation Safety Board determines that the probable cause of the accident was the captain's failure to exercise positive flight management during the execution of a non-precision approach, which culminated in a critical deterioration of airspeed into the stall regime where level flight could no longer be maintained."*[12]

This crash was pretty spectacular. Remembered more than the crash itself was the fact that there were a number of well-known people on the flight. Among those killed were Dorothy Hunt, wife of Watergate conspirator E. Howard Hunt, U.S. Congressman George W. Collins of Illinois, Michele Clark, a CBS News correspondent, and Alex E. Krill, an ophthalmologist from the University of Chicago.

Dorothy Hunt became the focal point of this crash from the standpoint of publicity. She was carrying $10,000 in $100 bills when the plane went down. It was alleged that Mrs. Hunt supplied the money for the legal expenses of the Watergate defendants. This led to rumors and conspiracy theories related to the Watergate scandal. The conspiracy theories indicated that the plane was targeted due to Mrs. Hunt being a passenger and that sabotage of the flight was covered up by government agencies. In some instances, there were direct accusations that the CIA caused the accident.

The end result of the conspiracy rumors was that the NTSB, as stated, did not find them creditable, and placed the blame on pilot error.

Another crash contributing to the anonymity of my crash was one that occurred nine days after mine on December 29, 1972. Eastern Air Lines Flight 401 was a Lockheed L-1011 Tristar jet that was only four months old. It was on a regularly scheduled flight from John F. Kennedy International Airport (JFK) in Queens, New York to Miami International Airport in Miami, Florida. This was to be the first crash of a wide-body aircraft, and at the time, this was the second deadliest single aircraft disaster in the United States. A wide-body aircraft is described as an aircraft large enough to accommodate two aisles with seven or more seats abreast. This means a typical fuselage of 16–20 feet in diameter. The typical narrow-body aircraft is single-aisle, and only 10 to 13 feet across.

During Eastern Flight 401's approach to Miami International Airport, the first officer, Albert John Stockstill, noticed that after the landing gear was lowered, the landing gear light, which illuminates green when indicating that the landing gear was properly locked in the "down" position, had not illuminated. The landing gear could have been manually lowered, if necessary. It was later discovered that they were dealing with a burned-out landing gear indicator lightbulb. The captain, Hobert Albin "Bob" Loft, was operating the radio and told the tower that they would discontinue their approach. He requested that they enter a holding pattern in order to buy time to investigate the anomaly. The approach controller cleared the flight to climb to 2,000 feet and then hold west over the Everglades.

Loft dispatched Second Officer Donald Louis "Don" Repo to the avionics bay beneath the flight deck to confirm that the landing gear was indeed down. There was a small porthole there where this could be checked. Fifty seconds after reaching the 2,000-foot altitude for the holding pattern, Loft assigned Stockstill to put the L-1011 on autopilot. For the next 80 seconds, the plane maintained level flight. Then it dropped 100 feet and again maintained a level altitude for the next two minutes. After this, the plane began a slow descent, so gradual that the crew did not notice. In the following 70 seconds, the plane lost only 250 feet, but this triggered a chime from an altitude warning system under the engineer's workstation. The engineer, Repo, had gone below to check on the landing gear, and there was no indication that Loft or Stockstill heard the chime. In another 50 seconds, the plane had lost 1,000 feet of altitude.

The crew's preoccupation with the landing light indicator had distracted them from noticing that the autopilot had become disengaged. As the plane continued to descend, Stockstill noticed the discrepancy. He asked Loft if they were still at 2,000 feet. Loft verbally questioned what was going on. Less than ten seconds after the conversation, the L-1011 crashed into the Everglades, killing the three pilots, two of the ten flight attendants, and 96 of the 163 passengers. The plane was traveling at 227 miles per hour upon impact. The swamp helped to absorb some of impact, but still 101 people died. There were 75 passengers and crew that survived. All of the survivors were injured. Seventeen suffered minor injuries that did not require hospitalization. Sixty passengers received serious injuries, the most common of which were fractures of ribs, spines, pelvises, and lower extremities. Fourteen survivors had various degrees of burns. Two of the 60 died later. A rather unusual issue occurred in that the swamp mud may have slowed bleeding for some of the injured, but made the rescue more difficult. It also brought about the possibility of infection. Eight passengers became infected. Doctors used hyperbaric chambers to treat the infections in order to prevent gas gangrene.

The plane investigation led to issues such as two data channels, A and B, that display a switch from autopilot to control wheel steering (CWS) mode in pitch. In this mode, once pressure is released on the yoke (control column), the plane will continue from the last position held. Investigators believe that the captain accidentally leaned against the yoke while turning to speak to the flight engineer, who was sitting behind and to the right of him. The slight forward pressure on the stick would have caused the aircraft to enter a slow descent, maintained by the CWS system. The force required to trigger CWS in channel A was different from the force required to trigger channel B. This left the possibility that the switch to CWS in channel A did not occur in channel B, thus depriving the First Officer of any indication that the mode had changed. Channel A provided the captain's instruments with data, while channel B provided the First Officer's instruments with data. This along with not hearing the altitude warning chime after descending 250 feet from the assigned 2,000 feet holding pattern, and the fact that there were no ground lights from the swamp, meaning that it was pitch black, were additional potential causes of the crash.

The crash occurred 18.7 miles west-northwest of end of runway Nine Left (9L). The final NTSB report identified the cause of the crash as pilot error, stating: *"The National Transportation Safety Board determines that the probable cause of this accident was the failure of the flight crew to monitor the flight instruments during the final 4 minutes of flight, and to detect an unexpected descent soon enough to prevent impact with the ground. Preoccupation with a malfunction of the nose landing gear position indicating system distracted the crew's attention from the instruments and allowed the descent to go unnoticed."*[13]

This crash garnered publicity first in John G. Fuller's 1976 book "The Ghost of Flight 401." Fuller told of paranormal events aboard other Eastern aircraft and the belief that these were caused by salvaged equipment from the wreckage of flight 401. Eastern Air Lines CEO and former Apollo astronaut Frank Borman called the ghost stories surrounding the crash "garbage." All parts that were cannibalized from flight 401's airframe were eventually removed from other Eastern Airlines aircraft.

The crash was also the subject of Rob and Sarah Elder's 1977 book "Crash."

Two movies based on the crash were aired in 1978: "Crash", aired in October, was based on the Elders' book, and "The Ghost of Flight 401" aired earlier in February, was based on Fuller's book, and focused more on the ghost sightings.

The crash was featured in Season 5 of the Discovery Channel Canada / National Geographic TV series Mayday, in a 2009 episode called "Fatal Distraction."

Musician Bob Welch recorded a song on his 1979 album "Three Hearts" entitled "The Ghost of Flight 401."

It can be seen from the books, movies, music, and television programs that this crash into the Everglades attracted much national attention. Add to that the fact that this was the first wide-body jetliner crash, the numbers of people killed, the simple distraction factor, and it is easy to see why my O'Hare crash paled by comparison.

The final crash that I will discuss was the most famous of them all. It was the Uruguayan Air Force Flight 571, which was a chartered flight from Carrasco International Airport in Montevideo, Uruguay to Pudahuel Airport in Santiago, Chile. The flight was carrying members of the amateur Old Christians Club rugby team from Montevideo, who were scheduled to play a match with the Old Boys Club, an English rugby team in Santiago. The plane was carrying 40 passengers and 5 crew, 45 people in all. It is an interesting coincidence that my plane was also carrying 45 people, but with 41 passengers and 4 crew. The

Uruguayan plane was a Fairchild FH-227D, which was a twin-engine turboprop aircraft, made by Fairchild Hiller in the United States. The Air Force plane was piloted by Colonel Julio César Ferradas, who was an experienced pilot ,having flown over the Andes 29 times. His co-pilot was Lieutenant-Colonel Dante Héctor Lagurara.

The plane left Montevideo on October 12, 1972, but a storm front over the Andes forced them to stop at the Mendoza International Airport in Mendoza, Argentina overnight. Mendoza was to the south and on the eastern side of the Andes. The plane needed to fly south upon reaching the Andes Mountains to get to a pass where they could fly at a lower altitude than would be required if they flew directly. Flying directly would put them right at their maximum altitude and burn significant amounts of fuel. It was standard for a plane of this type to fly a "U" pattern, heading south to Malargüe, Argentina, then west to Curicó, Chile, and then north to Santiago.

The next day, the weather continued to be a problem, but it was supposed to clear up in the afternoon. At 2:18 PM on Friday, October 13th the plane took off. Co-pilot Lagurara, who was piloting the aircraft, went south to Malargüe, and then turned west. They were flying on instruments due to the cloud cover and could not visually confirm their location. He radioed the Malargüe Airport and told them that he would reach the 8,251 ft high Planchón Pass at 3:21 PM. The pass is the place where air traffic controllers from Mendoza, on the east side of the Andes, transfer flight tracking to Pudahuel air traffic controllers on the west side of the Andes.

At Planchón Pass, the aircraft had about 40 miles left to reach Curicó. They were still in heavy cloud cover.

Lagurara informed Pudahuel air traffic controllers that he expected to reach Curicó a minute later. Only three minutes later the pilot told Santiago that they were passing Curicó and turning north. The flight time from the pass to Curicó is normally about 11 minutes. The pilot requested permission to descend. The controller in Santiago provided authorization to descend to 11,500 ft., but he did not know that the plane was still in the Andes. The pilot had turned too early and used the wrong heading as well. As they descended, they were hit with severe turbulence. It was reported that one downdraft dropped them several hundred feet and out of the clouds. The rugby players had been joking about the turbulence, but then some passengers noticed that the plane was very close to the mountain. It is assumed that this was about the same time that the pilots saw a black ridge rising above them. Roberto Canessa, one of the rugby team members, later said that the pilot began a steep climb where the engine began to stall and shake. The pilot was able to get the nose to clear, but the right wing was torn off. The plane struck the mountain two or three times with the tail section, and two rows of seats were torn off. This left a huge hole in the rear of the plane. Three passengers, the navigator, and the steward were all lost at this point. The aircraft continued to fly for a few more seconds until the left wing struck an outcropping at 14,400 ft and was torn off. The left propeller sliced through the fuselage. Two more passengers were sucked out of the rear of the plane. The fuselage continued flying until hitting the steep downslope and sliding at over 200 miles per hour down the mountain for 2,379 ft. where the fuselage ran into a snow bank crushing the cockpit. Ferradas was killed at this point. Lagurara was badly injured and trapped in the crushed cockpit. Anchored seats broke loose and were hurled to the front of the plane, killing several more passengers. The plane ended up on a glacier in the remote Andes Mountains at an elevation of 11,710 feet. This glacier was unnamed, but later it was named Glaciar de las Lágrimas or Glacier of Tears.

At this point, 33 of the 45 persons on board were still alive. Some had compound fractures, and none of those individuals were to survive. The ordeal of the survivors was only beginning. They were to endure starvation until they reached a point where their only means of survival was by eating the corpses their fellow passengers. As good Catholics, this was very hard. One would not do it and died of starvation. Eight more were killed when an avalanche hit the fuselage, which had become their shelter during the cold nights.

A search and rescue was conducted, but was called off when the fuselage could not be found. The survivors were to battle the cold of the Andes for more than two months. They decided that they would have to climb out and preparations were made to begin the trek. On December 12th, passengers Nando Parrado, Canessa, and a third teammate, Antonio Vizintin, began to climb a peak to the west. Upon reaching the top with great difficulty, they saw nothing but mountains in all directions. They believed they would die. They were running out of food and so Vizintin volunteered to return to the tail section to leave more food for Parrado and Canessa. Parrado and Canessa followed the ridge and then began a long descent. They hiked for several days and were able to reach a narrow valley where they found a river. They followed the river down. Finally, they reached the snowline.

On the 9th day of their hike, they saw some cows. When they rested for the evening, it appeared that Canessa had reached his end and could not hike further. Then Parrado saw some men on the other side of the river. He wrote a note in Spanish explaining the crash, that they have hiked a long way, were weak, and didn't have any food. Can they please come and get them? Also, that there were 14 other survivors at the crash site. He wrapped and tied the note around a rock, then threw it across the river. Sergio Catalán, who found them, read the note and gave them a sign showing that he understood. He then rode westward by horseback for 10 hours to get help. Along the way, he ran into a person who transported goods by mule. He asked him to get the boys and bring them to Los Maitenes, where they would be fed and allowed to rest. The other person did bring Parrado and Canessa by horseback to Los Maitenes. The boys had hiked 37 miles in ten days. Canessa was down to 97 pounds, which was about half of his normal body weight. In the meantime, Sergio had been able to hail a truck and get to a police station in Puente Negro. The news of the survivors was relayed to the Chilean Army in Santiago. Another coincidence with my crash was that they first found help on December 20th, the day of my crash!

The rescue operation went like this:

December 20, 1972—Parrado and Canessa encounter Sergio Catalán.
December 21, 1972—Parrado and Canessa are rescued.
December 22, 1972—7 survivors rescued.
December 23, 1972—7 survivors rescued.

There were four books written on this crash:

Survive by Clay Blair, Jr. (1973).
Alive: The Story of the Andes Survivors (1974) by Piers
Paul Read and a reprint re-titled *Alive: Sixteen Men,
Seventy-Two Days, and Insurmountable Odds—The Classic
Adventure of Survival in the Andes* (2005).
*Miracle in the Andes: 72 Days on the Mountain and My
Long Trek Home* by Nando Parrado (2006).
*I Had to Survive: How a Plane Crash in the Andes Inspired
My Calling to Save Lives* by Roberto Canessa (2016).

There were six movies, television films, and documentaries about the crash:

Survive! (also known as *Supervivientes de los Andes*) is a
Mexican film based on Blair's book (1976).
Alive based on Read's book. This is narrated by John
Malkovich and starred Ethan Hawke. It is a major film
bringing significant attention to the story. (1993).
Alive: 20 Years Later is a documentary film narrated by
Martin Sheen (1993).
*Stranded: I Have Come from a Plane That Crashed on the
Mountains* is a documentary film (2007).
"Trapped: Alive in the Andes" is a Season 1 episode of
the National Geographic Channel documentary series
Trapped. (2007)
I Am Alive: Surviving the Andes Plane Crash is a documentary film first aired on the History Channel (2010).

There was also one play and three songs written about
the plane crash and story of survival.

I bring these three crash stories to the reader's attention to explain why my crash is less well known. I do not bring them up to minimize it. My crash involved hitting another plane on takeoff, crashing, burning, and escaping the flaming fuselage. Writing this book reminds me that time has a way of softening the edges of tragedy. I am finding that my crash was more terrifying and tragic than I had remembered before I started this endeavor.

CHAPTER 37

THE TRAUMA

There was an article among my collection of newspaper airplane crash stories that I believe I received from my mother. There was no date or newspaper identified with the article. I suspect that it came into my collection within five years of the crash.

The article reported that there had been a study of survivors sponsored by the National Institute of Mental Health (NIMH) and conducted by aircraft disaster experts from the major commercial airlines and the armed forces. The NIMH report brought to light that air crash survivors are prone to ill health. The report stated that survivors often developed symptoms of both emotional and physical illness, if they did not receive psychological support at the time of or shortly after the traumatic event. These might include physical symptoms such as rashes, high blood pressure, long-term fatigue, or heart disease. They might include emotional symptoms such as phobias, depression, an inability to feel either happy or sad, and even psychoses.

Survivors are not the only ones affected by an air crash. Anyone with a connection to a crash or to the crash survivors has a potential of developing symptoms. Rescue workers, ground crew members, firefighters, air traffic controllers, and airline management could feel responsibility. Survivors' loved ones are also potential victims. Any of these people or others may need counseling as a consequence of an airplane crash.

The report found an exceptionally unsettling situation. There were incidents discovered where survivors would not move from their seats, even though they were uninjured and physically capable of leaving. The reason appears to be a feeling that there is no hope for survival, so why should they try. This is the ultimate in experiencing a loss of control. It happens. I have read of other survivors who had to be jarred out of their stupor in order for them to escape. I do believe this to be a very real problem. The flight crew needs to be trained on how to urge people to evacuate. This should be done in such a manner as to be able to break through the locked-up minds of those that are seemingly frozen to their seats. On my plane, five passengers never left their seats. I presume that they were burned before they could undo their seatbelts, but it is possible that some or all of them gave up.

Here are some suggested ways to help survivors:

Create an aircraft disaster center to develop mental health programs. This might be done at a medical school.

Have the NTSB send specifically trained individuals to airplane crash sites. These individuals would be trained psychologists, psychiatrists, or other mental health experts.

Train other groups such as rescue workers, ground personnel, firefighters, airport personnel, flight crews, etc. on how to help survivors with trauma and grief.

Create a network between airports and local mental health professionals trained in air crash assistance. Airports are a good center since more than half of all crashes occur at an airport.

Clearly, I have suffered emotional difficulties, although I don't think that I recognized them immediately. My sister Nancy has said that I suffered from a rash in the days immediately after the crash. I don't remember it nor would I know for sure if it was caused by physical exposure to the crash, mental anxiety, or some other reason.

Post-Traumatic Stress Disorder (PTSD) is the likely culprit that needs to be dealt with after an airplane crash. This is the same mental health condition that often affects soldiers coming home from war. It used to be called "shell shock" or "battle fatigue." PTSD is much better understood these days. PTSD usually affects people in the immediate aftermath of a terrifying event. This event may affect those witnessing it as well as those experiencing it. The fear of death or shock of the event may cause people to have nightmares, flashbacks, and/or uncontrollable recurring thoughts of the event. Severe anxiety may also result from PTSD and, of course, a fear of flying when the event is an air disaster. Symptoms may last for many weeks, months, or years. Also, PTSD may manifest in interference with day-to-day living and/or avoidance of situations that could trigger great fear.

I definitely suffered from some of these symptoms in the days, months, and years after the crash. Particularly troubling for me were the recurrent nightmares. These dreams were different from my crash in that typically I would be flying at altitude when the plane would suddenly plummet from six miles up until crashing into the earth. My fear was living through the 40 seconds or so with my imminent death in front of me. Since I had my approaching death in front of me during the crash, this is understandable. Also, I was inside of a falling plane and had time to anticipate the impending crash. This dream seems to make sense, but why at cruising altitude? Why not on takeoff? I can only imagine that our takeoff did not appear to be much of a problem, even with the jolt we received. I knew it was a pretty good jolt, but I was hoping that the plane would just keep flying and take us to our destination. Once the plane began levelling off, I knew we were in trouble, because planes just don't do that at 50 to 100 feet into the air. Those dreams stopped occurring after about six months. My fear of flying did not abate with the dreams. I was quite literally a white-knuckle flyer for more than the next twelve years. I also suffered from depression, and I will go into some depth on that subject a bit later.

Another connection to the report came from sitting back, as the flames engulfed my entire plane, and knowing that I would not survive. This sitting back seems to correlate with crash victims being mentally locked up and unable to move out of a plane even if physically able to do so. I suppose that if I hadn't reversed course immediately, after seeing the flames recede, then I would have fit into that category. Luckily, I did move, and quickly.

Trauma from a plane crash is a unique experience. Air crashes are extremely rare and it is very unusual to be involved in a fatal commercial crash. When a crash does occur, it often gets worldwide attention. I am sure that some of the trauma can be attributed to the fact that as passengers, we are not in control. We are only in control when we make the decision to try to save ourselves. In addition, the range of emotions that I went through in such a short period of time was unusual, but I believe that it was the sheer terror that marks a plane crash survivor for life.

I went over 46 years before I was finally able to speak with another commercial plane crash survivor other than on the night of the crash. In 2019, I found and joined a Facebook group called "Plane Crash Survivors." I have had lengthy, one-on-one conversations with survivors from other crashes, such as the Tenerife and Lynyrd Sky-nyrd crashes. At times, writing this book and seeing other crashes, I have experienced emotions that can shake me up a bit. To this day, it is stunning to realize that something so monumental and terrifying actually happened to me. I can only say that surviving an airplane crash was, for me, such an overwhelming experience that it left an imprint on my life that will always be with me.

CHAPTER 38
1973

SPRING SEMESTER

Back at school, I had quite the story to tell. One of the first people that I contacted was Ralph. I confessed that I was the cause of his dented car door and told him that I would cover the cost of getting it repaired. He went out to a body shop or two and came back indicating that it would cost $500 to fix the door. I paid him and thanked him for being so understanding about the situation. That was one burden that was now off my plate.

Shortly after arriving back in Oklahoma City for my final semester, I stopped seeing Debbie, the blond beauty that I had been seeing casually for about six months and the woman that I was with the night before my plane crash. Something wasn't quite right between us. I wasn't sure exactly what it was, but she was pushing me by giving me an ultimatum to be exclusive. I walked away from the relationship.

Besides, sometime during the 1972 fall semester, I met Cindee, a beautiful girl with shoulder-length auburn hair. We were opposites in some ways. She was a sorority girl and I was a defiant GDI (God Damned Independent). Nonetheless, I liked her a lot and we started dating. She was just a sophomore, so I wasn't quite sure what would happen when I graduated.

It turned out that this was another relationship which moved pretty quickly, at least for me. Cindee had her sorority girlfriends, but she also had many male friends. Maybe it would be more accurate to say that she had men that she had previously dated and now held on to as friends. She also seemed to have more close male friends than female friends. Nevertheless, I ventured deeper and deeper into this new relationship. It appeared we were falling in love, but I was having difficulty reconciling my growing feelings of love with a feeling that Cindee was not falling as quickly or deeply as I was. As time went on, we would just have to see where the relationship would go.

Another interesting incident, which shows my ability to attract unusual circumstances, occurred at a tennis tournament somewhere in Texas. One of my early matches was on "satellite courts." That means that the group of courts where the tournament was being held were in full use, but the organizers had arranged for other clubs and/or facilities to use their courts for early tournament play. The organizers had also arranged for transportation.

Shortly, a car pulled up and another player and I got into the back seat. It was about a 20-minute car ride to where our matches were to be played. We were not playing against each other and I am not sure how our opponents got to the courts. The other player was a friendly guy and we got to talking. During our conversation, he told me that his dad was Ambassador to the United Nations. I must admit that I was a bit skeptical when he told me what his dad did, but I took him at his word. He had introduced himself as Jeb Bush. That Bush name didn't mean a thing to me in 1973, but clearly his dad was a big deal. He went on to tell me that he played tennis for the University of Texas. I am sure I explained that I was a Californian playing for Oklahoma City University. Obviously, Jeb Bush is well recognized today in political circles. He is the son of the late President George H. W. Bush and the brother of President George W. Bush. Jeb would go on to become the Governor of Florida.

Apparently, as a freshman in 1971–72, Jeb was dominating intramural tennis tournaments at the University of Texas with his friend David Bates. It turns out that the Texas tennis team was looking for a 12th player and Jeb was suggested by several team members. After one practice, Coach Dave Snyder decided that Bush was good enough to play with the scholarship players. He was added to the 1973 roster as a sophomore. Bush didn't travel with the team. Snyder said that he didn't know anything about the Bush family when Jeb joined the team, but he soon found out.

A side note to this story is that this is the same Coach Snyder that had been coaching at the University of Arizona and had offered me a full scholarship back in 1969. It's a small world!

My drinking was still a problem. My bar-hopping nights often led me to excessive drinking. After one such night I was returning to campus, and just before I got there, I moved into a left-hand turn lane. The median went from wide to narrow in order to accommodate this lane. As I turned into the lane, I went up over the curb, then onto the median, drove over a sign, and then back down into the left-hand lane. I made my turn, drove to my dorm, and went to bed.

The next day, I walked back over to that intersection. The sign was not a stop sign but it was a round pole that had been bent and flattened to the median. I lifted the sign and pushed it back into its straight-up position, although the bottom of the pole had clear indications of having been bent. I also found a strip of chrome on the median which had obviously come off of my car. I picked it up and walked back to the dorm.

I took the car into a body shop to have the chrome reattached and to check out the car for any other damage. The bumper, oddly enough, was none the worse for wear, but I was told that the major issue was that the car frame had been bent. The mechanic told me that they could put it on the rack and do their best to straighten it. They were successful and the car drove normally after that. This was just one more incident where my drinking was causing problems, but I was not yet ready to stop.

My final semester of my senior year of college should have been the finest hour of my college tennis career, but it wasn't. Two more young Australians had been recruited to join our team. While this made our team stronger, I found myself losing to both of them. Make no mistake, these were excellent players. Dale Power and Tony Dawson were trading off as our #1 players. Dennis Maddern, from Melbourne, Australia, was an excellent player with a number of big-time wins over top-ranked world tour players. Dennis had 18 scholarship offers to choose from when he came to OCU. He ended up playing #3. Steve Wedderburn, from Sydney, Australia was another of the young Australians with playing experience and wins against world ranked players. The year after I left, Steve had an excellent NCAA tournament. As a sophomore, playing in a field that often features a draw of 256 players, he made it all the way to the semi-finals achieving All-American status. As a freshman, Steve would play #4 for us. I was relegated to playing #5 of the 9 players that OCU carried

on the tennis team. This is particularly disappointing because each team is limited to entering four players in the
NCAA tournament, and usually these four team up for
doubles. So I was the odd man out.

CHAPTER 39

1973 TENNIS SEASON INTERRUPTED

I was playing in a match in southern Texas during the 1973 college tennis season. My right foot had started to hurt and I wasn't sure why. Luckily for me, my opponent was not at my level. I was basically playing on one foot, but I was still able to pull off the victory. Our team had brought seven players and I was able to sit out the other matches, although as I recall, that match was near the end of our road trip. The pain in my foot was becoming quite severe. As we traveled northward heading back to OCU from South Texas, we were forced to stop in a Waco, Texas emergency room. I don't remember exactly what they did, but I think it would have consisted of anti-biotics and pain medications. They told me to see a doctor when I got back to school.

After arriving in Oklahoma City, I went to the doctor's office the next day. It was a Sunday. My foot was swollen to about twice its normal size. My pain had started about a week previously and just got worse on our trip. The doctor took a good look at my right foot and leg. He indicated that I had a pretty severe infection. He said that he could see red streaks indicating the infection went from the foot up to my knee. I asked him how this could have happened. His answer was that even a very small cut could serve as an entry point for bacteria on the foot. The cut could heal leaving behind the start of the infection. Based on the severity of the infection, he had me hospitalized immediately.

At Mercy Hospital, my foot was packed in wet gauze and elevated. I stayed in this basic position for a day or two as the infection began to slowly drain out of the side of my foot at the base of the little toe. The doctor came to visit me and decided that the infection was not draining at a fast-enough rate and that it needed to be cleaned out. He suggested that we try right there and I agreed. The right side of my foot had a hole in it the size of a quarter. It was in this hole that he was going to try to soak up as much of the fluid containing the infectious bacteria as he could with the object being to keep the infection from destroying the ligaments and tissue any more than it already had. This was done without any anesthetic, which was very painful. After a few minutes, he gave up and said that he needed to put me under.

I believe that it was the next day that my wound was cleaned out under general anesthesia. I spent a few more days in the hospital and an additional week or two using crutches. I was on the second floor in Smith Hall. I thought that I knew what I was doing with my crutches, but one day shortly after I had left the hospital, I was coming down the stairs. I put the crutches out in front of me on the first step down and as you would on flat land swung out over the crutches. Now this works fairly well on flat land, but not in a stairwell. I found myself flying out and down to the bottom of the stairwell landing squarely on my recently operated-on foot. Boy, did that smart! I don't recommend using crutches this way for obvious reasons.

After a month of recovery from my foot operation, I was able to play again and took back my position on the team. As mentioned earlier, we played OU home and away that year. We won both team matches and I again won both of my individual matches. We were once again a powerhouse tennis team, both nationally and in the very strong Southwest region, where we won 21 matches against only three losses.

SUMMER

On May 19, 1973, I graduated from Oklahoma City University with Honors. I had been selected by the President of OCU to be a student representative on a committee to interview candidates for the next Dean of the Business School. I was selected as a member of Who's Who in American Universities & Colleges. At graduation, I was surprised to find out that I had been given an additional honor. The certificate read *"This is to certify that Todd H. Overgard has been elected to Beta Gamma Honorary Fraternity in the School of Business, Oklahoma City University, signifying outstanding scholarship, character and leadership which qualifies him to rank in the upper one-eighth of his graduating class of 1973."* It was signed by the Dean of the School of Business and also by Dolphus Whitten, Jr., President of OCU. Besides the certificate, I was given an Honors Cord to be worn during the graduation ceremony. I was feeling very grateful for being honored in this manner.

Now that I had graduated, my big problem was that I needed to find work. I would have loved to go out on the tennis tour at this point and see what I could do, but I had no money. My jobs during the last few years provided pocket change, but not much more.

I hung around Oklahoma City for a month or two. I moved into a fraternity house with a few other guys that

I knew were staying around for the summer. I was sleeping on the sofa in the living room because no beds were available at that time and I wasn't sure how long I would be staying. I checked for work in the area and found that OCU was hiring for janitorial services on the graveyard shift. I took the job. Clearly, I was overqualified for this position. My first night on the job, I cleaned toilets, mopped floors, and ran a buffer machine. My coworkers did this for a living. They were a little surprised when I joined them. I am pretty sure that none of them had a college education. In the morning, I was exhausted. I went back to the frat house to get some sleep. Everyone was just getting up and since I was in the living room on the sofa, I could not get any sleep. I knew this graveyard shift was not going to work as long as I was living at the frat house. I had to quit the job after just one day. I needed to get some sleep.

As the summer wore on, I left OCU and headed home to see if my job search might be better in Wisconsin. I played in a couple of tennis tournaments that summer prior to finding that first career job after college. Since I was initially driving to my folk's home in Madison, I decided to play in the Missouri Valley Men's Tennis Championships. This was the premier tournament for the five-state United States Tennis Association (USTA) Missouri Valley section, which consisted of the states of Oklahoma, Kansas, Missouri, Nebraska, and Iowa.

The 1973 version of this tournament was being held at the Homestead Country Club in Prairie Village, Kansas. This is a suburb of Kansas City, Kansas and is pretty centrally located in the Missouri Valley Section. Colin Robertson, the man who authorized my scholarship and had been my boss at the Oklahoma City Tennis Center, was the top seed. He had the reputation as the top player in the section for quite a few years. This tournament had 80 players with 16 seeds. I was not seeded which I thought was a pretty big mistake by the tournament director. I considered myself just a notch behind Colin in playing ability and therefore felt I should be highly seeded. I definitely considered myself better than Arnold Short, my OCU coach who had garnered the #12 seed. Arnold was 40 years old at the time and I was quite confident that I could beat him. The tournament director must not have seen it this way or perhaps he didn't recognize my name and skills. In those days seedings were often done based on one's reputation. The tournament chairman's seedings would be only as good as the information that he had.

I do not remember the first couple of rounds. I either won both matches or more likely got a bye into the second round where I won that match. In the third round, I played 11th seeded Randy McGrath. Randy was ranked seventh in the Missouri Valley USTA Section for 1972. This tournament was loaded with excellent players. In the prior year's championships, McGrath had made the quarter-finals where he lost to Colin Robertson, 7-6, 7-5. Considering that Colin won this tournament in 1972 and that Colin was ranked #1 in the Missouri Valley section, Randy would not be an easy match. As was reported in the newspaper the next day, Randy McGrath was to be the highest seed to exit the tournament, as I beat him 6-4, 6-3. The 11th, 12th, and 13th seeds were all beaten in that 3rd round, meaning that Arnold Short was beaten as well.

In the next round, I played Rick Lashley from Muskogee, Oklahoma. I am pretty sure that I had played and beaten Rick while I was at OCU and he was playing for

OU. When he joined OU, he was a year or so younger than I was and played #5. He had improved a lot since those days. He had lost to Colin Robertson in the semi-finals of the 1972 tournament, 7–5, 6–4. I know Rick wasn't one of the top two seeds in 1973, even though he was ranked #2 in the Missouri Valley section behind Colin for 1972. He must have been the third or fourth seed. We played a tightly contested round-of-16 match which I lost 6–4, 4–6, 7–5. Rick would go on to reach the finals, where he would once again lose to Colin. This time though, the score was 6–7, 6–2, 6–4.

I was playing right at the same level with these guys, but I couldn't head out on tour. I would have had to try to fight my way through qualification draws in an attempt to earn enough money to pay for my travel and hotel bills. It just seemed like a huge uphill battle and I didn't have the money to even get started. It seemed better to get a job and earn some money first. That may have been the wrong decision, because once I started working for a living, my playing skills would drop. I had strokes that take quite a bit of practice to maintain. That practice would be hard to come by with a full-time job, but I didn't recognize all of this at the time.

The second tennis tournament that I played in was the 1973 Wisconsin State Open Tennis Championships. I think it was played near Milwaukee, Wisconsin. This draw was smaller than the Missouri Valley tournament had been. They had eight seeds and again, I was not seeded. Since I had spent a lot of time in Oklahoma, and Wisconsin was in another section, this wasn't very surprising. Once again, I thought that I should have gotten more respect and been seeded. The top seed was Mike Cahill who was playing #1 for the University of Alabama and would go out on the pro tour a bit later. The local newspaper had posted a header that said "Top Ranked Cahill Bows." This seemed to be a bit of a mixed metaphor. You see, I had drawn the seventh seed in the round-of-16 and it was Mike Cahill's younger brother Tom. This was the second round of the tournament and the paper got it right that Mike was top seeded, but Mike didn't lose, his brother Tom did. I posted the day's only upset beating him 6–3, 6–3. My next match was in the quarterfinals against Mike Cahill where he turned out to be too tough as he beat me 6–0, 6–4. He went on to win the Wisconsin State Championship.

My relationship with Cindee had gotten to a point where I felt that I was in love with her and could consider marriage. For the most part, Cindee reciprocated these feelings, but she had problems of her own. She was debating whether to stay in Pueblo, Colorado, where her parents lived, and go to Southern Colorado State College (SCSC), or to go back to OCU. Part of Cindee's decision was monetary, and whether or not credits earned at OCU would transfer. I am assuming that SCSC was a less expensive alternative for her. As far as love went, Cindee was uncertain about a long-term relationship and/or marriage. Yet, she wrote to me that she loved me and didn't want to lose me. I was in a quandary. I wanted her to be fully committed and just didn't get that sense. There always seemed to be a hesitation. I proposed marriage, which would have to stand the test of time, because Cindee still had a couple of years of college left. She didn't accept, but still wanted the relationship to continue. This was all very confusing for me. We wrote letters back and forth throughout the summer.

Thinking back on this relationship, why would I propose? I wonder about the impact of my relationship with

Kathy and the heartbreak that came from that betrayal a year earlier. Was this a rebound relationship? Did my jetliner crash have an impact? From Pam to Kathy to Cindee, I was seeking a deep and long-lasting relationship. I suspect my proposal was just another way to find out if Cindee was ready for a long-term relationship with me. She wasn't.

HEAD TENNIS PROFESSIONAL

As fall approached, I continued my search for jobs. My tennis work at the Oklahoma City Tennis Center meant that I had a solid background for seeking a full-time teaching position at a tennis club. I visited an indoor club in Minneapolis to interview for a tennis pro job and also one in Rockford, Illinois. I was offered and accepted the job as the head tennis professional at the brand-new Victory Tennis Club in Rockford, Illinois. Starting in the fall of 1973, my career as a teaching tennis professional began.

Rockford, Illinois, is located about 90 miles northwest of Chicago and about 75 miles from O'Hare. It is the county seat of Winnebago County and the third largest city in Illinois. Rockford was a blue-collar town with quite a bit of manufacturing. It was good for me in the respect that I was within 70 miles of Madison and could see my family fairly often.

My relationship with Cindee was to continue for a short while longer. I went to her home in Pueblo, Colorado that Thanksgiving to give the relationship one last chance. We were living over 1,000 miles apart now, and from my standpoint, if there wasn't going to be a commitment, then I needed to be free. At the end of that Thanksgiving nothing had changed, and I broke off the relationship with Cindee.

The Victory Tennis Club was a seven-court indoor tennis complex with a two-story section about the width of a tennis court in the middle which had a tennis pro shop, the check-in and court assignment desk, offices, and a bar area on the mezzanine level. The mezzanine level was ground level with the parking lot. Heading downstairs led to locker rooms and the courts.

The three owners of the club were interesting. Two of the owners were men who made their money as partners in a construction firm in Chicago. They owned another indoor club in Chicago, so this was their second venture of this kind. Each of the men owned 30 percent of this Rockford club. The third owner was a woman who owned 40 percent of the club.

Within a couple of months, the owners brought in a woman, Linda, to be their Director of Tennis. The Director of Tennis managed the club with the exception of certain tennis activities such as tennis lessons, racquet stringing, and the pro shop, which I handled. Linda was the daughter of the woman club owner. She was a capable manager. We both reported individually to the owners. Linda was also a very attractive woman who was a few years older than I was. We kept our relationship on a professional level and went on to become very good friends while working together at the club.

I had picked up a roommate, Tim, who was a disc jockey at a local radio station. Tim was in the process of getting divorced and was looking for a place to live. He wore coke bottle glasses which I think gave him an odd appearance. He was a few years older than me. Tim also was very personable, which was a great asset for his job, and likely the reason that he had it. Unfortunately for me, Tim liked to drink. I was all too willing to be his accomplice in crashing the bars at night. As I said earlier, "wine, women, and song" were to lead me down a path that I wish I had not taken, but I have no one to blame but myself.

When Linda joined the staff of the Victory Tennis Club, Tim was already my roommate. Very quickly they began seeing each other romantically. Since Linda and I were friends and seeing each other at work every day, she began to tell me more about her past. Linda told me that her father had been shot-gunned to death in their living room. She had indicated that she thought it was a mafia hit. That was a shocking revelation and a bit concerning.

Linda went on to tell me that when her father died, her mother inherited his 40 percent stake in the Victory Tennis Club. She said that her mother was looking to get away from the club because she was having trouble making the payments. To make matters worse, the other two owners were working together to make the sale of her portion of the ownership difficult. Linda told me that they were hoping that her mother would default and they would able to pick up her 40 percent for less money.

I taught tennis lessons as my primary source of income. I would collect for the lessons, but then I had to pay for the use of the court. Also, the owners and I would split the profits on items sold out of the pro shop. Most items were marked up 100 percent. I also would string racquets for the club members as needed.

That winter, I ended up teaching a local businessman named Frank. He liked me and my style of instruction. He told me that he was going to be building a new tennis club in San Jose, California, and he wanted me to come and be the professional once the club was built. I told him that I would like to return to California where I could teach outside the year round. So it looked like I had future employment very close to where I grew up. San Jose was only about ten miles southeast of Sunnyvale. Since the club was not yet built, I would have to bide my time until I could make that move.

That winter, Gordon McKellen came to me for tennis instruction on his serve. Gordie was a figure skater who was on the verge of winning three consecutive US Men's Figure Skating Championships from 1973–1975. He was just 20 when he came to see me. He was working with his coach, Slavka Kohout, at the Wagon Wheel ice rink in Rockton, Illinois, which was about 13 miles north of Rockford. How he got interested in tennis or how he found me, I don't know. Gordie was an athlete and very coordinated. He was having trouble with his serve. I put him through some basics and added few minor corrections. That was all it took. He started banging big serves into the court with a good deal of control. We worked for the rest of the lesson on his being able to hang on to certain keys that would allow him to repeat the successful serve consistently. I am sure that Gordie was very satisfied with his new serve. I loved working with athletes because my tips were immediately accepted and translated into productive strokes.

With beginners, most would progress pretty rapidly, but some would struggle with the very basics. This is why more advanced players were more exciting, but not the typical people that I was teaching. My libido remained high and I was always interested in the ladies. Normally I was wary of involvement with my clientele. On one occasion, that broke down when a very cute housewife began flirting with me while taking a tennis lesson. After the lesson, we went for a drink with one thing leading to another. We ended up at my apartment. When we were finished, she told me that she wanted to leave her husband to be with me. It was clear to me that this had been a mistake. She had been flirting with me because she was not happy with her home life. She had two children and a husband. I had to tell her that I couldn't start a new life with her and her kids. I also had to hope that this wouldn't blow up on me and create problems at the club or with the husband. Nothing further happened, so I guess I dodged a bullet.

Around the start of the new year, 1974, I met a young woman who was the niece of a woman who worked at the club. Lori, the niece, was very attractive. I was a bit concerned with her age, because she was still in high school, but she was 18 years old, a senior, and just a few months away from her graduation. So we started dating. At this point, I was 22, and I didn't view the age difference as that dramatic. She was a very sweet girl. I know she had strong feelings for me and she wrote me a letter in April where she expressed them. I do believe that I was concerned that we were not on the same level emotionally. Also, I was only two years past my breakup with Kathy and a few months past my decision to leave Cindee behind. Both of those relationships had been emotionally draining. Little did I know that other circumstances were soon to change, which would further discourage the relationship.

My teaching at the Victory Tennis Club continued through the spring. The difficulties between the owners continued while I was getting the inside scoop from Linda.

Sometime in the spring, Linda was removed from her position by the owners. She was replaced with Lorraine, who was probably in her 40s. She took over as the club director. Her husband was a United pilot and he came around the club quite a bit. It was clear that Linda's removal was motivated by the desire of the two owners to be rid of any acrimony that might have developed from the way the ownership situation had proceeded. On top of this, neither Lorraine nor her husband were particularly friendly. I let my displeasure that Linda had been fired be known to the two male owners. Linda had done a very good job prior to being let go, but clearly this had to do with divesting themselves of those that may have been aligned with Linda's mother. Shortly after this time, the two construction owners bought out Linda's mother. My understanding was that she received a fair price for her portion of the ownership. My letting the construction owners know that I disapproved of their firing Linda was not a good career move. I think they recognized that Linda and I had become friends and that I was disapproving of their judgement concerning how the club was run. In the late spring, prior to the slowdown that inevitably happened in the summer months at indoor clubs, the owners informed me that we needed to part ways. Clearly, they wanted a clean slate with no one who may have supported Linda and/or Linda's mother still working there.

I took the pro shop supplies that I owned and put them in my car. I was done with this club and these owners. The first thought was that I should return to San Jose because of the head tennis pro job that Frank had spoken to me about. I went to Madison to say my goodbyes to my family. Then I left my apartment and started the trek back to California by car via Highway 80. This was the same route that my dad and I had taken 12 years earlier. I know that Lori wanted to continue going out with me before I left, but I did not expect to return to the area and did not want to lead her on. I was off to start a new adventure.

CHAPTER 42
1974–1975

CROCKER BANK

I was a bit worried about how my former bosses might react. Emptying the pro shop would prevent a few days of sales unless they wanted to move items from their Chicago tennis club pro shop. Otherwise, they would have had to order them wholesale which could take a few days. I had left them a letter explaining that these items were mine and I was taking them. I didn't think they knew that I was over 2,000 miles away. I wasn't hiding from them and could easily have been found, but I assumed that they would just be glad at that point that I was gone. I am pretty sure this turned out to be the case.

I also had to see what would happen with my draft status in 1974 and 1975. Luckily, my numbers in the draft lottery were good enough to keep me from being drafted. The Vietnam War was winding down, and it just wouldn't have been good to be killed in action at that anti-climactic stage of the war, not that it is ever good to be killed, particularly when forced to serve by your government.

Upon arriving in California, I contacted Frank. He told me that the club was still in the planning stages and that they had not yet broken ground. He wasn't sure how long that would take. I told him that I was in California and that I would seek employment while I waited for the club to be built.

1974 was not a good year to be looking for work in Northern California's South Bay. Actually, the entire western world had suffered an economic downturn from 1973–1975. There was a gasoline crisis. In response, President Nixon had instituted both price controls and rationing. Price controls do not work and exacerbated the situation. The gas crisis was addressed by rationing the gas sold at gas stations. Odd-even rationing was instituted, which meant that if your license plate carried a last digit that was an odd number, then you could only buy gas on odd-numbered days of the month. Even numbers had the gas buying privilege for even days of the month. The fuel shortage created long lines waiting to buy gas at gas stations. All of this contributed to declining economic growth. Although the US economy began to grow in 1975 while President Ford was in office, the growth remained slow through President Carter's four years until 1982 under President Reagan.

Job hunting was difficult. I decided that since I had an economics degree, I would begin to look at banks. Crocker Bank did not have openings that would utilize my degree, but offered me a position as a teller. I decided to take the job, assuming that I would be promoted when I showed them how good I was. Little did I know that it wasn't going to work like that. Besides, I figured that I could use this job as a stopgap measure until I was able to work at Frank's new club.

I did spend a lot of my free time in bars and discotheques. This combined two of my favorite activities, drinking and chasing women. I thought of myself as a ladies' man, but I think the memory of my high school days and not dating much made me want to push that narrative. Despite that, I was really looking for long-term companionship. Maybe bars weren't the best places to search for that, but they were good places to find alcohol. While I was working at the bank, I did not have a single girl that I would date for any length of time.

I didn't play tennis. Having taken a year off of playing to teach tennis, I had lost the precision in my strokes. It was going to take a lot of time to regain that precision, which seemed like too much effort. I would also likely have to suffer losses to lesser players and that was never pleasant.

The bank did not promote me. They had been looking for a bank teller and that was the job that I had taken. Most of the bank tellers only had high school degrees and certainly not business degrees with honors and an emphasis in economics. It was frustrating.

I stayed in touch with Frank into 1975. He was happy that I was in the area and that I was waiting to take the job. By the summer of 1975, he had still not broken ground and I knew it would be another year or two before the reality of the club could happen.

The economy was in the tank, the bank teller job that I had with Crocker Bank was going nowhere, and Frank was not making much progress on building his club. It was a depressing time for me. I decided that what would be best for me was to get out of the teller job, go back to school, and get a Master's degree. I talked to my folks about it and they suggested coming to Wisconsin to pursue a Master's in Business Administration (MBA). I thought that it was a good idea on several counts. It would give the economy more time to recover, meaning more job prospects, and it would give Frank more time to build his club. I would be in school for at least a year and a half. Best of all was that after I graduated, I would be able to pursue a career path which I was not able to do at Crocker Bank.

UNIVERSITY OF WISCONSIN—WHITEWATER.

I drove back to Madison. I now had a Ford Pinto, which I had bought in Wisconsin while working at the tennis club. I had determined that the best course of action for me would be to pursue an MBA through the University of Wisconsin—Whitewater (UWW) located in Whitewater, Wisconsin. Whitewater was about halfway between Madison and Milwaukee and just a bit south of both of them. It was roughly 45 miles from Madison. Whitewater was a small community of about 12,000 at the time, but the University had about 10,000 students as well. I had a small advantage in that my mom's brother, Fred Hoffmeister, and his wife Mary, both taught at Whitewater. Fred was in charge of the Driver Education/Motorcycle Safety Department, which meant that he was instructing future high school teachers on how to teach these skills. He had his PhD. I believe that Mary had a Master's degree and she taught in the Business Administration school.

To get into graduate school, I had taken the Graduate Record Exams. I applied and interviewed at the University of Wisconsin—Madison to see if I could get into their PhD program in economics. I was informed that my undergraduate grades were not quite as high as they required, so I was denied admission. I was able to get into Whitewater and had applied for in-state tuition. I argued that my folks lived there and I was using their address. Also, I had bought my car in Wisconsin and was intending to live in the state after my graduation. I was given in-state tuition, which was much lower than out-of-state tuition. I used student loans to pay for tuition, books, room, and food. Still, it was incredibly cheap by today's standards. I was also able to get a job, which helped to defray the expenses.

I had taken a pause in my drinking before coming to UWW. It didn't last long. Although I had not wanted to identify myself as an alcoholic, I clearly thought that it might be better not to be drinking so much. When I arrived on the UWW campus, I quickly discovered that the student union had its own bar, which served beer on tap. I learned that not only was the drinking age in Wisconsin 18, but that Whitewater had a colorful array of seven bars downtown. These bars catered to the UWW students and were only a short walk from the campus. I began drinking again. Drinking had always made social interactions, particularly with the opposite sex, a little easier.

I took a side trip to Rockford to see if Lori would like to continue dating. It had been over a year since I had left. I went to the Victory Tennis Club one evening and saw her aunt. There didn't seem to be anyone else around that I knew. I know I was a little concerned about walking back into that club, particularly if the owners had any animosity toward me. Luckily, I didn't see them, probably because they weren't usually around the club in the evening. I got Lori's phone number and called her from the club. Although her letter from a year earlier had said that she could not imagine falling for anyone else, and if I was ever to come back to the area, she would want to start up our relationship again, she told me that she was now in a relationship and did not want to see me. I was a little surprised, but I was the one who had left the area, and I was the one who told her that she was likely to find another guy that she would love. Although I was a little disappointed, I told her where I was and that she could contact me if things didn't work out. She never did.

I had a job as a teaching assistant for one of the Management Professors at UWW. Mostly this consisted of helping the professor with anything he needed, such as correcting papers. One day, he said he wasn't going to be able to teach his beginning management class and he wanted me to teach it. I wasn't familiar with the specific material or his method of teaching, but he gave me a few instructions and off to class I went. As I said, it was a beginning management undergraduate class in the business school and it had 30–40 students. Boy, was I thankful that I had taken Speech and Debate classes in high school. The teaching of the class went well and that turned out to be the first and last collegiate teaching experience that I would have.

Classes in graduate school, as you might expect, were difficult. We had an advanced mathematics professor whom I believe was from India. He had a heavy accent. I remember that when he was telling us a story once, I couldn't tell if he was referring to a "Police Chief" or a "Polish Chef." Understanding this professor was going to be a challenge. I think this was the class where I was to meet Marty B., who was from New Jersey. Marty B. had gone to UW—Madison for his undergraduate studies. Marty and I had a good time with laughing at the different interpretations we would get from the professor's pronunciations.

It also appeared that everyone in the class was struggling early on with the class content. None of us were living up to the professor's expectations of graduate mathematics work. He got so mad at us one day that he asked every student in the class to identify themselves and where we got our undergraduate degrees. I think this was his attempt to understand our background, but I also think of it as displaying his prejudices. If a student had gone to an Ivy League school or a prestigious university like Marty had, then I suspect that the professor would automatically assume that their background and training would be better than those of us who had not gone to schools rated as highly. I knew I had gone to one of the top schools in the Southwest, but I suspected that the professor would not recognize this. The real question that he should have been asking was, "what background mathematics classes did we pass in order to be able to understand his course content?." He never asked that question. Listening to the undergraduate colleges identified, I learned that most of my fellow classmates had gone to UW affiliate schools from around Wisconsin. These schools, in my opinion, were not as good academically as OCU. Despite this, I dropped the class after finding out that I was on my way to a "C." The university demanded that all MBA candidates must maintain a "B" average. This means maintaining a 3.0 on a 4.0 scale with an "A" being worth 4.0, "B" being worth 3.0, "C" being worth 2.0, "D" being worth 1.0, and an "F" being worth 0.0. If the student didn't maintain that 3.0 average, they were dropped from the program.

Marty and I were to become great friends. Marty loved to drink and so we would go out to the bars. My dating life picked up as there were quite a few young women that I met in the bars who were willing to head home with me. Marty and I would also often catch a beer at the student union. I was simply amazed that they sold beer right in the middle of campus. I wasn't in Oklahoma any longer, that was for sure. I was still looking for that one woman who would eventually become my wife. I actually thought this was a great place to potentially find her. Young women would come to a town like this finally liberated from their parents and able to go to the bars at 18.

I was older than most students including Marty. UWW had a large undergraduate population on campus with a much smaller number of graduate students. Most graduate students went directly from completing their undergraduate work into Master's or PhD programs. I had taken two years off from academics, which accounted for some of the age difference.

On one night of heavy drinking, an attractive woman, whom I shall call Samantha, was very aggressive. A group of men and women that I was with decided, after the bars had closed, that it would be a great idea to go skinny-dipping in one of the nearby lakes. We all jumped into the cold lake, leaving our clothes behind. Samantha made a beeline for me and left no doubt as to her intentions. I am sure some of the other skinny dippers must have noticed, but it was nighttime and there were only minimal lights. Samantha had a brother whom she told me had played, or was playing at that time, in the NFL. That was about all of the personal information that I ever learned about her. She sought me out at the house where I was living and sharing a room with another student. She came straight into the room and again, it was clear what she wanted. My roommate barely had time to clear out. I may have had one more encounter with her, but she was almost too much for me...almost.

So I was having quite the time in Whitewater dating quite a few young women. I felt like this was a complete reversal of my high school days where I couldn't get dates or was too shy to ask back then. I wanted to find companionship, a relationship, and eventually true love. I didn't see the harm in enjoying myself during that pursuit.

There was a woman, Lena, that I dated a few times. I would have considered continuing to date her except for the complications. She had a boyfriend and I think he had become her fiancé. She appeared at my door one last time a month or two later. She was very nice-looking, smart, sexy, and we got along. She wanted to see me just one last time. I tried to talk her into giving us a chance, but she hesitantly decided to leave. I am pretty sure that she wanted to stay and was in a bit of turmoil. My guess is that her fiancé would have seemed like the safer, but less exciting choice.

The fall of 1975 went by with my completion of just three courses and nine credits. To graduate with an MBA from UWW, one had to complete 36 credits which was 12 courses. These courses had some variability based on the major selected within the MBA program. The recommended "full-time" curriculum was three or four courses per semester which was nine or twelve credits. The maximum allowed coursework was five classes in a semester. It looked like my studies could take two years at the rate I was going. Marty and I often studied together. I remember having to study for a business statistics math course that he and I were in together. We would go out, buy a 12-pack of beer, bring it back to his place, which was a fraternity house, where he rented a room. We would study and drink all night.

As the late fall arrived, Dad had mentioned that I had better consider whether I wanted to file a lawsuit against the airlines and the government, based on my involvement in the crash. It was time-critical, because there was a three-year statute of limitations on a suit of this nature, and my three-year period would expire on December 20, 1975. I had received compensation for my suitcase and my letter jacket. I had received something like $800 shortly after the crash. My Dad had a lawyer in Madison that he recommended. I contacted the attorney and we discussed the situation. There was very little time left before the statute of limitations would occur. We agreed to file a suit for $10,000. It would have been more, but I had never reported my neck injury. I know that my lawyer had some problems serving North Central Airlines, but finally did get the suit filed against North Central Airlines and the United States Government. The suit was settled in April of 1976 by my lawyer for $2,000 of which I was to get two-thirds or about $1,333.33 with the rest going to the lawyer. To look at that in 2019 dollars, the suit was for $44,675.22, was settled for $8,935.04, of which I was to receive $5,956,68. I was ticked at the very low settlement. I thought it was way too small, but it was my own fault for waiting so long to act. Also, the amount was based on the fact that I was not injured in the crash. My neck pain, which I first had from the jolt of my North Central plane hitting the Delta plane, has never gone away. It is not severe and cracking my neck helps. I also suspect that the lawyer was agreeable to this smaller amount in order to just get it settled. It seems that there should have been a way to get more, but I had settled, and North Central Airlines no longer exists today.

During the winter, I knew that I would have to get used to the cold again. I must have sold my car, because I remember walking everywhere. There was an incident where I had walked downtown from the house where I was staying. The distance was a little over a mile. The temperature was cold, but seemed OK. It was still daylight, but after 4 PM, when I started walking. I arrived at the store where I wanted to shop for a few items. Across the street, I saw a digital bank sign that said the current temperature was 10°F, and the sun had just set, so it was getting dark. The time was also displayed and I casually noted it. When I came out of the store 20 minutes later the weather had changed dramatically. The bank sign across the street showed a 20°F. drop. It now said that the current temperature was -10°F. That alone would not be so bad, but the wind had picked up a lot. A strong wind plus a low temperature drives the wind chill lower, sometimes significantly.

Although I was 156 miles south of Shawano, Wisconsin, where I had experienced some frightful temperatures on my paper route, I did not take the situation lightly. I started to walk back to where I was living. I may have walked for a few minutes, but it quickly became apparent that even though I had a coat on, the temperature was feeling extremely cold. I became frightened because I was quickly experiencing numbness of my ears and fingers. I started to run which would provide a little heat, but this was a race to get to my lodgings before I was seriously compromised. This may seem dramatic, but believe me, it was not. I covered the remaining distance as fast as I could, which may have been about five minutes. Once I was inside and away from the extremely cold wind, I began to regain feeling in my extremities. I was shocked by how quickly the temperature had become dangerous. I turned on the TV news which reported the local wind chill temperature as -57°F. No wonder I was so cold. That temperature requires very special clothing and I just had a jacket and maybe a hat, which was not nearly warm enough. Wisconsin was once again telling me that it was too cold of a place to live.

In the spring of 1976, I signed up for 12 credits as I had for the previous fall semester. Again, one of my courses was not going well, and I couldn't chance that I would get an "A" to offset a potential "C" grade. I dropped that class, virtually assuring me that I would need two years to complete my MBA.

Also, in the spring I played in a tennis tournament for all Whitewater students, and won that handily. I also talked to the coach of the women's tennis team. I don't remember why I wasn't involved with the men, but maybe they already had enough help. The coach invited me to assist with his players. I accepted because I didn't mind helping young women to improve their tennis.

Often in the bars, my friends and I would run into a fellow named Willie. Willie was a bit of a troublemaker. He was periodically challenging any of us to fight. My position had always been that what he said didn't matter, but if he got physical, then that would change everything. To be honest, he was frightening. He was a 6'6" ex-convict with an intimidating reputation. We had heard that he had been in prison for some sort of altercation that left a man dead. He would verbally attempt to get us to go out in back of the bar to fight him, but he never physically started an altercation. He would threaten us despite the fact that nobody had paid any attention to him or caused any kind of issue with him. I concluded that once he had been drinking, he was ready to fight.

I was in the student union one day when he came up to me and apologized for having tried to start a fight. The whole left side of his face was very swollen. He said that he shouldn't have done that and he wouldn't do it again. I found out that he had threatened one of the Wisconsin farm boys in one of the bars the night before. I guess they went out back and he had picked on the wrong farm boy, but maybe there wasn't a right one. He got the hell beat out of him. I saw Willie occasionally after that, and he was back to his old tactics. I was torn between trying to teach him a lesson and taking an unnecessary chance in a fight with a felon. He would never stick around very long after his threats if he wasn't getting any takers, and he never put his hands on any of us. I decided my best course of action was to defend myself only if I was physically assaulted, which never happened.

Another adventure was playing foosball in the bars. I met Gary, who became a friend. He was really good at foosball. We started playing together. I was the goalkeeper and he was the forward. I used the two rear handles and he use the two front handles. The competition was high level and I became pretty good. We decided to enter a local tournament together. I don't remember how well we played, but we didn't win it. Gary and I would also drink together. I know, what's new about that? Well, sometimes we would drink a shot of 151 proof rum. If you have never done this, don't. It takes a lot to keep the shot down since it was almost pure alcohol.

Drinking had become a very common occurrence. One night, Marty and I had a lot to drink. It must have been a weekend. After the bars had closed, we were bored, and not ready to call it a night. We had a six pack of beer, and since neither of us had a car, we decided that we would walk to Madison. Now this is not something that most people try and I don't recommend it. So somewhere around 2:00 AM, we began the approximately 45-mile walk. As dawn came and went, we entered Fort Atkinson. Fort Atkinson was ten and a half miles from Whitewater. So we had probably walked at a pace of about two and a half miles per hour. By the time we reached Fort Atkinson, we were getting pretty tired. We hadn't slept, we had been drinking all night, and we had walked over ten miles. We decided to go back to Whitewater, but we were too tired to walk another ten miles. Now, the question was, how in the hell would we get back to Whitewater? There was virtually no traffic at that early hour of the morning in this small town. Well, we got lucky. We spotted a group of teenagers. We stuck out our thumbs and they stopped. We told them of our predicament and they gave us a ride back to Whitewater. Another adventure was in the books.

During the summer and into the fall, I was seeing a young woman named Mary Carole who had graduated from UWW. She was a pretty brunette with very long straight hair. Mary Carole's parents lived pretty close to where my folks lived in Madison. While I was in Madison during the summer, I would go to a local liquor store and buy a case of beer a few times a week. One day, I was in there and saw Mary Carole's dad. I can't remember if I spoke to him, but he was not the least bit friendly. Maybe everyone runs into this, but parents of the girls I dated either loved me or hated me. I am sure he was just being protective of his daughter and with some justification. I certainly hadn't decided where any of my relationships were going, and didn't currently have any that I seriously considered might lead to marriage.

Mary Carole was working up in Neillsville, Wisconsin, as a school teacher. Neillsville was almost 200 miles north of Whitewater and in one of her October letters to me, she had mentioned that there was snow on the ground. Well, that's Wisconsin for you, very cold. Although we were staying in touch, things were changing that semester.

When the fall semester of 1976 arrived, I had a predicament. I felt some urgency to get on with my life and finish my studies. Originally, I had intended to be finished with my MBA by December of 1976. Now, I was short credits. I had scheduled 12 credits in each of the first two semesters and I had dropped a class in each. I had finished exactly half of the curriculum and still had 18 credits, which was six classes, left to finish. If I went an extra semester, I would have higher expenses for room and board while in school. I decided to check into the possibility of taking all six classes in the fall semester. The rules said that three classes was a full load. The maximum allowed was five classes. I did find out that if I could get the administration's approval, I could attempt to take six classes. So I went to them and did get approved. Now I was going to attempt to complete half of a two-year program in a three-month semester. I definitely had my work cut out for me.

For this fall semester, I had moved to an apartment just off campus. I had some roommates, at least one of whom was a fellow MBA student, Richard. Richard and our other roommates were guys from Ashland, Wisconsin. Ashland was about as far north as you could go and still be in Wisconsin. It was 340 miles north of Whitewater and right on Lake Superior. It was definitely colder territory than southern Wisconsin.

Richard and his roommates enjoyed showing me that they were acclimated to cold temperatures. As winter approached, the three of them went off to their early morning classes in their T-shirts. It was 15°F outside. They were only about a third of a mile from classes and could get there in just over five minutes. Still, I wouldn't have done it and I assumed they were just displaying their cold weather machismo. It was either that or they were truly crazy.

It was in this early fall semester when I walked into a bar and saw the most stunning blonde. She caught my attention immediately without even trying. She was with her girlfriends sitting in a booth. I don't know how I did it, but I found a way to talk to her. Her name was Mary Lee. We hit it off from the start. She was a senior and would be graduating in the spring semester. The only downfall to a relationship that I could see was that she was a smoker. We spent most of the semester together and I thought that this was a pretty serious relationship, more serious than any that I had had since Cindee. Based on how my "serious" relationships had gone in the past, this one was probably doomed as well. That seemed to be my pattern. As we came to the end of the semester, we were at a bit of an impasse with our relationship. She needed to stay at UWW and I needed to find a job. My first thought, assuming that I could get my MBA, was to look for a job in the big cities of the upper Midwest, preferably close to Madison and my family. I had made no commitments to Mary Lee and I think she had completed her semester and gone home, which was in a smaller city quite a distance north of Whitewater. I think that I had suggested that she come out to California with me once she graduated. She did not like that idea at all. I think it was more that she didn't want to leave Wisconsin. After she headed home for the Christmas holidays, I suspected that I would never see her again. That turned out to be the case.

I wasn't lonely for female companionship, though. One of the members of the female tennis team was still around campus. I think she might have been a junior. We got together and she was another one that I thought, given enough time, we could have had a longer-term relationship. The problem was that she had even more time left at UWW and I had no idea where I would end up after this semester.

From an academic standpoint, I was very proud of having forged through this crazy amount of work to complete my Master's degree. We had a choice of a master's thesis or a comprehensive exam as the final hurdle of the MBA program. I took the exam and passed. I finished that semester with two "A"s, three "B"s, and one "C." It was enough for me to receive my diploma.

After I got my MBA, I moved back to Madison with my folks and worked some odd jobs while I pursued a career. One of those odd jobs was working at a Madison JCPenney auto department as a tire salesman. Now I had another pattern. As soon as I got a degree, it seemed that the first jobs that I ended up with were jobs that didn't require a degree, but I wanted to work. In those days, there was no commercial internet. The way jobs were pursued was by creating a resumé with a personalized cover letter, and then sending that resumé to potential employers. Finding potential employers with the "right" jobs was usually done through the classified section of newspapers. I was getting newspapers from Madison, Milwaukee, Chicago, and Minneapolis, and I started sending out dozens of resumés with cover letters.

Keep in mind that there were no personal computers. My former classmates Steve Wozniak and Steve Jobs hadn't yet invented and introduced them to the world. In those days, a typewriter, preferably an electric one, was used to create the resumé and the cover letters. The resumé could be taken to a print shop where copies could be run off. Again, there were no printers which typically accompany today's personal computers and can be used for multiple copies. I would read the classified ads in these major city newspapers and look for the right jobs. When I found a possible fit, I would have to type up a cover letter and envelope without mistakes. I would take the cover letter describing my interest in the job, add my resumé, put them in the envelope, and send them off. Much of the time, if I was dealing with a major company, I would get a typed letter back. The letters that I got back said thank you, but no thank you. Jobs were very hard to come by, even with my new credentials. After a few months, I decided that I would go back to the West Coast and resume my search for work there. Who knows, maybe Frank would be getting close to completing his club and would hire me as the well-educated head tennis professional.

CHAPTER 44

1977–1979

ADVANCED MICRO DEVICES

So, in the spring of 1977, I had decided to go back to California. I had a friend, Dick, who was a tennis-playing dentist. He and his wife Faye had two children, but they graciously agreed to let me stay in their Mountain View home until I could get settled in the area.

I had always previously driven back and forth between Wisconsin and California. Typically, the 2,122-mile journey between Madison, Wisconsin, and Sunnyvale, California, would take about 4 days of driving. I didn't have a car, so I looked at public transportation with low cost in mind. I saw that I could take a Greyhound bus for $50. The trip would only take two and a half days as the bus would travel almost continuously with only short stops for food and change of drivers. I knew this would be interesting. These buses did not have reclining seats or any of the amenities of today's buses. Thankfully, the bus did have a bathroom.

Well, my first priority upon arriving back in California was getting a job, and this time, hopefully, a potential career as well. Initially, I got a job at a Sunnyvale Radio Shack. Again, it was a temporary situation for me. I was just going to work there until I could find a job with a future. I was riding the bus to get there in the mornings. During the first day or two of work, the manager had told me to slow down, apparently because I was working too hard. It didn't make sense that he wanted to slow me down. Maybe it showed up the other clerks. One morning I boarded the bus in Mountain View after a late night of drinking. The next thing I know, I'm in San Jose. I had fallen asleep and missed my stop. I got off at the next stop and caught a bus back to Sunnyvale. I must have arrived about an hour late and the manager immediately fired me. I was on a 90-day probationary period, so he had every right to do it, but I suspected that he didn't think that I quite fit in there. I was unhappy with the manager and so I sent them a letter saying, "You can't fire me, because I quit."

It was for the best. I got my resumé together, had copies made, and located some local potential employers. I walked to companies such as Signetics, Advanced Micro Devices (AMD), and National Semiconductor. They were all in the same vicinity and it was about six miles from where I was staying in Mountain View. I dropped off my resumé at a lot of companies and I received a call within a few days to come to AMD for an interview. I interviewed and was offered a good-paying job as a production control planner. This was in May of 1977. I was able to get an apartment and a car a short while after that.

AMD was a company that was started in 1969 by Jerry Sanders, who was an engineer/marketeer. He had previously worked at Fairchild Semiconductor as the Director of Marketing. Fairchild Semiconductor was also in the Santa Clara Valley. He had broken away from their very conservative leadership, and founded AMD, a semiconductor manufacturing company. AMD had been growing as had other high technology companies in the area. These companies became known as "hi-tech" companies and

Santa Clara Valley was fast becoming "Silicon Valley," because silicon is a primary element in semiconductors. I didn't really know it at the time, but I had just caught an early wave in the tsunami that was to become the hi-tech capital of the world!

I used to take a lot of my work breaks with a couple of married women, one of whom worked in the production control department with me. Cynthia was quite attractive, but I figured there was no chance for any relationship since she was married. At one company party she asked me to take her to my place, which I did. That was the only time that we were together. It was just as well that this didn't go any further.

I worked in the production control department as a scheduler for about 16 months. I was getting burned out because our department was working at least three Saturdays every month. These Saturdays were just as long as the ten-plus hours that we put in every day as exempt employees. Years later, I was informed of a law suit against AMD for not paying overtime when our salaries were commensurate with non-exempt pay. My feeling was that I didn't have much to complain about since I had agreed to the salaried position and the salary meant that you worked until the job was done. The issue was whether or not the job was defined properly. Along with the notification of the suit was a check in settlement for $100. Now that was humorous. It was as if that $100 was to cover the minimum of 40 Saturdays of extra work that I had put in, not to mention the extra hours every workday.

In September of 1978, I moved into a position as a Production Test Supervisor. It meant more money, more responsibility, and less hours per week. As a Test

Supervisor, I was supervising the electronic testing of
die on wafers to see if they performed correctly electri-
cally. Die, or dies, are integrated circuits, also known as
chips. A wafer is a round, thin slice of crystalline silicon upon which small squares of die are manufactured.
AMD had just set up a work schedule so that production
would continue around the clock. Well, 21 of 24 hours,
anyway, with 3 hours reserved for maintenance. There
were two day shifts and two swing shifts. All four shifts
worked three long days and a partial fourth day. My initial production shift was a partial work day from about
6:00 PM until 2:00 AM on Wednesday, and three full days
from 3:30 PM until 2:00 AM on Thursdays, Fridays, and
Saturdays. Now for a single guy like me, who was out
at the bars on Friday and Saturday nights, this was an
inconvenient schedule. Also, since I wanted to date, the
weekends were shot.

I did this work for about six months and then I was
asked to move to Diffusion Supervisor. This got into the
heart of how silicon chips were being made. It also meant
a change in shift times. I was now required at work from
5:00 AM until 3:30 PM on Sundays, Mondays, Tuesdays,
and on Wednesdays, I would work from 5:00 AM until
12:30 PM. The Complementary Metal-Oxide Semiconductor (CMOS) rectangular chips were made by duplicating
the chip design on a wafer.

As many small chips (die) as possible were designed
onto the three-inch wafers used back in 1979. The size of
each individual chip depended upon the design. Elements
of the process of depositing materials onto the wafers included etching areas of the chips to remove material and

masking areas of the chips that were not to receive a deposit of certain materials.

For some operations, the wafers were configured into a row of about 20 of them and placed vertically, at a slight angle off of perpendicular, into a holding container called a wafer boat. The boats, which were essentially holding trays, went through a number of processing steps in order for the correct materials to be placed in the correct areas. One of the steps was for the boats to be put into small round diffusion furnaces which were of a size capable of holding a boat filled with vertically stacked wafers. These furnaces would get up to 2500°F.

There were many dangers in the diffusion production areas. The furnaces were fed with oxygen, nitrogen, and hydrogen. During the late 1970s, we experienced a number of earthquakes which were up to about 5.7 on the Richter scale. During these earthquakes, we would evacuate the production areas. My fear, which thankfully was never realized, was that hydrogen tubes might be pulled loose from the furnaces, filling the production area with hydrogen, which, when combined with the heat provided by the furnaces, could cause an explosion.

Another danger was sulfuric acid. The wafer boats would go through alternating processes of deposition of materials onto the wafer and then acid baths to remove or etch specific areas of the wafers. Deposition was the depositing of materials onto the wafers. The production workers would have to pour sulfuric acid into a sink-like area designed for that specific acid. Sulfuric acid was kept in rather large glass containers since it would not eat through glass. One day, one of my female employees was taking the glass container out of a larger plastic box with slots used for the storage of ten to 20 of the glass containers. These sturdy plastic boxes were roughly three feet by three feet and resembled a larger version of the old milkman delivery containers. The glass containers fit into their individual slots to keep them separated from the other sulfuric glass containers. This employee had lifted the container out of the plastic storage box, when it slipped out of her hands, hitting the plastic container, and then breaking on the floor. She started screaming immediately because sulfuric acid splattered onto her and it will eat through shoes, clothing, and body parts.

Our procedure was for me to get the employee to the emergency shower located in our production area in order to apply water to all affected areas. I ran to her aid, but as I stepped into the sulfuric acid now spread on the floor, I slipped and almost fell into it. The acid was very slippery on the cement floor that we had. Luckily, I did not fall. I did get the sulfuric acid rinsed off the employee's shoes, feet, and any clothing that it may have splattered on to. I also had to put my feet and pants into the shower as they had gotten acid on them during my efforts to help her. She was not burned with the acid and neither was I. My shoes and pants were ruined. Her shoes were also ruined and maybe some of her clothing. The company reimbursed us for these losses.

Another dangerous chemical was hydrofluoric acid (HF). This was another of the acids used in etching of the wafer boats. The production workers would lift the boats into sinks or tubs filled with hydrofluoric acid. They would wear latex gloves to prevent contact with this acid. If a pinprick hole developed in a glove, then the acid would seep into it. This was dangerous because of the unique properties of this acid. HF would penetrate the skin and it interfered with the nerve function which meant that initial exposure was not painful. Hydrofluoric acid would continue through the skin to attack the bone. At this point, the affected person would begin to feel pain, and it was urgent to get the person to a critical care clinic as soon as possible. I had this happen with one of my employees. I took them immediately to a nearby clinic where calcium shots were injected into the affected area. Without treatment, Hydrofluoric acid will eat away enough bone to deform and cripple fingers and hands. This injection treatment had the effect of drawing the hydrofluoric acid away from the bone and, by diffusing the acid, preserved the integrity of the fingers and hands. The employee was saved from any permanent damage.

In other areas of diffusion, there were large pieces of equipment. One was a gold deposition vacuum centrifuge. Wafers would be put into the device, typically around the inside wall of the roughly four foot round centrifuge, with gold held in place at the very center. The air would be vacuumed out and then the centrifuge would spin while the gold would be hit with a laser which would melt it. The melted gold would fly around the centrifuge being diffused evenly on all unmasked areas of the wafer. The masks would define where the gold would be deposited.

One evening, this particular gold centrifuge had a problem. A couple of technicians, who were trained to work on the equipment, were brought in. While they were testing the circuitry, one technician would turn the power switch on or off at the command of the other technician who was working on the equipment. They must have gotten their signals mixed up because the technician working on the centrifuge went to work on it when the power was on. He was instantly electrocuted. Even though the paramedics got there within a minute or two of being called, they could not revive him. Yes, it was a dangerous place.

Another issue that I had to deal with was a female employee who came in to work with a black eye. I was immediately suspicious, because her live-in boyfriend had recently been released from prison, where I was told that he had served nine months for beating her and putting her in the hospital. The woman claimed that her black eye was an accident. Her boyfriend, at some point after that, showed up at AMD. I don't remember the pretense upon which he came to see me, but we were talking in the lobby and he asked me to accompany him to the parking lot. There he went to his car and opened the trunk to show me something, while continuing to talk to me about the pretense. In the trunk was a large machete and I had the distinct feeling that I was being subtly threatened. I did not react to the machete. The boyfriend closed the trunk and we finished our conversation. I was not happy about the veiled threat, but it really only served to make me more vigilant when I went to my car. Nothing further ever came of this situation for me.

AMD was not that big back in the late 1970s and I went to one of the parties that AMD put on. Jerry Sanders was one of the founders and the initial president of AMD, and remained so until his retirement in 2002. Jerry was known as a flamboyant marketeer. Sanders used his marketing skills to push company sales even when AMD was not the strongest semiconductor company in terms of manufacturing and particularly technology. Based on this approach, Sanders used company growth targets as a way to make AMD a success and he shared his success with his employees. After one of his target goals had been met, he had a drawing for his employees. A production worker won $1,000 a month for 20 years. At $240,000, that was not a bad prize! Jerry also held expensive blowout Christmas parties for the employees.

At one company event that was set up for management only, I got a chance to talk with Jerry, one on one. You know the company was small if I, as a production supervisor, would get a chance to talk to the living legend. Back in 1978 and into the early 1980s, inflation was a pretty big problem. Employees wanted raises to cover the inflation factor. Jerry was complaining to me that his engineers all wanted annual ten percent cost of living pay increases and it really put him and the company in a difficult position. I had to agree. I understood that if the employees didn't get ten percent it was like losing salary. By the same token, the fierce competition in the semiconductor world was forcing companies to reduce their prices in order to compete. Large employee increases and falling sales prices were an untenable combination. Without increased sales, this situation would likely lead to large losses and the possibility that the company would fold. I could certainly empathize with Jerry's dilemma. Nevertheless, he somehow resolved the situation, and was able to keep AMD as one of the foremost semiconductor companies in the world. Jerry was an excellent example of leadership.

CHAPTER 45
1978

CLIMBING IN YOSEMITE

In May of 1978, my apartment roommate at the time, who had been one of my high school tennis teammates, Scott, talked me into buying climbing gear such as shoes, straps, and carabiners. Scott had ropes, nuts, and other climbing equipment needed for rock climbing. He wanted us to go climbing on the walls of Yosemite National Park in the Sierra Nevada Mountain Range. Another friend, Paul, was going to join us. I had never done this, but I was in pretty good shape. I weighed about 155 lbs. and could do 16 pull-ups with my knuckles toward me. So I thought, why not? It sounded like another exciting adventure. The plan was to go up to Yosemite for nine days.

Scott and I practiced by going to Pinnacles National Park which is 90 miles southeast of Sunnyvale, California. We did a number of climbs and I learned the techniques. This was called "free climbing" because the equipment is only used for protection from falling and not to assist in the progress of the climb. All of our climbs were to be free climbing. We practiced bouldering and short climbs just to master the techniques of belaying, which is holding the rope in case of a fall, setting nuts, and looking for hand-holds and footholds.

I had never been to Yosemite Valley before. The valley is about 190 miles east of Sunnyvale. It is a very beautiful place. The valley floor was carved out leaving 3,000 feet of sheer granite cliffs on either side. The Merced River runs down the center of it bringing water through the valley from the higher Sierra elevations to the east.

We slept in our sleeping bags and stayed in Camp Four, which was the campsite where most of the serious climbers stayed. It snowed lightly on us one night. The first couple of days we tried easier nearby climbs to work on techniques. On these climbs, I had been fearful of rappelling on the descent. When rappelling, the climber has the rope around him, but he must stand and then, while leaning backward, step off of the cliff. The climber's body was now nearly perpendicular to the rock and close to parallel to the ground. I remember one of the guys saying "Are you ready?" I responded, "There's no time like the future!" Nevertheless, I learned to overcome my fear and to do it. Then we went to El Capitan. This is the majestic wall that expert climbers often try to scale. Climbing to the top usually took days and requires further specialized equipment and extraordinary climbing skills. We had no desire to do that level of climbing.

There is a system of climbing called the Yosemite Decimal System which was developed in the 1930s and modified for rock climbing in the 1950s. Essentially the first digit goes from a 1.0 for easy walking to 5.0 where vertical or near vertical walls require ropes and other equipment for protection and descending.

Originally, a 6.0 was going to mean aid climbing. It was later dropped. Aid climbing is climbing with the use of equipment such as ropes or rope ladders, and sometime jumars, which are also known as ascenders. Ascenders are tools that can grab a fixed rope so one can pull oneself up. They come in pairs so that one can be used to grab the rope while the other is free to slide up the rope before it becomes the grabbing device and the other ascender is free to slide. In aid climbing, the fixing of a rope or ladder is accomplished through the use of pitons, which are metal spikes driven into the rock wall. This approach negatively impacts rock walls and decreases the difficulty.

In the Yosemite Decimal System, the second digit designates the difficulty of the climb. Rock climbing requiring ropes starts at 5.0 and originally continued to 5.9, which was supposed to represent the most difficult climbs capable of being scaled. As time went on, unscalable climbing routes began to be successfully completed and were given designations of 5.10, 5.11, 5.12 etc. for increasing climbing difficulty. These latter three were pronounced "five-ten," "five-eleven," and "five-twelve," thus denoting levels of difficulty beyond 5.9.

Climbs almost always follow cracks up the granite wall. Climbing nuts (the equipment, not the climbers) come in a wide variety of shapes and sizes, often with a preset looped wire. The lead climber will wedge the appropriate nut into the crack in the rock in such a manner that a downward pull locks them in and they will not come out. Typically, a carabiner is attached to the wire loop and then the rope is placed into and through the carabiner. With the climber below belaying, the lead climber will ascend and set these nuts on his way up. If the lead climber falls, he will fall twice the distance of the last nut that was set. Assuming that the nut holds, his fall will be stopped at that point as the rope is firmly held from below. The belayer will tie themselves into a permanent preset anchor or set a nut such that the belayer is kept from being pulled off the rock by a falling companion.

At the end of a pitch, the lead climber will stop, anchor himself in, and he then becomes the belayer. The pitch is the section of a climbing route between two belay points which is less than the length of rope being used. The following climber will remove the nuts as they climb so that the nuts can be used on the following pitches.

For our first Yosemite climb beyond the smaller, closer climbs, we decided on a one pitch climb on El Capitan. Back in the late 1970s when we climbed, the ropes that we used were 50 meters, which is about 164 feet. Today, the ropes are typically 60 or 70 meters which is 197 or 230 feet in length. The climb we chose was called "The Footstool" which was classified as a 5.4 and was 120 feet up. Two interesting things happened on this climb. First, it was at least a 20-minute hike to the base and when we arrived, it was snowing. This was not good because it makes the rock slippery. It was a light snow that soon stopped as we ascended.

At the top is a ledge, which is how The Footstool got its name, the second interesting incident started with me being alone on the ledge. The rope ended up six feet below me. I don't clearly remember how that happened. It must have fallen to the last placed nut. To get back on the rope, I was going to have to climb down, which is tougher than climbing up or rappelling. I had no choice but to climb down without protection. With great fear I slowly descended, having to traverse one tricky section, until I was able to retrieve the rope. At this point, I must have tied back in and climbed back to the ledge. The rest of the climb and descent was uneventful.

I should point out that I had a great fear of heights which I did not have to the same degree before my plane crash.

So why in the world would I take on rock climbing, particularly in Yosemite? Part of it was because my friends were asking me to climb with them, but I think part of it was to try to overcome my fear of heights by confronting it directly. This may be a sort of self-imposed exposure therapy. I was facing my PTSD head on, but since I didn't really know anything about PTSD, I was not cognizant of anything other than climbing through a fear of heights.

Paul had joined us shortly into our stay and Mark, Scott's brother, had also joined us. Mark had ridden his motorcycle up to Yosemite with his girlfriend in tow. All four of the guys were going to climb and Mark's girlfriend just came up to be with him. I remember there was one climb that I didn't participate in because I was too hung over. Clearly the drinking thing was still interfering with my life.

Another climb that all of us did was called Munginella, which had a 5.6 rating. It has three pitches for our rope length and went up 350 feet. It is the far left of what is known as the Five Open Books. This climb was challenging for me since I was a relative novice. It had portions where you used finger holds, jamming, and even a lie back move where your feet were against one wall where an overhang came out and allowed for hand pressure on an opposing lip. Holding oneself parallel to the ground and edging around this overhang using just opposing hand and foot pressure was quite difficult.

When I got up toward the top, I tied in and wrapped the rope around my waist and then yelled "On Belay!" to signify that I had the rope so the next climber could start his climb of the pitch. I was sitting with a tree right above me and gravel at my feet. At one point, the climber following me fell. The rope pulled tight around my waist and dragged me sideways into the gravel that was at my feet on this pitch. I held tight to the rope with my face in the gravel. The climber who fell was also secure, as long as I kept the rope tight around my waist, which I did. After a few seconds, the rope slackened, meaning that the climber had recovered and resumed his upward ascent. Quite exciting!

One day, the temperatures in Yosemite Valley rose. It was about 95°F out. We had gone from snowing one day to very hot within a week. After a day of climbing, we were looking to cool off. The Merced River running through Yosemite Valley looked mighty refreshing. We were in our climbing shorts and decided to go for a swim. There was a large flat rock out in the middle of the river. It looked to be about 50 feet out. We dove in and swam to the rock. We had forgotten one little item. It was May and the Merced River flows from higher elevations in the Sierras where the snow was melting. To put it mildly, it was icy cold. We hit that water and went through shock while swimming rapidly to the rock where we scrambled out of the river. The rock was significantly warmer. We sat there talking about it a bit and sunbathed some. Then we realized we were going to have to do it again to get back to shore. We finally worked up the courage to dive back into the water and swim quickly to the shore. Nothing quite like a refreshing dip in an icy river!

One day we were climbing a short technical climb on a rock near Camp Four, which had a technical difficulty of 5.8. As we were climbing, we noticed that the Yosemite Mountaineering School & Guide Service instructors had stopped with their students and were watching us climb. I assumed they were watching us in order to point out to the students how climbs like this were handled. This was a proud moment. I had gone from novice to instructor by example!

There was one more climb that just Scott and I took on. It was a climb on Glacier Point called "The Grack." This is what is known as a friction climb meaning that your stability on the rock is best if your shoes are the typical soft rubber that will help to grab the rock. Sometimes on these climbs, there are indentations, but not really any solid fingerholds. We were following a crack, but it was still balance and friction. The Grack is rated a 5.7 climb. It is about 350 feet of rope climbing with three pitches. I remember looking down at the evergreen trees very far below me and thinking it was beautiful and scary at the same time. Geez, those trees seemed a long way down!

As I followed Scott up the sharply sloped granite cliff, I came to one of the final nuts that he had set and this one just fell out. This sometimes happens as upward pressure from the lead climber's rope can loosen a nut. Although this was frightening, the nut was likely sufficient for a downward pull, and there were other points of protection. I am sure that we were safe. It is just that for a novice, that can be unnerving. Falling hundreds of feet to our deaths flashed through my mind. Nevertheless, we did get up and down this climb which was actually scarier than it was difficult.

Rock climbing is not a sport for the faint-hearted. Most rock-climbing deaths are the result of carelessness, overconfidence, or distraction. Between 1970 and 1990, there were 51 climbing deaths on the granite walls of Yosemite. We had heard about some climbers dying during our nine days in Yosemite. Still, that only averages 2.5 deaths per year and considering all of the people who climb there, that was not a particularly high figure. That is, unless you are the one falling.

On the following pages are some photos of other climbers doing the same climbs that we did during my nine days in Yosemite. I am including these to offer the reader a view of what these climbs are like.

Kristen Shorette climbing The Footstool, located on El Capitan. Photo by Bryan Gohn—February, 2011.

*Kelly Mcguire climbing Munginella with another climbing group ahead.
Photo by her husband Andy Johnson—May, 2018*

Lisa Stefke climbing Munginella. Photo by her husband Elmar Stefke—July, 2013.

Climber on The Grack. You can see the route crack winding to the upper left. Photo by Bill Olszewski—May, 2009.

Climbers Shawn Swenson and Scott Sellers on The Grack. This view of the evergreens far below is what I remember from this climb. Photo by Marissa Christman—September 2011.

DOLORES

In 1977, while I was working at AMD, I met a woman named Dolores. She was a 33-year-old, 5'1", dark-haired Hispanic divorcee. I was doing a lot of running at the time and ran in a company race where she was helping the race officials. She had beautiful exotic looks and I asked her out.

While we were seeing each other initially, we were not exclusive. I found out that she was having an affair with one of the AMD vice presidents who happened to be married. I told her that I could not continue to see her if we were not going to be exclusive. It took a few weeks, but she came to me and said that she had broken it off with the VP. From there on our romance was exclusive. We seemed to be quite compatible and I was thinking that Dolores might be my future wife. She had two daughters, one that was about 13 years old and the other was about ten. The girls' father was not in the picture. Dolores and I continued to see a lot of each other and the relationship grew.

We continued to date for over a year and then we decided to move in together. As we started living together, something was not quite right. I was still drinking too much. We began to argue a lot. Living together was not working out the way that I had hoped. I felt bad for Dolores's daughters and the nice couple that we had rented our apartment from because we were on a month to month lease. Exiting from the apartment went pretty smoothly considering the circumstances, but I know it was frustrating for our landlords. We had only been in the place for a few months.

Dolores and I went on to live separately and to try to date, but the relationship was continuing to break down. I became very frustrated. Here I had what I thought was going to be a long-term relationship, but once again, I had failed to find a way to make it work. It seemed as if the prospect of a wife and family was never going to materialize.

GROUP THERAPY

My frustration turned into something deeper and darker. I was severely depressed. All of this was happening in early 1979. I wasn't eating and I was losing weight. I was down to 148 lbs. At 155 lbs., I was at my collegiate tennis playing weight. I didn't have much weight to lose. On top of that, my stomach was in knots and I wasn't hungry. Depression is a black hole. As you sink into it, nothing looks good. There appeared to be no way out of this quagmire. It was truly awful.

I thought about ending my life, but I had always been such an optimist that it just didn't make sense. There had to be a way out of this. I had to do something because I just couldn't keep going on like this. I felt like I was being torn apart. I searched the phone book and found a Santa Clara County Mental Health telephone number. I called it. I was told that there was a Men's Group that met weekly and that I could join it for a moderate cost. I agreed to go. What did I really have to lose?

Upon arrival, I found out that the group was led by two men who had us use their first names. There was a psychiatrist named Dr. Don and a psychologist named James. I was in a group of about six to eight men. As we began to discuss our problems and the issues that led us to the group, I began to realize that there were people in this group who were significantly more dysfunctional than I was.

The Don and James team were quite adept at calling the attendees out on their bullshit. Since it was always easier to see the problems of others more clearly than your own problems, the group would often talk about their observations of fellow group members. Gradually, I began to feel better. I began to recognize that my problem was centered around my unwillingness to let go of my relationship with Dolores. This was so even when I knew it was not going well and even when I knew it was unhealthy for me to continue to see her.

My own assessment is that this was a bit like an athletic contest. I wanted to "win at all costs" because this was my life. However, to continue to hang on meant to continue to feel bad, because I was not able to change my relationship with Dolores. It became clear that I needed to break it off completely with her. That was the only way that I would be free of the frustration and depression. In October of 1979, I paid a visit to the apartment where Dolores was now living. We talked about the future, made love, and I left. It may be an odd way to say goodbye, but seemed appropriate based on where our relationship had been. I have never seen her since. This was the best solution, since the relationship was toxic for me.

I went back to what I was comfortable with which was visiting the bars and chasing women. I did not play tennis. After a year of therapy, I was feeling that I was doing much better. I suggested to Don that I was ready to leave the group. His response was that I was not. I ended up staying another year.

As I neared the end of my second year of weekly group therapy meetings, Don invited me to come to see his home with a pool in Los Altos. I didn't think much of it at the time, assuming that it was just a nice gesture. I did go over to see it one evening. He gave me a drink and invited me to swim in his pool. I told him I didn't have a suit. He said that was OK, that I should swim in the nude. I don't know why I accepted this invitation, but I did. While I was swimming, Don was on the side of the pool. He asked me if I had any physical issues that were bothering me and I told him that I had a hamstring pull that had occurred recently. He offered to massage it. At this point, a light bulb went off. I started to believe that he was trying to have sex with me. I was not gay and not interested in experimenting. This was not the first time that I had been hit on by a male. It was the first time that someone I thought I knew well and trusted was hitting on me. Don did not press the issue any further. I exited the pool, dried off, got dressed, and left his home as quickly and gracefully as I could. A hindsight observation was that this was a huge violation of the doctor-patient relationship. I continued with therapy for a few more months before I was released. I don't think James knew about this situation. He was married and his wife was a psychologist as well.

One of my friends in the group, Tom, told me later that Don had divorced his wife and began to have homosexual relations with a variety of young men. In August of 1999, it was reported that Don had died of complications from diabetes. Tom had told me that he had died of AIDS. It was common to avoid the stigma of AIDS, which would lead to a conclusion that the person was either an IV drug user or homosexual, by attributing death to a more socially acceptable reason. It wouldn't be that unusual. Did Don die of AIDS or diabetes complications? I don't know. All I know for sure is that I don't think his behavior, in inviting me to his home, by myself, was appropriate.

My second hindsight was that air crash survivors are more prone to illness and mental health issues. I don't think my time in group therapy is attributable to the crash, but it can't be completely discounted.

Once I left the group, my approach to life was more balanced. I was never given anti-depressants or prescribed any medications as a part of the treatment. I am surprised that neither of the doctors had made a strong push for me to give up alcohol.

I also knew that I didn't want to go through life with a series of one-night stands or yearlong love relationships that didn't work out. I was still searching for my love partner and future wife.

MEETING MYRA

As the years passed, I continued through a series of relationships, most of which ran their course in three to four months. There was a nightclub, located in Cupertino named The Sandpiper that I would sometimes go to. The Sandpiper had a band that played regularly called Sundance. Sundance played oldies tunes from the 1960s which, in 1981, was not that long ago. Sundance was a three-person band. Dan played guitar, Bill played bass, and Jan played drums. All three of them would sing. Dan took the lead on a lot of male vocals while Jan handled the female vocals. Bill and Jan did a tremendous Sonny and Cher imitation. Jan had been with the Vejtables and the Mojo Men in the 1960s and had cut albums. Her most famous song was "Sit Down, I Think I Love You" with the Mojo Men, which was a cover of a Buffalo Springfield hit. She sang lead and the song made it to Number 36 on the Billboard Top 100 in 1967. For my money, the Mojo Men cover was the better version. Jan was also particularly notable as one of the very first female drummers.

The three members of Sundance would mingle with the crowd, which I am sure was an effort to build the fan base. Bill and I would talk during some of these breaks. I got to know him the best. It appeared to me that he was the least comfortable of the three when it came to mingling. Maybe he recognized a kindred spirit, but in any case, we hit it off. He would come over and sit with me during some of the breaks. The music was really great and the club had a fun, relaxing atmosphere.

In February 1981, I went to the Sandpiper. As I was sitting at one of the tables, I spotted a couple of women who were both very attractive. The music had started and people were dancing. I got up and asked one of them to dance, which we did. It turned out that the woman that I had asked to dance was Karin and she was from, of all places, Wisconsin.

We went back to her table where I sat down. Karin introduced me to her girlfriend, Myra. Karin was excitedly telling Myra that I was from Wisconsin. Myra said that everywhere that Karin went, she seemed to meet people from Wisconsin. I asked Myra to dance and we did. Myra was about my age with long black hair that hung down to her waist and exotic good looks. I was definitely intrigued.

Around 1980, I had met another woman, Cathy, who was a few years older than I was. She was a divorcee with one child. We became good friends. Yes, I know that was not my modus operandi, but we were just friends. She had come to California from Minnesota, so we had that upper-Midwest upbringing in common. We got along well, and would sometimes go out together as friends. Our relationship remained platonic. On these outings, we would each look to see if we could find people that we were interested in.

A few weeks after meeting Karin and Myra, Cathy and I went to The Sandpiper together. I saw Myra sitting with a group of people. I tapped her on the shoulder and asked her to dance. She invited me to sit at her table, although it was a bit crowded. She was concerned about Cathy, but I told her not to worry. If Cathy was alone at our table, I was pretty sure she would have no problem making male friends.

It turns out that Myra was there with members of her family. I got her telephone number and would soon ask her out. We talked on the phone and dated over the next few months. Our relationship became more serious. She had recently gotten out of a seven-year marriage and was now divorced. She had a 12-year-old daughter, Michelle, from a prior relationship. Myra had gone to an all-girls Catholic high school in San Francisco, where she graduated in 1968.

Myra and I were to quickly become close. We talked at length, got along well, and shared a common set of values. Would Myra be the answer to my quest to find a lifelong partner, a loving, caring wife? As time went on, we would see.

At the time that I met Myra, she and her ex-husband were selling the home that they had lived in. It was in Sunnyvale about a mile from where I grew up. The housing market was not particularly good at the time and they were having trouble selling it.

On September 20, 1981, I moved into the house and began living with Myra. This helped to defray the expenses for her. Myra's main concern with our relationship was that she had never really spent a lot of time on her own until her marriage ended. She had a new group of friends and had been looking forward to facing the world on her own for the first time.

As our relationship moved forward, Myra and I wanted to separate ourselves from her ex-husband. We came up with a plan to buy him out which he accepted. Suddenly, I was a home owner. Together, Myra and I could handle the new mortgage.

One of her good friends was Jan, the drummer from the band Sundance. Soon after Myra and I had moved in together, Jan met Paul, with whom she was falling in love. Their relationship continued to advance and we would get together with them from time to time.

In the spring of 1982, Myra and I were looking at the back yard of our .22-acre lot from the dining room. Beyond the sunroom was dirt. There was an old garage on the right and a shed on the left and lots of dirt in between. We talked about doing something with the yard by perhaps putting in a lawn. In the middle of our discussion of putting in a sprinkler system, I asked Myra to marry me. I took her by surprise. She agreed. I had found the love of my life! We were looking toward 1983 for a possible wedding. Sprinklers and love, who knew they could be paired in such a romantic way!

THE WEDDING

Myra and I continued living together through the spring and summer of 1982. The relationship just kept getting stronger. In August, Jan called Myra and said that she and Paul were going up to South Lake Tahoe to get married. She asked if we wanted to come along with them and get married at the same time. Myra and I agreed. Myra and Jan got matching antique dresses while Paul and I wore suits.

Paul and Jan drove up to South Lake Tahoe in Paul's car while Myra and I drove up in mine on the day after Labor Day, which was September 5th. The next day, we drove across the California state line into Nevada. We went to one of Jan's favorite places, Virginia City.

Virginia City, Nevada was an old silver mining town. It is located about an hour out of South Lake Tahoe, California. It is over 6,000 feet above sea level. Virginia City became a boomtown in 1859 with the discovery of the Comstock Lode, which was the first major silver deposit discovery in the United States. By the mid-1870s, Virginia City's population had grown to 25,000 residents. There were numerous mines in the area at that time. After 1878, silver mining output declined and so did the population. The 2010 census showed only about 855 residents. Virginia City is the county seat of Storey County, Nevada. The county has about 4,000 residents. Back in 1980, there were only about 600 residents in Virginia City. Mark Twain has a historical tie-in to the city since he lived there from 1862–1864. It was during this time that Samuel Clemens adopted the moniker "Mark Twain." Today, the city is a tourist attraction with wooden board sidewalks and saloons that look like they came straight out of the Old West. Among the attractions are the Red Dog Saloon, the Brass Rail Saloon, the Delta Saloon with the Old Globe and Suicide Table, the Bucket of Blood, and the Silver Queen.

We talked about getting married in the Bucket of Blood Saloon, but we finally selected the Silver Queen Hotel and Wedding Chapel, which is famous for its large picture of a woman whose dress is made of silver dollars. The wedding chapel was located as a room in the back of the saloon. The Reverend John Galley conducted the service for the double wedding. For years afterward, our wedding picture, taken in the chapel, was on a bulletin board near the front of the saloon, as the only double wedding ever conducted at the Silver Queen Wedding Chapel. Our picture was there along with a picture of the Captain and Tennille, the famous singing duo, who had also been married at the chapel. Unfortunately, they were divorced a few years ago after 39 years of marriage.

On the way back to South Lake Tahoe, we took our wedding picture with the four of us, having Lake Tahoe provide the backdrop. Arriving back in South Lake Tahoe, we walked through Harrah's wearing our wedding duds. We saw many people staring and it was a fun time.

The next day, we headed back to the South Bay. As we started our drive, my car engine began to overheat. We were caravanning, so the two cars pulled over. I tried turning the heat on to dissipate as much of the engine heat as possible. Because of the heat, my new wife Myra rode back with Jan and Paul, while I trailed with the heat on and the windows open. While traversing a pass near Sunol, my car conked out. I climbed in with Myra, Jan, and Paul to finish the ride to Sunnyvale. It turns out that my car problems were due to my attempts to save money by tuning my own engine. Not being a mechanic and having no internet to turn to, I had forgotten one step which was to also change the fuel filter. Once that filter had become blocked, the car's overheating and eventual failure to run were inevitable. I no longer change my own oil.

Myra and I flew back to Wisconsin in 1985. My folks had not met her yet. It was not a problem. They loved her. Myra also got to meet my 89-year-old grandmother and that turned out very nicely as well.

Flying back home was a bit more difficult. It had been over twelve years since I had crashed. On the flight back, we were going from Wisconsin to Denver and then Denver to the Bay Area. Leaving Wisconsin, the pilot announced that we were going to head north to avoid a line of thunderstorms. This would make the flight longer and have a potential impact on making our connection in Denver. We didn't go just a little north. We must have headed north for a half hour. We did not get another announcement from the pilot, but I could feel the plane turn west and we were pretty far up over Minnesota, almost to the Canadian border. I think the pilot realized that he couldn't get around the line of thunderstorms, so he decided to go through them. We entered complete cloud cover with rain and the plane started rocking and rolling...a lot. I was quite literally white-knuckling this one. It was bringing up too many memories and the plane was bouncing all over the place. The flight attendants were calm, but I knew that either it had to be an act or they felt that there was no chance the plane could go down. Of course, I knew differently!

After 10–15 minutes, we broke through the western edge of the storms and entered sunshine with level and smooth flight. Finally, I could relax a little. Myra was a comfort to me on this flight. So, it turns out that I wasn't quite over my fear of crashing again just yet.

Our Wedding Photo: Todd, Myra, Jan, & Paul with Lake Tahoe in the Background

CHAPTER 50

OTHER SPORTS

After reaching my mid-thirties, I was running regularly in 10,000-meter (10K) races. 10Ks are 6.2-mile races. I ran the San Jose Mercury 10K in 39m:15s, which was a pace of 6m:20s per mile. That is not bad. I also ran as much as 17 miles in a single day. I remember running a 5K, which is 3.1 miles, at a pace of six minutes per mile, or just over 18½ minutes.

In two consecutive years, I ran the Martin Luther King Half Marathon at Stanford. It was a relatively flat run, which allowed me to post good times. I ran both of them in almost exactly the same time. In one of those races, I was trying to beat a couple of my training partners. I was ahead of both of them for the whole race and I thought I had left them well behind. Little did I know that they were working their way forward and slowly catching up. They tried to stay behind other runners so that I would not see them and try to pick up my pace, which was particularly important in the last few hundred yards of a race. During those final yards, they both went sprinting past me before I had a chance to try to prevent them from coming in ahead of me. Oh, well! I finished both of these races in about 1h:28m:30s, which is a pace of 6m:45s per mile. I am proud of those times.

In the early-to-mid-1980s, I took up bowling. As with most sports, I was very good, but not great. I bowled in a couple of leagues and I would bowl competitively for prize money on Saturday mornings. I had achieved a high season average of 184. In one of my games, I threw a 278 which was 11 out of 12 strikes. I remember during one of the league games, one of the other competitors came up to me and told me that he recognized me as a very good tennis player from high school. I hadn't played tennis in over a decade, so it was kind of nice that I was recognized for my tennis game so many years after I had stopped playing. I was still drinking at this point, which probably didn't help my scores, but I know that I was sober on Saturday mornings, and the lanes weren't much kinder to me.

After a few years, I gave up bowling and drifted toward other sports. I had skied from the late 1970s on. This was not terribly dangerous, but then I often took unnecessary risks. I remember one of the very first times that I went skiing. This was with my high school friend, Jeff, and some of his friends. This skiing was in the Sierra Nevada Mountains at one of the top ski resorts. Jeff and the others took the ski lift to the Black Diamond Runs. Not knowing what I was doing, I went up with them. Once I was up there I had to ski down. Black Diamond Ski Runs are the steepest and toughest runs at the resort. This is not a place learn how to ski. I tried to replicate what the others were doing as they skied down. As you might have guessed, on my initial run, I fell about eight times before getting to the bottom. Eventually, I became a very good skier. I haven't skied for years now, because as you recall, I am never particularly thrilled with cold weather.

In the early 1980's, I was invited by my manager at work to go on a company river rafting trip. Families were invited and so I talked Myra and Michelle into going along.

I understood that we would be on the South Fork of the American River north of Sacramento. The river was extremely dangerous this particular year because there had been a large amount of rain and snow in the mountains. The runoff was making these rapids very treacherous. There had already been at least one river rafting death on the river that year. As Myra was seated between Michelle and me in the back corner, the rough water dumped her into the river. She was there one second and gone the next. Michelle and I were screaming as the raft moved into a calmer section of water. She did not come up for about 30 seconds which really had us frightened, but apparently, she had come up under the boat and had to fight her way to the surface. This trip was not fun. The water was cold and Myra's experience was very scary. The rapids, where Myra was knocked out of the boat, was named Satan's Cesspool. How fitting!

In 1986, I turned 35. I had enjoyed riding bicycles and thought that bicycle road racing looked like something that I could get interested in. In 1987 or so, I joined a local Sunnyvale bicycle racing club and started riding a lot. When it came to road racing, I was starting in the 35 and over age group for Category 4 riders. Category 4 was the lowest category of racing reserved for beginners or for the worst riders.

I rode up to 250 miles a week. The problem was that at an average of 15 miles per hour (mph), 250 miles ties up almost 17 hours a week. I was riding my bike to work which was about 9 miles from home. On my way home, I would take excursions into the nearby hills to add miles. I did make it to work in as little as 22 minutes, which was about a 24½ mph average speed.

I also used to train up and down Highway 9. Highway 9 went from Saratoga, California, to Skyline Boulevard, which was a cross road at the top of the nearby Santa Cruz Mountains. It is a seven-mile ride rising over 2,100 feet. I would ride up as fast as I could, which was in less than an hour. I could get down in 12 minutes, averaging about 35 mph. There were lots of twists and turns and I could never reach a high speed of much over 40 mph.

I would also do rides where the goal was to complete the course and speed was irrelevant. Still, I liked to go fast. I went on a 200K ride, which was just under 125 miles with 10,000 feet of climbing. It took me about eight and a half hours to complete. One highlight was leaving Gunn High School in Palo Alto, going over the low mountains to the west, coasting down to Highway 1 at about Pescadero. Highway 1 runs along the coast with the beautiful Pacific Ocean on my right while heading south toward Santa Cruz. On one long stretch of very straight downhill, I registered a maximum speed of 49 mph. About 2/3 of the way to Santa Cruz, we made a left turn and headed up Bonny Doon Road, which is very steep. I remember being slowed to five mph as I struggled up the road for a half hour. Near the top, we stopped for lunch. Then we were winding up and down through the Santa Cruz Mountains until we finally ended up at the bottom of Highway 9 on the Santa Cruz or west side of the Mountains. Again, a lot of climbing was required to reach the top, and then descended through Saratoga in order to take Foothill Boulevard back to Gunn High. Now that was a tiring ride.

Another ride that was not a race was bicycling up Mount Diablo in the East Bay. It is 3,849 feet high and one of the tallest peaks in the San Francisco Bay Area. After making the climb, which was relatively easy for me at the time, we had lunch at the top, and then started down. I was watching a male bicyclist ahead of me when he suddenly lost control. His bike jerked, and then went straight ahead across about 20 feet of shoulder, and over the side. The mountain, at that point, went down at about a 45-degree angle. I went over to the edge, noting that he had luckily hit a manzanita bush, which was rather large, about 100 feet down the side from where he went over. He hit it with a lot of speed and went over the handle bars, landing on his back. I imagine he got scratched up pretty good, but at least he survived without breaking bones or getting killed.

I also did some interesting rides with my road racing teammates. On one ride, three of us rode as fast as we could from Sunnyvale to Morgan Hill, which was about 30 miles away. Racing was, however, a different story. Although in great shape, I was heavier than most of my competition. A lot of these riders were toothpicks. Being very thin helped them on the climbs. Because I outweighed most of them by about 20 lbs., I had to carry that extra weight uphill, creating a disadvantage.

On one ride in the Livermore area, the pack went along at an average of 21 mph for a full hour before the race turned up into some steep hills. I was quickly in last place as the pack left me in the dust. I rode criteriums in quite a few cities, but I never did very well. A criterium is a race that runs around a closed circuit with the object being to complete a certain number of laps. Most of my criteriums were circuits located in cities and would run from one-half to one mile per lap.

One highlight was riding a road race in Brentwood. The pack had climbed quite a few hills together and I was still with them. The descent was very steep and had some twists and turns. After the race, I checked my speedometer and found that it had recorded a high speed of 51 mph in the middle of a pack. In the middle of those packs, there were riders within a foot or two of each other with riders in front, back, and both sides. The pack would all lean the same way through the turns, but one wrong move and quite a few riders would go down. I thought about what it would be like to hit the pavement at over 50 mph, and the thought was frightening. A year or two later, that happened during this same race, although, luckily, I was not in it. I heard that a number of riders went down and were off to the hospital. Landing on your face on cement at high speeds, even with a helmet, is very dangerous.

Another adventure that I had was riding on Saturday mornings from a nearby Los Altos bicycle shop. They had advertised that a couple of Race Across America (RAAM) winners would ride with the local riders. I guess that there were no more than 20 of us who showed up to make that ride.

The RAAM is just what it seems. The racing, of course, is done on bicycles. The object is to ride a prescribed course from the Pacific Ocean across the United States until the race ends at the Atlantic Ocean. To win this race requires a lot of long-distance riding experience. It also requires a team to follow the rider in a recreational vehicle to be used for stops and to carry equipment that may be necessary along the route. Another attribute is the necessity to live on very little sleep for about ten days while being exhausted for much of the race. These riders often get only a couple of hours sleep per day.

This was about 1988 when I rode with Pete Penseyres of Huntington Beach, California. He was the 1984 men's winner of the RAAM in 9 days, 13 hours, and 13 minutes. In 1986, Pete won the 3,107-mile race in 8 days, 9 hours, and 47 minutes, setting a record that wasn't broken until 2013. I also was able to ride with a former women's champion, Elaine Mariolle. Elaine won the women's RAAM in 10 days and 2 hours in 1986, setting the women's record at the time. The records today show the men in the 7-day range and the women in the 9-day range. Pete Penseyres and Elaine Mariole were pioneers of the new sport and were clearly very strong endurance riders. That day we rode into the mountains on a short 20-to-30-mile ride. It was truly an honor to ride with them.

VARIAN ASSOCIATES

In 1979, prior to meeting Myra, I had been working the Sunday–Wednesday fab diffusion day shift at AMD. I received a call from a headhunter who asked for my credentials. When I told her, she offered me a job pending an interview with the company that she was representing. The pay would be a sizable bump to my current salary. Also, I would be able to return to a more regular work schedule. I told her that I would be willing to interview.

The company was Varian Associates, which was located in Palo Alto. The position was a Production Control Supervisor. I went and interviewed with their general manager and was offered the job. This meant that I could work a Monday through Friday, 8:00 AM to 5:00 PM workweek. This was a vast improvement over the working hours of any of my first three jobs at AMD. I accepted the job at Varian. The AMD fab production manager asked what I was being offered and when he found out he wished me the best, which meant to me that he couldn't do better.

Varian Associates was an old-school technology company. It was one of the first high-tech companies in Silicon Valley. The company was started in 1948 by brothers Russell and Sigurd Varian, along with William Hansen and Edward Ginzton. Initially, the company was formed to sell the klystron, the first vacuum tube which could amplify electromagnetic waves at microwave frequencies, and other electromagnetic equipment.

When I joined Varian in October of 1979, my initial production control group had six or seven planners in it. I was to make a fairly fast ascension while at Varian. Over the next five years, I was to be promoted from supervisor, to manager, and then to a manager of managers. All of this was within the production control groups.

As my staff grew, I was eventually in charge of a group of 58 people including myself. I had three or four managers, each of whom was managing three or four supervisors. In addition to the managers and supervisors, there were analysts, master schedulers, coordinators, planners, expeditors, and others. It was quite a group. I was managing production control for over ten separate product lines with sales in those days of $110 million. In 2019 prices, that would be over a quarter of a billion dollars. By the mid 1980s, Varian Associates' tube division was what's known as a "cash cow." Merriam Webster defines a cash cow as "a consistently profitable business, property, or product whose profits are used to finance a company's investments in other areas." Because there was little further invention, it was expected that moving into the future, sales would decline and that meant that profitability would also decline. How long the profitability would last was not clear, but what was clear was that efficiency of production operations was needed to reduce costs and thereby maintain profitability at maximum levels.

One of my primary achievements while at Varian was inventing tracking charts that I referred to as "The Canopy Reports" because, like a canopy on a four-poster bed, they were meant to cover the planning and production areas that I was responsible for and reveal where problems existed. I was able to set up charts for each manager, supervisor, and planner that would tell them where to concentrate their efforts. Shortages and late delivery of kits to the manufacturing floor were key. Once these charts were set up, they were graphed weekly to illustrate improvements or deteriorations. The system was a good one and resulted in vast improvements to manufacturing.

I remember flying once for the company while I worked at Varian. A new materials manager, who was in charge of purchasing, production control, and the stockrooms, took a number of the managers on a one-day trip to Salt Lake City. I do not remember if flying affected me at that point. I suspect not, because I don't remember being nervous about it.

One notable event about 1984 was a production conference. The American Production and Inventory Control Society (APICS) invited me to be a panelist. There were a number of others with expertise in production who were with me that day. It was a large audience and one of my fellow panelists was the moderately famous economist Elliott Janeway. Janeway was a prolific author and informal advisor to Presidents. He was featured in television advertisements and mentioned on TV shows. Although I am sure that his politics were quite distant from mine, I ended up with a signed autograph of his 1983 book "Prescriptions for Prosperity."

As time went on, assemblers, technicians, and managers were starting to be laid off. I, along with my immediate manager and the general manager, were all removed from our positions. The other two were laid off. I was placed into a software group initially. I had worked with the software group to achieve the accuracy of the canopy reports. I knew how the Varian manufacturing software system worked, but I did not know how to program. My rock-climbing buddy Paul had come to work for me as a supervisor in one of my production control groups. As the layoffs started, he had been moved into programming. Since Paul knew how to program, I absorbed as much as I could from him in the short time that I was there.

After losing my managerial position, and noting that the Varian tube divisions were steeped in company politics, I started my job search. To aid in this search, I went on to get my APICS certification. APICS certification meant paying money to take classes and then tests. I didn't take the classes because I didn't need them, based on my work experience with Manufacturing Resource Planning (MRP) systems. I used their study books and just took the four tests of about three hours each on different production and inventory control aspects. I had hoped that obtaining my Certification in Production and Inventory Management (CPIM) would make me more acceptable to hiring companies. Still, the marketplace for production control managers was extremely difficult. Most companies used their own MRP systems or standardized versions that were tweaked for the individual company. Because of the differences in applying MRP systems to the products being built, most companies hired their management from within.

In the meantime, Varian had moved me into a training group. My family background had a lot of teachers and I was very skilled at teaching. After all, I had taught tennis for quite a few years. One of the assignments that I had was to create a computer program to track personnel statistics to be used in garnering government funding on a project to instill quality in the workplace. I wrote a program in dBase that handled the statistics.

I was also asked to write a Varian-oriented training program using basic quality techniques. I did that and used that program to train all 1,500 remaining employees of the tube groups. I was the sole trainer for all of the classes, which held about 25 students per class. It was a lot of training, but very successful.

I was still struggling in my search to find a new, high-paying job. I knew the company had placed me in these positions to give me the opportunity to become gainfully employed elsewhere. After at least five years of being out of my management position, I was finally laid off in December of 1992. When I joined Varian, the three tube divisions had about 2,200 employees. When I was finally laid off, there were only about 800 employees left. In some ways, I was thankful. I really wasn't doing work that was commensurate with my MBA, work experience, and skills. Leaving Varian was good for me, but I was worried about finding another job because the job market was very tight.

MY RETURN TO TENNIS

I didn't play tennis very much at all in 1970s, at least after the summer of 1973. In the 1980s, I played industrial league tennis for Varian. There were some good players at Varian during the years that I was there. I was the #1 player on the Varian ladder and won their annual tournament every year.

In 1989, Leigh Olson, whom I knew from Varian, asked me to play doubles in Northern California class tournaments. We were eligible to play "B" singles and doubles, which was the third level behind "Open" and "A" tennis in Northern California. The first six months of 1989, competing at the "B" level, I was terrible. I won nine matches and lost six. Six losses to players that I should beat in my sleep. I was very distraught. But suddenly, my game started coming back to me. For the second six months of that playing year, I was 28 wins and only one loss. The only match that I lost was to a French player who didn't know which division he should be playing in, and even that was a close match. There was a Grand Prix, where the top eight players for the year played a tournament. I won that as well. I finished the season ranked #1 in singles and in doubles with Leigh. I was named the Player of the Year. Maybe this shouldn't be so surprising, but I was 38.

The way these divisions work is that if you do well enough in an adult division, they boot you out of that division for five years. I was tossed out of the "Bs" and forced to play "As" or "Opens." Of course, I was always eligible to play the age groups. Age group tennis starts at 25 or 30, but I think it should start at 35 years old. If the player turns that age or older during that calendar year, then they are eligible to compete. The age groups are typically five year increments up until one reaches the age of 90 and over.

I did OK in the As, but not as well as I expected. Surprisingly, though, starting with the 1991 season, I played a ranked Open player in Stockton and beat him. Later that year, I won three rounds in the Mountain View Open, winning two of those matches in three sets. I lost to a very tough San Jose State player 7–5, 7–5. I ended the year being ranked in the Men's Open Rankings for Northern California at #50. That is not a particularly high number, but I was competing at age 40 against players from colleges throughout Northern California, including Stanford and the University of California, all of the club pros, and all of the up and coming juniors. It really was quite an accomplishment. Starting in 1992, I was booted out of the "A" level based on my performance in the Opens. I was only allowed to play Opens or the age groups when it came to Northern California tournament tennis for the next five years.

In 1991, I was also ranked #3 in Men's 40s and over in the Northern California section. Over the next 13 years, I would win 15 age group tournaments, including the 1998 Northern California Sectional Championship for Men's 45s, and I received three national rankings. In 1993, at the age of 42, I was once again ranked in the Men's

Open Rankings at #61. I drove to Tucson, Arizona to play in the USTA Men's 40s National Hardcourt Championships, where I went through the #2 seed's bracket getting to the quarterfinals. In 1996, I played in the USTA Men's 45s National Hardcourt Championships in Westlake Village, California. I lost in the first round, but then played in the consolation tournament, which is sometimes known as the losers' bracket. Still, there were about 40 national-caliber players in that secondary tournament. I got to the final and played a very tough Texan named Carl Morris. It was a very hot day with temperatures around 95°F. Carl won the first set 7–6 and I came back to take the second set 6–4. In the age groups, a ten-minute break was offered after two sets had been split. I went into the locker room soaked in sweat and I don't generally sweat that much. I was drinking plenty of fluids, but I knew that I was going to have to go and compete for what could be another hour in that heat.

I was in excellent shape, running up to six miles a day when I wasn't competing. Still, this was a scorcher of a day. I took off my shirt and soaked it in a sink full of cold water. Then I wrung out the shirt and put it back on. It would dry out quickly, but it helped keep my body temperature cooler at least to start. I went on to win the deciding third set 6–4 to take the consolation championship.

My tennis game was not where it had been, but that was a bit much to expect at my age. A bigger problem for me was that between 1973 and 1989, racquet technology had changed immensely. Wood racquets were the primary tennis racquets in the late 1960s and the early 1970s. There were some innovative metal racquets just starting to be seen. The Wilson T-2000 was a metal racquet that I used some during my high school days. In college, racquets were provided to us for free, but they were only offering wood. With a wood racquet, the serve could be struck very hard, but it was difficult to hit hard groundstrokes. Generally, most top players in the United States were coming to the net in those days, employing a "serve and volley" style. As the racquet technology changed, most players played from the back court. The serve and volley style was becoming a thing of the past.

In age group tennis, most of the players were still serving and volleying as that was what we had grown up learning to do. In Open tennis, although I still had some success, powerful topspin groundstrokes presented a problem that was hard to overcome. It was almost like two different games. I played in the age groups until age 52. In the Men's 50s in 2003, I won two out of the three tournaments that I played in. The Northern California Section had changed its method of ranking players to a point-based system like the pros used. I ended up in a three-way tie for #6 in the 2003 NorCal Men's 50 and over rankings. I didn't like the system and stopped playing tournaments. Besides, I was in the midst of a new sport, mixed martial arts.

CHAPTER 53
1989

THE LOMA PRIETA EARTHQUAKE

On October 17, 1989, Leigh Olson and I were getting ready for the Grand Prix men's doubles tournament where we would be top seeded in the Bs. I was also top seeded in the Grand Prix singles event. The Northern California Section Grand Prix was the end of the year tournament where the top eight players or teams were invited to play against one another.

In preparation, Leigh and I had scheduled a tennis match at Marymeade Park in Los Altos. I do not remember who our opponents were. We were to meet at 5:00 PM and play two or three sets. Also, the Bay Area World Series was getting ready to start. The San Francisco Giants and the Oakland Athletics were going to play the third game of their World Series clash which was getting ready to start at 5:35 PM at San Francisco's Candlestick Park.

At 5:04 PM, the Loma Prieta Earthquake hit with a magnitude of 6.9 on the Richter Scale and a maximum Mercalli Intensity level of IX (Violent). It was centered in The Forest of Nisene Marks State Park, approximately ten miles northeast of Santa Cruz on a section of the San Andreas Fault system, and was named for the nearby Loma Prieta Peak in the Santa Cruz Mountains. The quake was to be responsible for 63 deaths and 3,757 injuries, 400 of which were serious. The effects caused heavy damage in

Santa Cruz County and then north to San Francisco and Oakland.

We were approximately 25 miles from the epicenter as the crow flies. That was not nearly far enough. As a Northern Californian, I had been through many earthquakes. Some of them had reach 6.0 on the Richter Magnitude Scale. This scale is logarithmic meaning that every full number increase is a ten-fold increase in intensity. This means that this earthquake was roughly 100 times more intense than a 5.0 earthquake and about ten times more intense than any earthquake that I had previously experienced. The quake hit very hard for about 15 seconds. It felt like a lot longer. The ground was rocking and rolling, so much so that I had to sit down for fear of being knocked off my feet. The light standards on the three tennis courts started swaying violently. These light poles were thick at the bottom and tapered to half their starting circumference or less as they extended to their height of 15 to 20 feet. On all three courts, all of the light standards started bending from their straight up and down position to about a 90° angle. I had no idea that they could bend so far. There were maybe four light standards on each side of the court and evenly spaced apart. Looking from my sitting position, I could see about 12 of these standards moving back and forth in unison from one side to the other about every second or two. It was fascinating to watch. After the shaking stopped, the light poles continued to move in unison, gradually losing a little of their angle on each side until they eventually stopped.

We stood up and looked around. The lights at the nearby intersection, which we could see from the courts, were out.

Traffic was already backed up past our location. We did not have cell phones yet. It wouldn't have mattered, because if we had them, the cell towers would have been flooded with calls and getting through would have been next to impossible. In any case, after assessing the situation, we decided to play tennis as we had originally intended and try to let the traffic clear a little bit before heading home.

Myra was at work at the time that the earthquake hit. She remembers diving under a desk or table and then heading to the parking lot where the cars had all been moved around by the quake. She found hers and was able to drive home. She was terribly worried about me, because I had not called, but she was unaware of how bad the traffic was near the tennis courts. I had assumed that she would be stuck at work or in her car for hours.

The World Series game must have saved lives, since traffic was lighter than usual around the Bay Area, and many people were in their homes getting ready to watch it. Also, a four-year drought limited the potential for landslides, but even so, there were up to 4,000 landslides that occurred. Forty-two of the deaths occurred in Oakland when the Cypress Street Viaduct collapsed on the Nimitz Freeway (Interstate 880). A 50-foot section of the San Francisco-Oakland Bay Bridge collapsed, leading to one death. Three people were killed in the collapse of buildings along the Pacific Garden Mall in Santa Cruz, while five more died in the collapse of a brick wall on Bluxome Street in San Francisco. With a normal Tuesday rush hour instead of the lighter traffic due to the World Series, deaths could easily have been significantly greater. Once again, I was in the middle of another historic event and yet safe from injury. Granted, several million people felt this earthquake, as I did, but it is still remarkable to have experienced the event. I am grateful that Myra and I escaped injury.

UNEMPLOYMENT

After Varian laid me off, I applied for and received unemployment, which was to last for 26 weeks or until I found a job. Myra and I bought a $1,500 laser printer so that I could print off cover letters, resumés, and envelopes. I knew this would be helpful. That was very expensive at the time. In 2019 dollars, that was a $2,732 purchase and today you can get a laser printer for a tenth of that price.

I would check the local newspapers and send out resumés for any jobs that would fit my background. Over the next year or so, I sent out about 250 resumés. Often, there would be more than 20 applicants to a job. The unemployment checks didn't make up for my salary, but at least it was something. Just when my 26 weeks were about to end, Congress passed an extension and I was able to sign up for an additional 26 weeks. I had never imagined that I would be unemployed for this long.

I went through all of 1993 unemployed. We were living off of Myra's checks and my unemployment insurance. It was getting quite frustrating. I had grown up with the expectation of being the breadwinner. Here I was just out of a highly salaried position, and now I was not having luck finding a new one.

Someone gave my name to the *Sacramento Bee* Newspaper as one of the unemployed executives among many. The reporter called me and asked me a series of questions. Then the article on unemployment came out portraying my situation and struggles to find work. This was a prominently displayed article. I was proud to have described the situation that quite a few Silicon Valley executives and workers found themselves in after so many companies had cut back their workforces with layoffs during this recession.

I was to be unemployed for 14 months. You would think that having 14 months off would be like having a 14-month vacation. Believe me, it was not. Growing up as poor as I did, I had a great fear of being without money. This period was very stressful for me and I could not relax. Intellectually, I knew that I should enjoy the time off, since I was doing all that I could think of to find a new job. Emotionally, I was very stressed. All of that was about to change.

SPACE SYSTEMS/LORAL

At the beginning of 1994, I received a call for an interview at a Palo Alto company. The company was Space Systems/ Loral, which was also known as SSL. SSL is a manufacturer of satellites that were primarily launched into geosynchronous orbit. That orbit is 22,000 miles from earth. As of 2018, SSL has built more geosynchronous satellites, currently in orbit, than any other satellite manufacturer in the world. They have launched over 270 satellites. This includes spacecraft for services such as direct-to-home television, video content distribution, broadband internet, and mobile communications—the technologies that billions of people use every day. SSL took over as the commercial satellite leader during the last ten plus years of my career there. This was a formidable achievement considering that SSL's primary competitors were the very powerful companies of Boeing Satellite Systems, Lockheed Martin, Thales Alenia Space, and Airbus Defence and Space.

I went to an interview with a gentleman from their planning department. It turned out that several of my former employees were working in the procurement wing of the company. The manager was an old former Navy officer. He checked out the names of Paul, my old climbing and running buddy, who had been a supervisor of mine at Varian, and a few of my other Varian employees. There was Tom, who had been a supervisor, and Ron C. who had been a planner, supervisor, and manager in my groups at Varian along with Rich. There was also Janet who had worked in purchasing at Varian. There were times, at Varian, where I had 200 people reporting to me in my collective groups when I sat in for a higher-level manager. Sometimes that would last weeks. This SSL manager got the thumbs-up from my former employees and I was offered the job.

In late February of 1994, I was back to work. The job was just a planning job, but they were starting me at my Varian salary, so I couldn't complain. I found out that my resumé had come to SSL and been sent over to Program Management by Human Resources in the summer of 1993. There, my resumé languished for at least six months before it was uncovered and sent to the manager that could and did hire me.

One of the first things I found in a supposedly cleaned-out desk was a 20-year pin left behind by a person who had been laid off. I knew from this that I could potentially be laid off again. All of these Silicon Valley companies struggled to stay competitive and when business dropped off significantly, then the remaining workforce was just too large for the work. Layoffs were just a part of doing business and I accepted that. These companies were non-union and operated under "at will" employment rules. This means that either the company or the employee may sever their relationship without having to establish just cause, as long as the reason is not illegal.

Shortly after taking the job with SSL, I was asked to provide support in resolving a serious problem with a set of parts that needed to be replaced on about ten in-process satellites. A couple of these satellites were close to the launch schedule. I was asked to fly with Subcontracts and Production personnel to a couple of suppliers to work out a schedule that would accommodate all of the satellite replacements. I made a number of trips to the East Coast to meet with one New York supplier and then another group of trips to Southern California to meet with a parts supplier to the New York supplier. It was complicated scheduling work. It took quite a few months to rebuild, retest, and replace all of the hardware. Once we were past the first two satellites, then the rest gave us a bit more time.

In April of 1995, I was asked to go to Paris with the Vice President (VP) of Operations, the production control manager, the subcontracts specialist, the engineer for the product, and the newly hired supplier management manager in a few days. Wow! This would be my first trip overseas. Not bad work if you can get it. I knew that I would not likely get to see much of the sights, but I had taken a couple of years of French in high school, so I was looking forward to it.

However, there was a big problem. I didn't have a passport. It was Thursday and the flight was to leave on Sunday, land on Monday, with meetings to start on Tuesday. I went to the Vice President of Purchasing to explain my dilemma and he wrote a letter to support my passport application. I was told that I would have to go to San Francisco's passport office, located on Market Street. The next morning, I headed up to San Francisco wearing the SSL uniform of the times, a full suit. I found parking and began my trek to the passport office, which was at least six blocks away. The streets were filled with vagrants and other sketchy people. Here I was looking like a potential target for robbery or attack. I was carrying a hardcover briefcase. I was ready to swing it at the first sign of trouble. There must have been 20 of these derelicts per block, so I was constantly ready. No one attacked me or even spoke to me. Maybe it just looked like I was ready to fight or maybe no one was interested in me. Either way, I was thankful.

I went into the passport office at about 9:00 AM. They took my application. They told me it would be quite a wait and it was. At just about 5:00 PM, when they were supposed to close, they called my name. When I went up there to pick up my passport, they told me to come back on Monday to pick it up. I told them in no uncertain terms that I had been waiting all day and needed the passport in order to fly on Sunday. I was quite forceful and they acquiesced. They told me to have a seat again. After another 20 minutes, they came back with my passport. I was none too happy with them. They had made me waste an entire day and then tried to screw me in the end. Government agencies are the pits. They control your business and you can't go elsewhere.

That weekend, I flew to Paris with the engineer. We flew through O'Hare which, of course, carried special memories for me. The engineer and I met the others when we got to Paris. The supplier was outside of Paris and we took a taxi to get there in the mornings. It took about an hour to get to their plant. We spent the day laying out the schedules. This supplier was to deliver 48 identical subassemblies per satellite and was running late. The production control manager was in charge of my planning group and therefore my direct line boss for this trip. He and the VP had come to SSL recently and were trying to change things. The production control manager wanted me to produce computer schedules of the work that we were doing. I remember that it was an awful lot of computer work.

In Paris, we would get up at about 6:00 AM, eat breakfast, and go to the company by taxi, arriving at about 8:00 AM. Then we would spend all day working on improving the schedules. At about 6:00 PM, we would catch a taxi back to the hotel arriving about 7:00 PM. The VP wanted everyone to dress in full suits for dinner every evening, so we did. We would meet in the lobby at about 8:00 PM and then find a restaurant. As is the European way, these dinners had many courses and did not end until about 11:00 PM. Then we would come back to the hotel to sleep. Sleep was for everyone except me. The production control manager had required that I put the schedules from our discussions into a computer format. These were thousands of entries and I would have to work on them for three to four hours each night. I would get to sleep about 3:00 AM only to have to get up by 6:00 AM to repeat the pattern. At the end of the week, I was exhausted and not too happy with that production control manager.

At about this same time, I was being recruited into a new group at SSL called Supplier Management. It reported into the Subcontracts group which was part of the Procurement group. Basically, Supplier Management would report on the status of all schedules to our Program Management group and troubleshoot suppliers who were having delivery problems. I was the first hire of the newly hired Supplier Management manager. I don't think that initially he wanted to hire me, but my former employees had spoken to the Subcontracts manager about me and I think she forced him to hire me. He changed his mind about me during our first year together as he came to realize what an asset I was to his group.

Since this manager was on the trip to Paris with me, he pulled me aside and told me that he wanted me to come back to Paris in a couple of weeks to check on the schedules. He didn't have to ask me twice and without the production control manager looking over my shoulder, I could actually get some sleep while I was in Paris. I did make that second trip, and a month after that, I was back for the third time. I spent the next five years or so reporting schedules and troubleshooting suppliers whose schedules were not meeting our satellite requirements. I started traveling even more.

I was very glad to get away from the corrosive company political atmosphere that was the fabric of Varian while I was working there. In my job as a supplier management specialist, I would sometimes end up flying to the same location over and over again, checking on supplier schedules or on a particular issue. I was visiting a company in Chandler, Arizona almost weekly for a long time. From July of 1995 through March of 1997, I took 49 trips to and from Phoenix, Arizona. That is 98 individual flights. For five consecutive weeks, I was even requested to fly down on a Monday, back on a Tuesday, report to our program offices and vice presidents on Wednesday, fly down on Thursday, and come home on Friday. I had other companies that I would visit a number of times, but this was the one that I had to personally troubleshoot the most.

For a guy who had survived a jetliner accident, this was a lot of traveling, but it had been over 21 years since the crash when I took the SSL job. I really wasn't bothered anymore, including flying through Chicago's O'Hare quite a bit. I was always thinking that an accident like mine could not happen twice. True or not, I felt safe. I had learned to relax while flying by treating it as a vacation in the sky. It was particularly nice flying overseas. For overseas trips, I always ended up flying business class, with the exception of one trip. As far as flights and miles flown go, there was more flying to come.

In the fall of 2001, the satellite industry as a whole was suffering. On average, the satellite industry was getting about 35 large commercial satellite orders per year. These were won primarily by the big five satellite manufacturers. These were Lockheed Martin, Hughes (which was to be bought out by Boeing), Alenia (which was to be bought out by Thales), Astrium (which was to be bought out by Airbus), and Space Systems/Loral (which was eventually to be bought out by McDonald Dettwiler Associates (MDA) and later renamed Maxar Technologies), then renamed yet again in 2019 as Space Solutions. The number of satellites sold had dropped dramatically around this time and just after. At one point, the industry saw only two commercial satellite orders for an entire year and SSL didn't win either of them.

SSL began an employee reduction strategy where most weeks there were layoffs of employees. The problem with this strategy was that the employees were constantly worried about being laid off. At least with a larger layoff, the employees would usually get a few months before the next layoff might come. This pattern of layoffs almost weekly went on over a period of two to three years.

By late 2002, the Supplier Management group, that I was a part of, was disbanded. There were about 15 employees at SSL headquarters in Palo Alto, California, and another ten in various locations throughout the United States. Also, there were Supplier Management personnel in Europe and Japan. Two of us, Doug and I, were recruited to fill vacancies in the Subcontracts group. Although I had supported Subcontracts for years, I had dealt primarily with the scheduled deliveries and our satellite schedules, not with the contents nor the methodology of contracting. Nevertheless, I was honored to be kept on when everyone else in that group's U.S. contingent, except for Doug and myself, was laid off. I went into the RF Subcontracts group and Doug went into the BUS Subcontracts group. RF and BUS were different sections of the satellite. RF stands for Radio Frequency and BUS represents the infrastructure of the satellite upon which multi-satellite models are based. These two groups bought distinctly different products.

The first company that I had to handle for Subcontracts was a Canadian company in the Toronto area. This company could be a bit difficult to interact with. Two months prior to this, one of SSL's better purchasing agents, known as buyers, had been given the opportunity to handle the subcontracts for this company. I didn't know the individual, but I understand that he did not succeed and was laid off. The Purchasing group is different from the Subcontracts group. Buyers typically buy standardized products and the work is often routine. There is a lot of variety in Subcontracts. In Purchasing, prices and schedules are negotiated, but the legal contracts language is preset for the most part. In Subcontracts, all terms of a contract are potentially negotiated and the language is often written to accommodate the results of these negotiations. This considerably widens the scope of the work and the required flexibility. I was a bit concerned about the purchasing agent's dismissal, but I had an advantage. I was very willing to ask questions and I asked plenty of them.

There was a Subcontracts co-worker who sat across from me. His name was Bob. He was hired into Subcontracts at about the same time that I came into the Supplier Management group in 1995. It turns out that we went to high school together at Homestead with Bob graduating a year ahead of me. I didn't know him then, but he became my go-to contracts guy. My favorite lead-in for any question that I had for Bob was "You're an expert on this!" which was followed by my question. It still took me between three and six months to feel that I was fully up to speed.

The RF Subcontracts group had been about a 40-person organization. As the layoffs during the preceding and following years continued at SSL, the group got smaller and smaller. I was very worried that I would eventually be laid off. After all, I was new to subcontracts even though I had a world of experience in other areas. Many of my fellow RF subcontracts specialists had been working for more than ten years with some having 20 years of working experience specifically in Subcontracts. As the group became smaller and smaller, my workload increased. I picked up all RF active assemblies. These were more challenging. My concern over layoffs was not just in the hopes of keeping my Subcontracts job, but SSL was heavily staffed with engineers and the engineers were the core of the company. This meant that those of us without an engineering degree would be laid off at a higher rate than those in the engineering jobs of the company.

Eventually, the RF Subcontracts group was reduced to just three of us. The lucky three out of 40. I must say that I was astounded to still be working. The BUS Subcontracts group had around ten people working on crucial satellite assemblies which were often bought under Long Term Purchase Agreements (LTPAs). Most of these veteran Subcontracts people were kept. On July 15, 2003, SSL had declared Chapter 11 bankruptcy, which cost me about six figures in lost stock that I had been accumulating since I joined SSL. The end of the layoffs showed that SSL employees went from approximately 3,400 to 1,400 employees, or roughly 2,000 layoffs, but I had survived.

In 2005 I was moved into the BUS group. I spent the next 12 years buying high-priced assemblies for our satellites from U.S., European, Japanese, and Canadian suppliers. I bought the largest and most expensive subassembly on our spacecrafts as well as the controlling computer for our satellites. My work also took me into unusual locations including the National Security Agency. I ended up negotiating contractual agreements with them.

In February of 2009, I was on a trip to Buffalo with the propulsion manager, Ron K., and a subcontracts specialist that I was training to take over the Propulsion contracts that I had been managing. At the conclusion of our visit to three suppliers in the area, Ron and I was scheduled to go to the Buffalo Niagara International Airport to catch our flight back to San Francisco. The subcontracts specialist in training had left earlier and was no longer with us.

Our United Airlines flight was scheduled to go to Washington, D.C.'s Dulles International Airport, where we would transfer to a flight headed to San Francisco. Our flight from Buffalo was scheduled for a 6:42 PM EST departure. Upon arriving at the airport, we noticed that the snowy conditions had forced a delay in our flight to Dulles.

Our flight out of Dulles was scheduled to leave at 9:50 PM EST and arrive in San Francisco at 12:47 AM PST. As the flight delays out of Buffalo continued, Ron and I wondered if we were going to be able to make our connection.

We finally were able to take off close to 10:00 PM. We could only hope that the inclement weather would delay our flight to San Francisco until we could arrive. About a half hour into the flight, one of the passengers, a row or two in front of us, was receiving current news on her phone. She said that there had been a plane crash in Buffalo. Another crash at the same airport that I had just left was getting a little spooky.

The plane was a Colgan Air Flight 3407 marketed as Continental Flight 3407 that had been delayed for two hours at Newark Liberty International Airport before taking off on February 12, 2009 at 9:18 PM for Buffalo Niagara International Airport. The plane was a twin-engine turboprop Bombardier Q400. Shortly after being cleared to land on Runway 23, the plane disappeared from radar. At 10:17 PM, the plane went into a stall and plunged into a house killing all 49 people on board and one on the ground. That was too close for comfort.

On February 2, 2010, the NTSB issued its final report. Their conclusion as to cause was as follows: *"The National Transportation Safety Board determines that the probable cause of this accident was the captain's inappropriate response to the activation of the stick shaker, which led to an aerodynamic stall from which the airplane did not recover. Contributing to the accident were (1) the flight crew's failure to monitor airspeed in relation to the rising position of the low-speed cue, (2) the flight crew's failure to adhere to sterile cockpit procedures, (3) the captain's failure to effec-*

tively manage the flight, and (4) Colgan Air's inadequate procedures for airspeed selection and management during approaches in icing conditions."[14]

I was to discover that Joe Tolland, one of the SSL field quality engineers, almost boarded that flight. Joe worked out of Massachusetts, flying every week to supplier locations to examine and clear hardware for final shipment to SSL. He was scheduled to go into a New Jersey company to examine some power dividers that day and then on to Buffalo. At the last minute, he changed his plans. The weather was horrible, so he took an earlier flight to Buffalo from Boston. When the plane went down, he was sitting in the Buffalo Holiday Inn, located at the end of the runway at the airport. If he had gone to examine the parts in New Jersey, he would definitely have been on that flight. Joe and I often spoke about this incident based on his knowledge of my having survived a plane crash and his very close call.

When Ron and I reached Dulles at around 11:00 PM, we found out that we had missed our flight to San Francisco. We got in line at a United help desk and were told that the next available United flight bound for San Francisco was at 5:30 PM the next day. We booked it. After that, I called our emergency travel center and they were able to get both Ron and me on a Virgin America direct flight the next morning at 7:00 AM. They also took care of cancelling the 5:30 PM United flight that we had just booked. So we were set, but we still had about six hours to kill. We weren't comfortable leaving the airport and booking rooms at a nearby hotel with such an early flight. We scouted out the airport and finally decided to sleep in the baggage section of the terminal where there were chairs. We slept sitting up for the most part and it was not comfortable. We made the flight that morning without any further issues.

Over the years, my air travel is what ties my work life most closely to my air crash. I was able to get beyond my fear of flying that had developed after the accident. During my 23 years at SSL, I kept all of my travel records. They told my story of flying during those years and it varied. In five different years I flew over 40,000 miles each year, with the high being 58,324 miles in 1995. In 2003 and 2013, I didn't fly at all.

Phoenix, not surprisingly, ended up being the city that I flew to the most, a grand total of 52 trips, 104 flights. Forty-nine of those flights were to the supplier mentioned earlier. I had another supplier in the Phoenix area, accounting for the other three flights. I also flew to Florida, Orlando, and Tampa, a grand total of 24 times. I flew to New York's Long Island and Buffalo a total of 15 times. And I flew to the Washington, D.C. area 13 times.

All in all, I flew 611,294 miles for work at SSL, using 13 airlines, with 426 separate takeoffs and landings, in 173 business trips. I flew to Canada seven times, to Japan six times, and to Europe 11 times. Flying to the East Coast often resulted in going through cities in the middle of the country. I flew through Houston 12 times and Denver 15 times. I did have a couple of suppliers in Denver, making it a destination on a few occasions rather than just a pass-through city. Interestingly enough, leading the pack of pass-through airports was O'Hare in Chicago, where I landed and took off 16 times. O'Hare served as a reminder of my crash, but I was not any more fearful there than I was at other airports. My most frightening flight was taking off from Phoenix's

Sky Harbor International Airport when the temperature had reached 118°F. With the temperature providing reduced lift, we seemed to roll down the runway forever and then lift off very slowly, but lift off we finally did.

I didn't fly much at all between the crash and my marriage to Myra, but once we married, we were also flying. We would fly to Hawaii. We went in 1983 on a delayed honeymoon, and in the 1990s started making it our vacation of choice. We probably went to the islands about 20 times. We also took a few trips to the Midwest and Southern California. My personal flying must have exceeded 100,000 miles making a total of over 700,000 miles or about 2 months in the air. I can confidently say that I got past my fear of flying.

In February of 2017, I left SSL to begin a new chapter in my life, namely retirement.

THE BUCK STOPS HERE

On November 3rd, 2000, my excessive drinking finally caught up with me. I was at a company going away party in Palo Alto for two of our executives. Both were leaving SSL to go to one of our Southern California competitors. The party was held at a bar in Palo Alto where I had a number of rather strong European beers. I left the bar a little before 9:00 PM and headed home via El Camino Real. I was driving toward San Antonio Road at the Los Altos/ Mountain View border. I was in the right-hand lane of the three lanes headed south when an unseen car raced out of a driveway to my right. I am pretty sure that the driver, a man, was heading for the left turn lane and going directly across all three lanes to get into the left-hand turn lane. He had gunned his engine because he either thought he could get out before I arrived or he didn't see me until it was too late. I could not avoid him. I hit the back end of his car which kept his vehicle parallel to the road. He raced across all three southbound lanes, the beginning of the left turn lane, over a curb high median, across the three lanes headed north, and into a parking lot across the street. Luckily, there was virtually no traffic on the usually busy road.

I was ticked off and had no doubts that the other driver was at fault. He had pulled out of a relatively blind driveway right into my path giving me no time to avoid him.

I called 911, drove into the left-hand turn lane, made a legal U-turn and went into the parking lot where the other driver was waiting. I informed him that I had called 911. The police arrived shortly after that and interviewed us both. They noticed that I had been drinking and gave me a breathalyzer test which showed a .13 level of alcohol in my system. California state law allows up to and not including a .08 alcohol level. My car was searched, I was handcuffed, and driven to the Los Altos Police Station where I was booked on a Driving Under the Influence (DUI) violation. My pockets were emptied. They thanked me for being cooperative. I was allowed to make one call before I was placed in a small holding cell. It must have been about 6 feet by 4 feet. There were no bars, only one wired glass window on the door. I don't remember how long I was there, but I am pretty sure that it was more than an hour. Myra came and got me, since my car had been impounded, and I was not allowed to drive in my condition anyway.

When I looked later at the DUI ticket that I was issued, the Los Altos officer had indicated that I was traveling in the far-left lane. I know that I told him that evening that I was in the far-right lane. About a week later, I went to the Los Altos Police department to talk to the arresting officer about the error. He said that he saw debris in the far-left lane. I surmised this was a taillight that might have fallen off when the other car hit the meridian. I asked if he would change the ticket to reflect the correct lane. He declined. I suspect that he didn't want to make changes because it looks like he was unsure of the facts. I was also trying to make the case that the accident itself was the other driver's fault. He said it didn't matter even if I was right. Once one party is cited with a DUI, then in almost all cases, that party is declared at fault for any accident that occurs.

The DUI cost me more than twelve hundred dollars in fines, plus another thousand or so for an attorney. The attorney did me absolutely no good. I went to court and was found guilty. I had to take a class provided by the California Occupation Health Services (OHS) DMV DUI program, which I had to pay for and attend weekly for ten weeks. I had to forfeit my license and I was formally booked at the Elmwood Correctional Facility in Milpitas where I was fingerprinted and assigned to a weekend work program known as community service. For about five weekends, I worked from 7:30 AM–3:30 PM at the San Jose International Airport. My only concern about this assignment was that I didn't want to be seen by any of my coworkers, many of whom were flying a lot. It was February of 2001, and I wore a sweatshirt hoodie with the stereotypical orange vest. I kept the hoodie up and my head down as I and the others on the same assignment went through the entire airport emptying trash barrels. No one spotted me or at least it was never brought to my attention.

This whole experience was painful, but it turned out to be a very good thing. I stopped drinking the night of the arrest and have been sober ever since. It took me about a year to get past the psychological desire to drink. I did not go through physical withdrawal symptoms. It seemed strange to go through life sober. After about a year, I lost all desire to drink, and I realized that it is strange to want to drink all the time. This was a revelation and total change of perspective.

I did not go to Alcoholics Anonymous. I had done that in the past and failed. I realized that the revelation of having been given a DUI was a clear indication of a drinking problem. In April of 2002, I was back in court reviewing my record. I had completed all aspects of my misdemeanor sentencing except for the three-year probationary period. I asked the judge if he would waive the balance of the probation and expunge my record. The judge indicated that it was unusual to make this request after just one year, but he granted it. The action cleared my record with one condition, which was that the police would keep that record on file to be used should I get another DUI. I did not. I gave up drinking completely that night and have been sober for the last 18 years.

MARTIAL ARTS

In 2003, Myra asked me to come to a Martial Arts class with her at Ernie Reyes West Coast World Martial Arts (WCWMA). We stayed in classes together through the first year, each of us achieving a blue belt in the school's system of progressive belts. I like to say that Myra was ok with martial arts until she found out it was fighting. In fairness, she was getting whacked pretty good during sparring, particularly by teenage boys who could not control their punches and kicks. After about a year, Myra was not enjoying the classes enough and decided to quit. We were still at least three years away from the goal of becoming a black belt. I had an overlap with tennis during the first year, but I didn't think that I could do both effectively.

Grand Master Ernie Reyes, Sr. has the credentials to lead a big school. In 1977, Master Reyes was the U.S. National Tae Kwon Do Champion and won a bronze at the World Taekwondo Championships. Along with Grand Master Tony Thompson, he co-founded the West Coast World Martial Arts (WCWMA) Association. As of 2019, the WCWMA has 41 schools across 10 states with thousands of students.

Ernie Reyes, Sr. has also had roles in the movies "Surf Ninjas" and "Secret Bodyguard." He has choreographed martial arts fight scenes for a number of movies along with the TV series "Sidekicks." "Sidekicks" starred his son Ernie Reyes, Jr. who was one of the original "Teenage Mutant Ninja Turtles" and starred in the sequel." Ernie Reyes, Jr. has a very good fight scene in the 2003 movie "The Rundown."

The martial arts school that Myra and I attended was the Sunnyvale School. That school left the Ernie Reyes family of schools shortly after I stopped my training at the end of 2011. Originally WCWMA was a Tae Kwon Do school, but expanded into a Mixed Martial Arts or MMA school. The curriculum incorporated aspects of Tae Kwon Do from Korea, Muay Thai from Thailand, Brazilian Ju-Jitsu from Brazil, Escrima from the Philippines, Grappling or Ground Fighting, Kick Boxing, and American Boxing. Currently WCWMA is headquartered in Campbell, California.

After Myra left Martial Arts, I decided to continue my quest for a black belt. In the fall of 2007, after learning thousands of moves in various forms and memorizing inspirational texts along with many Korean Tae Kwon Do terms, I passed my test and became a 1st Degree Black Belt at the age of 56. In preparation for the testing, all black belt candidates had to come to Santa Clara University on Saturday mornings for six months and train with Master Reyes and his instructors. Black Belt Testing at WCWMA consisted of a full day of activity and a nighttime show where we would demonstrate our abilities to an audience made up mainly of the black belt candidates' family members. Nonetheless, these shows often had 2,000 people in the auditorium audience. I continued on because I had made many friends at the school, including older adults, such as Curt, Marty G., Linda, Carol, Kow, Lisa, and others. Marty

G. had the distinction of being the only person training with me that was older than I was. He was often mistaken for me and vice versa by our instructors since we both had gray hair and gray moustaches. Another reason for staying with martial arts was that it was nice mentoring students in the advanced classes.

In the fall of 2009, I successfully tested for my 2nd degree black belt. My partner during the years after my 1st degree black belt was Curt. It was fun even though Curt was much taller and bigger than I was. This was a larger issue when I had to carry him on my back during training. Not that he was exceptionally tall, but he reminded me of a gentle giant. 2nd degree training also involved training directly with Master Reyes at his Campbell School, two times a week, for six months. The Saturday morning classes were also in effect. At the presentation show, we had to perform an Open Form for the audience. This was a form that we designed and put to music.

Michelle, Myra's daughter, had graduated from Fremont High School in 1987. We lived within the boundaries for Fremont High School, which was the chief rival of Homestead High School where I had gone. Michelle subsequently worked in the area for a couple of years and then went to New York City to seek her fame and fortune in 1989. In 1992, she called home. She was pregnant and wished to return home and raise the child with us. Myra and I welcomed her back and in March of 1993, Rain was born. Soon after Rain was born, Michelle started training at WCWMA's Sunnyvale School. She was the inspiration for all of us who were to follow her. Michelle went on to get both her 1st and 2nd degree black belts. Rain started working toward her black belt at age three in 1996. Initially she didn't like it and stopped for about a year and then went back. At age 11, in 2004, Rain was able to get her black belt.

Rain watched me take my 1st degree black belt test in 2007 and she was inspired to come back to pursue her 2nd degree black belt. Particularly enjoyable for me was taking my 2nd degree black belt test at the same time as Rain did. I think we are the only grandfather-granddaughter duo to test together. Rain was much smoother than I was, particularly in her Open Form, while I was better at the board breaking.

In the fall of 2011, Curt and I tested for still another pair of black belts and, lo and behold, at the age of 60, I received my 3rd degree black belt. We had learned knife defenses, close quarter gun defenses, advanced boxing drills, advanced Tae Kwon Do, Brazilian Ju-Jitsu, and Muay Thai drills. We had to go to both Master Reyes' classes in Campbell and the Saturday morning Santa Clara University classes for six months. On top of that, we had to develop and perform an Open Weapons Form to music at the Black Belt Show.

For my weapon, I had chosen tonfas, which are very similar to police batons. They are about 20 inches long with a longer end piece that extended out perpendicularly, about five inches from one end. Two of them are used with one in each hand initially held with the short end toward the hand and the longer end running toward the elbow. I learned to use them through online videos and incorporated the maneuvers into a music piece. Toward the end of my Open Weapons Form, I would go into a forward roll holding my tonfas in both hands and using my knuckles on the mat for stabilizing the roll. I would come out of the roll and flip both tonfas simultaneously into the air in a

360-degree circle and catch them as the routine ended. I had to perform this form in front of Master Reyes himself, prior to being declared a candidate for 3rd degree. I successfully completed that evaluation, which can be intimidating.

My last year of testing was filled with injuries. Age may have played a role, but the injuries themselves could have happened to youngsters as well. During tonfa practice, I whacked my own right elbow three times in one session and pretty hard. The next morning, I got up and went to the computer only to find the skin on my right elbow hanging down by three or four inches. It was a skin sack filled with fluid and/or blood. I pressed it back to my elbow which seemed to work, but I ended up with a huge bruise on my right elbow, forearm, and triceps. My second injury was catching my index finger in Curt's uniform during grappling one evening at Master Reyes's class. It was pulled toward the thumb and sideways away from the middle finger next to it. That injury was still hurting during our testing and I occasionally still feel it today.

Kwan Jang Nim (KJN) means 5th degree and above at Ernie Reyes schools. My third injury occurred when my school's KJN Riz Angel performed a demonstration with me for 2nd degree candidates. He began showing them a maneuver, where one person is on their back and the other person, who is on top, puts a knee with full weight on the stomach of the person on the ground. KJN Riz's knee got a little high and caught the bottom part of my rib cage. To make matters worse, he bounced up and down. His estimated 225 pounds were too much and I heard a pop from inside me. I got him off of me and walked around a little bit. KJN Riz is a renowned martial artist and has a YouTube video that you should be able to find by searching his name. In the video he does an extensive brick breaking demonstration. It is worth seeing if you enjoy that kind of thing.

Curt and I did some grappling right after my rib injury occurred. I thought I might have cracked a rib. We did some Brazilian Ju-jitsu moves for about a half hour and I went home. The next morning, I had to get up to go to the Ultimate Boot Camp. This is an Ernie Reyes WCW-MA event that is held every year for black belt candidates. World class martial artists come and demonstrate their techniques for the candidates. Typically, these people are 7th degree black belts or higher and many have competed successfully on the world stage.

So Curt and I are at the event where groups move from master instructor to master instructor. When at the Judo demonstration, I had a question. The instructor was Mike Swain. Mike was on the 1980, 1984, 1988, and 1992 Olympic Judo Teams for the US. He won a Bronze medal in the 1988 Olympics. He also competed in the World Judo Championships where he was 2nd in 1985, 2nd in 1989, and was the 1987 World Champion in Judo.

When I asked my question, he demonstrated the technique on me. Of course, he didn't know that I had a cracked rib and I had not medically confirmed it yet. I didn't suffer any damage, but it was just the thought of tangling with this former world champion in my condition.

Some of what we saw at one of the first two boot camps that I attended was funny. Funny for Curt and me, but not so funny for one man. This gentleman was about 40 years old. We called him "Eager Beaver" because when they were asking questions his hand always shot up. This demonstration was from Pressure Point black belts. Pressure Point

Martial Arts is a style where nerve clusters in the body are attacked causing crippling pain and submission, when done properly. Master Charles Gaylord, 10th degree black belt and founder of the Kajukenbo Association of America (KAA) was running this demonstration. Master Gaylord was also in three Martial Arts Halls of Fame.

He was showing us how a very short strike to the back of the neck can disable an opponent. He asked "Do I have any volunteers?" Eager Beaver raised his hand. Curt and I looked at each other with question marks. Why would someone volunteer to be disabled? We didn't know. So Eager Beaver is placed on his hands and knees. Master Gaylord tells the audience that he will only strike the back of the neck from a short distance. He puts his knife hand (fingers extended) out and strikes from about one inch above the neck with the side of his hand. Eager Beaver went down like a sack of potatoes. He was completely unconscious. I don't think that Master Gaylord intended for that to happen. Eager Beaver was dragged off to the side where he was revived, but not able to go back to his seat in the audience for about 15 minutes.

I doubted that the Pressure Point masters could use a finger pinch to the side of the shoulder where it meets the neck and bring a person to the ground. I changed my mind when I questioned one of the pressure point masters and found myself on the ground in a split second.

In my Open Weapons Form, I became worried that Master Reyes might put us on the Santa Clara University Gym floor where the mats didn't quite cover. Then he did so. I went through my routine and when I came to the roll, I had decided that I would just tough it out which meant doing a forward roll by using my knuckles directly on the wood floor while my hands were holding the tonfas. I completed it, flipped my tonfas, and then caught them both for a successful demonstration.

I wore my 3rd degree uniform for a couple of months. I was now a Sa Bum Nim (SBN). At the end of 2011, I decided that three black belts were enough. Besides, I was getting injured too often.

HEALTH CONCERNS

As we get older, there are naturally more issues concerning health that arise. As with most things in my life, I seem to have had an unusual array of health concerns. Around 1987, I was noticing that I had a stuffed-up nose much of the time. I discovered that I had a deviated septum either from birth or from a very young age. I wanted a doctor to open my airways. The ear, nose, and throat surgeon said that he wouldn't do it if it were him, but I wanted this fixed. I went forward with rhinoplasty. It may have given me temporary relief, but I now believe that I was suffering from allergies which I confirmed on two separate visits to an allergist some years apart. I now agree with the doctor that the rhinoplasty was a waste.

About 1997, I was having quite a bit of pain in the bottom of my left foot. It was interfering with my tennis. I went to a podiatrist who diagnosed the situation as a Morton's Neuroma which is a pinched nerve between the metatarsals or bones of the feet. The first suggestion was to try a cortisone shot to handle the pain and damage. The podiatrist gave me a shot of the cortisone mixed with a numbing agent administered through the top of the foot. The shot was nearly painless, but alas, it was not successful. My pain returned. The podiatrist suggested a surgical neurectomy meaning removal of the damaged section of nerve. The operation was successfully performed. I was shown the nerve after the surgery and it was definitely damaged. Now I have a numb area between the 3rd and 4th metatarsals. Clipping toenails can be interesting since I can't feel half of two toes. After the operation, I was able to resume tennis with no residual pain.

In 2001, I had Lasik surgery and I was able to throw away my contacts. In 2005, I started having knee problems. The knee problem could be due to the pounding that the body takes in top-flight tennis or it could have been from extensive running, but probably both. I went to an orthopedic surgeon who diagnosed a meniscus tear. He said that arthroscopic surgery could be done and I would be up and moving without pain shortly after surgery. I had the surgery and it worked out that way.

In 2009, I had tooth implants put in. Now this is not actual surgery. It was worse. In order to have implants, they had to build up the bone mass where my upper teeth were. Some doctors use cadaver bone, but not the doctor that was recommended to me. It took a few months to get my mouth prepared for implants. The doctor drew blood, gave me Novocain to the lower jaw, and then proceeded to scrape bone material from the bottom jaw below the teeth and along each side. He would only do one side per session. He mixed a portion of growth material from my blood draw with the bone material scraped off of my jaw. Then more Novocain shots to the upper jaw. This time they would cut a small window in my upper jaw above the teeth and the bone floor of the sinus cavity. This is above where the new teeth would be. Then they injected the growth material/bone scrapping materials through the window and on top of the bone floor. After this procedure was completed on both sides, I had to wait about three months and take an X-ray to view the new bone material. In my case, there was good enough bone growth and two implants were put into the back of my upper jaw where the last teeth had been. Considering that I had lived more than 20 years with cantilevered false molars hanging off of the back supported only by bridges to the two teeth in front of it, this was a positive change. The cost for all of this pain was about $20,000 dollars and it was not covered by insurance. A few years later, I had a different surgical dentist provide an implant with cadaver bone. The work was done in a day and due to sedation, there was no pain. It only cost about $4,500 and was a much simpler solution, but again, it was not covered by insurance. It is true that the need to grow extensive bone material was going to complicate my original surgeries in any case, so maybe the prices are comparable. I have never regretted getting my dental implants. They are just like real teeth.

After I stopped Martial Arts, at the end of 2011, I was out running one day in early January of 2012. As I raced along on a sidewalk, I looked ahead and saw people in a driveway up ahead. Suddenly, my foot hit something. I think it was raised concrete. I went flying and upon hitting the sidewalk, my right thumb got caught on what I can only guess was another segment of raised concrete. Suddenly, my right thumb went back to my right wrist. I thought, crap, now I've broken it. I pushed it back to its normal position and I could bend it. Maybe I didn't break it? I wasn't sure. My hands and one knee were scrapped up quite a bit. My thumb was in a great deal of pain. I got to my feet and started running again. The people that I had seen in the driveway shouted as I went by, "Are you all right?" I yelled back, "I don't know. I'll have to go find out if my thumb is broken." I ran past them with my thumb throbbing. I kept running to the end of that long block. I was hoping that I could run the rest of the way home, which was less than a mile, but the pain just got worse. At the corner, I sat down and called Myra. She had guests, so it wasn't the most convenient time. She came and picked me up. As we drove home, I almost passed out. The pain was incredible. When we got home, I told Myra that I needed to get to the emergency room, and that I was OK to drive there since the pain had diminished a little bit.

At the hospital's emergency room they took X-rays, and it was determined that there was no break. They said that I should see my personal doctor. We were leaving for Hawaii in a few days and I put off the visit to my personal physician until we got back. One disturbing result of the accident was that I couldn't hold things securely with my right thumb which had an unusual ability to bend well past the stopping point of my left thumb when moving it away from the index finger. I learned to hold drinks with my pinkie finger underneath them to prevent them from slipping right out of my hand.

When I got back from Hawaii, I made an appointment with my physician to take a look at my injury. I remember that I had to wait a little more than a week to get that appointment. When I met with him, in less than 5 minutes, he sent me to their plastic surgery department because they apparently were the ones that handled hand injuries. I had to wait a few more days before I could get in to see the first plastic surgeon available. When I did get to see him, he took about a minute to diagnose "skier's thumb", so named because of the number of skiers that end up with this injury.

In skiing, the skier may fall holding on to the ski poles. As they fall, they hit the snow, the pole often lands on top of the snow and with the hands being palm down with the arms stretched out. The hand goes into the snow, but the pole does not which puts extreme pressure on thumb and this can cause damage to it. The doctor explained that I had a complete rupture of the ulnar collateral ligament (UCL) of the thumb. The UCL is a primary stabilizer of the thumb. He went on to tell me that once this ligament snaps, there is a concern that the ligament, which retracts toward the side where it is still connected could atrophy and therefore be unusable in the repair. He said that the UCL atrophy can take place in as little as a month, if not repaired. In that case, they would need to extract a ligament from my wrist to serve as the replacement thumb UCL. I was concerned about how this was going to affect my tennis game.

At the time of this appointment, it had been almost three weeks since the fall. The doctor said it was important to have surgery as quickly as possible. I went to get on the calendar right away, but there were no appointments available until after a little more than a week. The appointment was set for just over one month from the date of the fall. The day came and the surgery was performed. The doctor was able to reattach the damaged UCL to its original location. It had not atrophied enough that it could not be used. I attribute this to my old age making me a slow healer. I was grateful that I did not need to have a ligament taken from my wrist to be used as the thumb replacement ligament.

Now, I was in for a few months of recovery including wearing a cast and going through physical therapy. Michelle's good friend Nancy Y. was a skier who had also had this same injury. She had also needed surgery, so I had someone that I could discuss this injury with that knew what it was like. Nancy became my "thumb buddy." One thing that I had not been told was that since it was my right hand and I am right-handed, I would need to learn to write again. It took a while. The pen just did not want to go where I was intending it to go. With practice, I was able to write again. The surgery has not caused any other difficulties.

In late 2013, I went to the gym to work out on the weights and do a treadmill run. After I finished with the weights, I found an available treadmill. I always started my treadmill runs by just standing on the treadmill, grabbing the handles, and getting a heartbeat reading. Typically, it would register below 60 beats per minute. This time it was different. The machine said that my heart beat rate per minute was 155. The formula for a theoretical maximum heart beat was 220 minus your age. In 2013, my maximum heart beat would have been 158. The treadmill reading had me stumped. I figured the machine was broken. I went to three other machines all of which registered 155. I decided to run anyway. The heart beats per minute stayed at 155 for the duration of the run. This phenomenon continued for another month or so. I would try to check my pulse, but I couldn't feel a pulse anywhere. This was all very, very strange.

Myra and I had signed up for a new gym. At the new gym, I went through my regular routine and there was my 155 beats per minute on the first treadmill that I tried. All of these machines at the new gym were new treadmills. I awakened to the fact that maybe it was me all along and not the machines. I made an appointment with my doctor.

I had a new personal physician and she sent me for an electrocardiogram. When I finished, the technician looked at the results and said "It looks like you have Atrial Fibrillation." I went back and spoke to my doctor. She confirmed the diagnosis of an arrhythmia and set up an immediate appointment with a cardiologist.

The cardiologist indicated that I didn't have Atrial Fibrillation (AFib), but I did have the closely related condition called Atrial Flutter (AFL). So, what is the difference? The difference between the two appears to be that atrial flutter is a sudden onset, regular but abnormal heart beat and atrial fibrillation is a slowly developing irregular, abnormal heart beat.

The protocol prescribed was for me to take Pradaxa, which is one of several different kinds of blood thinners. Blood thinners are important to ensure that the blood passing through the heart doesn't coagulate, resulting in a blood clot. A normal heart moves the blood smoothly, which keeps it flowing so that it won't coagulate. In AFL or AFib, the blood is not moving smoothly, and is therefore potentially stagnant at times. Stagnant blood can coagulate, resulting in a clot that can then lead to a deadly or debilitating stroke. I went to a class on A-Fib with other patients before they told me that it was actually AFL. I was 62 years old and by far the youngest in that class.

The cardiologist told me that I was a good candidate for Cardioversion which is a procedure where the patient is put under anesthesia for about five minutes during which an electric shock is put through the heart in the hopes of returning it to its normal rhythm. This sounded good to me. As I was awaiting the procedure, Myra asked the cardiologist if sleep apnea could have caused the AFL. He said yes, which is what we had read. I would need to check with the sleep center after the procedure. I underwent the procedure in an area where there was a row of beds with curtains which resembled a post-operative recovery area. Since there was no surgery, this made sense. When my procedure was completed and I was awakened, the doctor told me that my heart rhythm was back to normal. I wasn't out of the woods. I still had to take blood thinners for another couple of months. I had researched the odds and found out that 50 percent of patients return to an abnormal heart beat in the first year and only 30 percent are "cured." I overheard a different doctor talking to the patient and the patient's wife in the bed next to mine. He told them that the procedure didn't work. Because of my age, I was cautiously optimistic.

I did go to be evaluated at the sleep center and it was determined that I did have sleep apnea. Myra went in within a couple of months after I did and she, too, was determined to have sleep apnea. We both now wear CPAPs also known as Continuous Positive Air Pressure devices. I am convinced that we sleep better as a result of using the CPAPs. It has now been over five years since my Cardioversion and my heart rate continues to be normal, so it worked for me and I am grateful.

In February of 2015, I was running up to 29 miles a week and losing the extra weight that the aging process had helped to put on. I was running at a pretty good pace for someone close to 64 years of age. I was doing 4 miles at an 8 minute-20 second per mile pace. I continued to run three to five miles a day through June, but I noticed that my left knee had gradually worsening pain. I stopped running for a month hoping that the knee would heal and

I could start running again, but no such luck. I went to my personal physician, who had X-rays taken, and then sent me to an orthopedist. The orthopedist told me that I had a bone-on-bone condition. This may have been accelerated by the meniscus surgery a decade prior. I told her that I needed to be able to get back on the tennis court, which had been my intention since leaving martial arts. I also needed to be able to run, since it was my get-in-shape exercising method. I asked her what could be done next. She said that I was not ready for knee replacement surgery, probably because I was not having pain when just walking around. She said besides, I couldn't run or play tennis on a knee replacement because the added stress would reduce the expected 20-year life of the knee joint. She said that a second surgery would be a lot more complicated and difficult than the first. I have since learned much about knee replacement surgery and she was right about the difficulty of a second surgery. Now what could I do?

Myra and I bought a very good recumbent exercycle which I could ride and not get knee pain. I could no longer use the treadmill. I had tried playing tennis, but every time I made a sharp movement to the side, I received an excruciating jolt of pain in the knee. There was no way to play without a fix to the knee.

I read up on the situation and decided that I would give stem cell therapy a try. I had to travel two hours each way from my home in order to receive the treatments. The key was the extraction of my own bone marrow stem cells from my back, which were then put through a centrifuge and a part of it was mixed with a portion of my blood. This mixture was then injected into my knee. There were about two sessions prior to when the stem cell injections were performed. All of the knee injections were extremely painful. I presume this is because there is limited blood flow to the cartilage of the knee and therefore it is difficult to numb.

The results were less than satisfactory. The knee might be slightly better, but I still cannot play tennis or run. My only choice now is wait for a breakthrough where cartilage can be added to the knee. Either that or have the knee replacement and play on it anyway. I had heard that one of our USTA National Men's 65 tennis champions won his championship with a knee replacement. I am not sure that I would want to risk the surgery repeat in just 10 years instead of 20, particularly since more bone up and down the leg would need to be cut. It is just not a good situation, so I wait.

As I got older, I started to have lower back pain, which is not all that unusual. In 2016, the pain suddenly got significantly worse. I felt pain moving from my back down the inside of my right leg to the ankle. Sitting wasn't so bad, but walking was excruciating. I went to my primary doctor who sent me to a back specialist. After X-rays had been taken, the back specialist diagnosed lower back spinal stenosis, which is a compressed nerve. He recommended an epidural steroid injection treatment, which might reduce the swelling in the nerve and relieve pain. We went forward with this plan. There was some slight temporary relief, then the pain returned. From what I had read, repeated injections did not typically eliminate the pain. Besides, my health coverage indicated no more than three of these steroid treatments were to be given in a year. I contacted the back specialist and said that I didn't want more injections so what was next? He sent me to a back surgeon.

The back surgeon reviewed my X-rays and asked me where the pain was. I indicated in the middle of my lower back and a shooting pain down the inside of my right leg. This latter pain was not sciatica, which runs down the back of the leg. The surgeon asked me to describe each pain. He then told me that there were two different causes. The pain in the middle of my lower back was due to disk deterioration. There was nothing he could do about that, based on the health organization that he and I belonged to. The pain down the leg, however, he told me he could fix. Since my middle of the lower back pain just felt like a sore back that anyone my age might have, I said my primary problem was the extreme pain from the compressed nerve. One thing of interest, when I looked at my X-rays, was my question to him concerning what appeared to be a squished disk. I asked him, "Do you mean squeezed like this?" while pointing at that disk. He said, "Yes, what's left of it!" indicating that the disk deterioration was severe. That concerned me a little.

We went forward with the operation and my leg pain from the compressed nerve was immediately fixed. I was very happy with the results of that back surgery. There has been no return of the leg pain from the compressed nerve. I was also glad that my back surgeon didn't operate on my middle back pain. I have friends, that I played in my younger days, that were top players, and both have had surgeries that required spinal fusion. That is something that I did not want since the fusion places more pressure above and below the fused area often leading to additional fusion surgeries.

GANG MURDER TRIAL

In 2013, I was called in for jury duty. How could jury duty lead to anything unusual? Well, based on my life story, it not only could, but it did. Years before, I had gotten myself off of a jury trial when the defense attorney asked me if I would want to be seated where the defendant was if I were the juror. This was an armed robbery case of five branches of the same bank with five tellers all coming in to testify that the defendant did it. On top of that, the defendant was wearing a leather jacket with his hair slicked back. I answered "Not if I did it!." I was the first person that the defense dismissed.

In March of 2013, I was called in along with many more prospective jurors and asked to fill out a questionnaire for voir dire. Voir dire is the questioning of potential jurors by the prosecution and defense in order to determine whom they wanted to sit on the jury. We filled out the questionnaire and left it for the court officials. I was not called in again for about three weeks. At that point, I was brought in with a group of about 24. We were getting our first view of the defendants. They were six gang members and one gang associate, each with his own lawyer. They were charged with the murder of a young man in 2007. Each of the potential jurors was individually questioned by the attorneys. There was one prosecutor and each defense attorney took several of the potential jurors for questioning. We were addressed by name which meant that the lawyers and the defendants knew who we were at that point. When I was being questioned, I tried to tell them that I didn't like gang members, but since few people do, I guess that didn't carry much weight. I even told them of an incident where some gang bangers tried to run our car off the road with Myra and Rain in the car. When asked if I could fairly judge their guilt or innocence, I said yes. The defense asked me about my black belts and whether I ever had to use them in a street fight, which I hadn't. I was also asked briefly about my DUI and my disagreement with the arresting officer as to who was at fault in that accident. This voir dire was tough on some of the potential jurors as they were questioned. We had several of the women crying. A couple of men expressed their fearfulness.

About a week after that, we were called back into Santa Clara County Superior Court. Now they were actually seating the jury. There were several of the groups of 24 sitting in the gallery seats waiting to be called. Mine was the last group. I was hoping that they would fill out the jury before they got to me. Time and time again, they would bring up a juror and then he or she would be dismissed.

When they finally got to me, I was called up to the jury box and assigned Juror Seat #10. The only female lawyer among the defendant's lawyers stood up and said that she wished to "Thank and excuse Juror #10." I stood up very much relieved, but I heard a lot of commotion among the defense lawyers. It looked like most of the female lawyers' colleagues were whispering to her and they were very animated. She said "I meant Juror #9 is thanked and excused." I sat back down, dejected. I had to tap the woman next to me in Seat #9, because she was confused about what had just happened. She happened to be one of those jurors who, during voir dire, had become very emotionally upset at the thought of being on this jury. She rose and left the jury box. They had not been excusing jurors in any particular order, so I was still hopeful, but looking back on it now, the writing was on the wall. Shortly thereafter, the last two seats of the 12-person jury were filled. Then the judge said "Congratulations, you are on the jury!" I was still sitting there a little shocked at these words that I didn't want to hear. The selection of six alternate jurors was next. When that was completed, we were told when the trial would begin.

This case was a gang murder trial, with gang enhancement charges potentially applied. The gang in question was Los Latinos Locos or Triple L. They operated out of the Evergreen area of East San Jose. During the early morning hours of July 8, 2007, during a house party near Silver Creek High School and Brigadoon Park, members of LLL attacked two partygoers who were outside of the house. The innocent partygoers had not provoked the attack, nor were they gang members. The LLL partygoers had crashed the party, but were allowed to stay. I am sure no one wanted to confront them about leaving. The attack was swift and deadly. Up to 15 members of the gang descended upon the two. One of them, 19-year-old Adrian Medina, was beaten with a baseball bat, fracturing his skull, and then stabbed 25 times by another gang member, piercing his heart and eviscerating him. Medina died at the scene.

The second partygoer was fighting off multiple attackers trying to get to his friend. When he finally reached Medina, he put his body over him to shield him as best he could, and in the process received multiple strikes with rebar. The rebar that had been found later at the scene and had left welts on his back and lacerations to his head while he attempted to protect his friend. Medina and his friends were actually part of a group of five. The commotion outside alerted the others to a fight and they went out to investigate. When the third friend of Medina tried to intervene, he was struck, with what was believed to be rebar, across the side of his face, breaking his jaw. The fourth friend came out next and got punched while entering the fracas. By the time the fifth friend had reached the fight scene, the gang members were fleeing, or had already left, so he was not attacked. Since the gang had prevented friends from intervening to help Medina, murder charges were issued against all of them, along with assault charges for the injuries to Medina's friends.

Once the trial had started, we fell into a routine. Eighteen jurors, twelve seated, and six alternates, shared a jury room where we would go for breaks, or during the many discussions that the lawyers and judge would have, when we were sent out of the courtroom. Every trial day we would come to the courthouse with our passes, which allowed us to move to the front of the line that formed outside of the courthouse at the security checkpoint. This checkpoint was run by Santa Clara County Sheriff's Department officers, and included passing through a metal detector. This pass was helpful in getting us through quickly. Next, we would go to the court offices to have our parking tickets validated. The parking garage was across the street, and the way to get to it was to walk up two to three flights of steps until we were about 20 feet above street level, where there was a walking overpass to the third floor of the garage.

In the jury room, we would read or converse with each other. We had brought in things to do during the breaks. There were darts that used Velcro to stick to the target. Some of us would play Hearts. Others put together jigsaw puzzles with many pieces. We got along well. There were at least two dropouts whose seats were filled by alternates during the length of the trial. In the jury room, jurors and alternates were all going through the experience, at least until deliberations.

A fellow juror, Dan Jacobson, is a pilot for a major airline who often flew the biggest planes on international routes. I told him about my crash and we would discuss aviation concerns during some of the jury room breaks. At one point during our trial, an Asiana Airlines jet crashed upon landing by touching down short of the runway at San Francisco International. We discussed the likelihood of that plane having missed all of its available approach windows thereby coming in too low. It was virtually certain.

Dan and I also discussed crew resource management (CRM). Initially the acronym stood for "cockpit resource management", but later became "crew resource management." The thinking is that the authoritarian nature of the cockpit, which may have come from military pilots moving into commercial piloting, put the captain in the position of being the only decision-maker. This is counterproductive. CRM maintains the command hierarchy, but provides for crew members to speak up. It allows these crew members to question the captain if they see that mistakes are being made. Although CRM grew out of the 1977 Tenerife crash of two 747s on a runway, the first formal NTSB recommendation came about as a result of the 1978 United Airlines

Flight 173 crash in Portland, Oregon. In the latter crash, the pilot was preoccupied with a landing gear problem and ran out of fuel. The resulting crash landing killed 10 and injured 24 out of 189 passengers and crew.

Dan and I talked about how the world of piloting has changed through the use of CRM. The authoritarian attitude in the cockpit led to accidents where obvious mistakes made by the pilot were never challenged by the co-pilots or flight engineers. CRM was aimed at changing this situation and it has been largely successful.

One of my problems during the trial was balancing work and the trial. I was trying to keep up with my SSL workload by working before trial in the morning, at lunch, and after the trial day ended. We would start our trial sessions at 9:30 AM, go until the lunch break at 11:30 AM, start the afternoon session at 1:30 PM. The afternoon session would run until 4:30 PM. Nevertheless, I could not keep up with work. The workload was always heavy and several subcontracts administrators (SCAs) were assigned to pick up portions of my SSL workload.

The entire trial was worrisome for me and for at least some of the other jurors, even though we knew that witnesses and two gang members, who turned state's evidence, were in significantly more danger than we were. I took steps to be able to defend myself, my family, and our home beyond my martial arts abilities.

The trial went on month after month. Each witness would usually be questioned by each of the lawyers during direct questioning, cross examination, redirect, and recross. Because each defendant's case had to stand on its own, often the same questions were asked repeatedly by different lawyers. It was very lengthy and usually very boring.

We learned a lot about many subjects, some pleasant and some distinctly unpleasant. We learned about DNA and that DNA belonging to Adrian Medina was found on some of the defendants' clothing during searches of their houses. We learned and saw graphically that intestines often slid through knife holes made in the outer wall of the abdomen leaving them on the outside rather than the inside of the body.

We learned that the LLL gang was associated with the Norteños. The Norteños (northerners) and Sureños (southerners) were initially groups that were part of a California prison gang known as the Mexican Mafia. The Southern California groups of the Mexican Mafia were apparently treating the Northern Californian gang members as inferior and calling them derogatory names associated with the agricultural farming more prevalent in the North. The Northern Californians formed their own prison group called the Nuestra Familia. The Norteños and Sureños both now have spread to other states and Mexico.

We learned that the Norteños use the number 14 and more often "XIV" to designate their loyalty and affiliation. This is because the "N" in Norteños is the 14th letter of the alphabet. The LLLs would sign with their right thumb and index finger so that others can recognize the "L." We learned a lot about gang culture, graffiti, and gang signs. We learned that if one gang member is in a fight, all nearby gang members have to help him. Any and all weapons are allowed. This is a lot different from the expectations of fights when I grew up, where weapons were not allowed and jumping in was an act of cowardice based on a fear of allowing a fair fight to take place.

We learned from the two gang members who turned state's evidence against the seven defendants that the LLL gang had chased two Sureños gang members one evening. After catching both of them, they were then knocked out. The gang member who had repeatedly stabbed Adrian Medina had then jumped on top of one of the downed individuals and repeatedly stabbed him. That individual luckily lived. We were also told of a murder in the driveway of a person in the Evergreen neighborhood who was just getting into his car when he was shot in the head. We also heard about numerous other fights, often against gang rivals.

The trial took a two-week break in July, which I presume was to allow the attorneys and the judge to take a vacation. It resumed until October, when final arguments were made, the judge gave us final instructions in the law, and we were sent into the jury room to deliberate. We deliberated for three and one-half days before reaching our verdict. The trial had gone on for six months and was one of the costliest in Santa Clara County history. The county ended up paying $2,000,000 for the lawyers of the indigent defendants.

Our jury convicted two gang members of 1st degree murder and the remaining five defendants were convicted of 2nd degree murder. The two individuals who were doing the stabbing and striking the victim with a bat were the two convicted of 1st degree murder. Gang enhancement charges applied where appropriate.

On the day that the verdicts were read, there were at least nine uniformed Santa Clara County deputies in the courtroom, presumably to ensure that order was kept. The defendants were sitting with their lawyers at three long tables. The prosecutor was at another table separated from the defendants. Behind these tables was a railing separating the general public from those involved in the court proceedings. My fellow jurors and I were seated in the jury box against one wall. The courtroom was packed with relatives of the defendants and others interested in the outcome of the trial. The District Attorney for Santa Clara County was in the audience to hear the verdicts read for this long and difficult trial. As the verdicts were read, sobs and gasps were heard from the audience, but the judge quickly put a stop to that by threatening to have anyone making a disturbance expelled from the courtroom. The prosecutor told the San Jose Mercury News that the San Jose Police Department never gave up in their pursuit of evidence. He also praised the jury for their unambiguous message that gang members involved in a violent and deadly attack will be held accountable.

This trial not only went on for six months, but over 950 prospective jurors were interviewed in order to arrive at the final 12 accepted jurors. Over 100 witnesses testified in the trial. More than 200 exhibits, including hundreds of photos, DNA evidence, and recorded interviews, were handed over to the jury.

I ended up being called back into the courtroom in January of 2014, along with three of the other jurors. Jurors were not supposed to discuss the case with each other during the trial and apparently court room cameras had shown that several of us were talking or showing our notepads at various times. For my part, I would show that in the upper corner of the notepad, I was keeping a count of the number of witnesses and how many were repeat witnesses. Sometimes I would show that to a fellow juror. The four of us had to go back into the courtroom individually in front of the defendants and their relatives in the audience. This inquiry went nowhere and we were dismissed.

Three years later, I was called for jury duty again. The law should offer us the option of opting out of the jury system since we had done several lifetimes worth of service, but they only told us that we could not be called for a year. I had to call in twice a day for ten days. I was never requested to come into court, so I did not have to explain that I really felt my service was done.

CHAPTER 60

THE FAMILY

My dad, Ted Overgard, had finished his work life in Wisconsin and retired to a cabin on Pigeon Lake near Drummond, Wisconsin in the northern part of the state. On his 80th birthday Dad received an honor that he treasured greatly. The Ojibwe Indian tribe bestowed an eagle feather on him in recognition of his service in World War II.

He and my mom, Joyce Overgard, who finished her work life as a teacher in the Madison, Wisconsin area, lived on Pigeon Lake from around 1992 until about 2006, when they moved to Harrison, Arkansas. Dad had wanted to move there to be the Secretary of the 5th Marine Division Association. The editor also lived in Harrison and they thought that it would just be easier to be closer together. While they were there, my dad effectively lost his sight. He could see, but only blurry shapes. Mom would have to drive him when he left the house. In 2012, my mother had a stroke and so we moved both of them to a Northern California city, where my sister Jayne lives.

In 2013, I arranged for and had their Harrison house sold. Over the next few years, they lived at a couple of retirement homes. These elder care facilities had food that was prepared for each meal and they had some access to emergency nursing care if they needed it. I would come up periodically and take my dad to the Silver Legacy Hotel and Casino in Reno, Nevada, which he loved. He really enjoyed playing Craps.

I had planned to take Dad back up to Reno on his 90th birthday, but nine days prior to that birthday he was found dead in his bed. We had expected Mom to die first, since she had seemed to be in worse shape. She had had a second stroke, was recovering for several months, then she went into the hospital and died just seven months after Dad. We buried both of them in a Wisconsin cemetery where many of my relatives are buried.

My sister Jayne played tennis, as well. At the age of 16, she was one of Wisconsin's top high school players and achieved a ranking of #7 in the Girls 16 and Under Doubles in the Western Section with Kathy Callen.

After high school, she was even offered a tennis scholarship to Brigham Young University, but she turned it down. She went on to attend the University of Wisconsin main campus in Madison and as a freshman took 6th year Spanish and 6th year German. At the end of her freshman year, she was effectively a junior because of credits associated with the previous years' language class completions. She then moved to California and had to work for a year in the state in order to get in-state tuition privileges.

She took a job as a tennis professional at West Lane Tennis Club in Stockton, California. She was to become the head tennis professional and she ran a very successful junior tournament with many age groups participating.

Once she had qualified for California resident tuition, Jayne quit working at West Lane and started attending school at the University of California at Berkeley (Cal). All of her language credits were not accepted at UC Berkeley, so she started as a Sophomore. She attended Cal for two years. She then went back to University of Wisconsin - Madison, where her credits were once again accepted. She graduated from the University of Wisconsin - Madison with a B.S. in Mathematics degree.

In 1981, Jayne had come to Myra's and my first Christmas together with her boyfriend John. A year later on Christmas Eve, John committed suicide. At the time of the suicide, Jayne was back in Wisconsin, but she was still very close to John. It naturally took a long time for her to move past this difficult situation.

In the early 1980s, she became an Air Traffic Controller, which was naturally interesting for me. She went through standard Air Traffic Controller training in Oklahoma City. She then worked out of the Monterey, California, airport for a number of years. There she met another air traffic controller named Lynne Ulicki. Together, they decided to embark on a great adventure. Since both were pilots, they got some sponsorship money and entered the 1983 Air Race Classic for women.

The 1983 Air Race Classic went from El Cajon, California, to Grand Rapids, Michigan, totaling 2,287.39 miles in eight legs. This was a handicapped event to account for the different types of aircraft that were entered. Lynn and Jayne were flying a Cessna 172P. They were two very good pilots, as they finished in 6th place out of 35 aircraft. Their success here encouraged them to enter in the following years.

The 1984 Air Race Classic went from Pasco, Washington, to Gainesville, Georgia, covering 2,213.92 miles in seven legs. Jayne and Lynn placed 2nd out of 31 aircraft. This year they were flying a PA-28-181, which was a single-engine Piper Archer airplane. Their achievement is truly noteworthy!

1984 Runnerup: Jayne Overgard and Lynne Ulicki, RDD-85

The 1985 Air Race Classic went from Redding, California, to Spruce Creek-Daytona Beach, Florida, a total of 2,559.78 miles in seven legs. Jayne and Lynn place 15th out of 36 racers. A higher handicap was placed on their aircraft, which was the same one used during the 1984 race. This handicap dragged down their overall scores and final position in the race.

In 1991, Jayne married Dan, who is the love of her life. I taught Jayne how to throw a ball when she was young and she throws really well. She says that's how she caught Dan, because they met at a softball game. I'll take credit for helping her throw better, but not for impressing the man who would be her husband. I am sure she did that all on her own. They have three lovely children, Maya, Ryan, and Haley, who are adults now. Maya, the oldest sibling, married Harrison in 2016 and they now have a baby boy, Nolan. Maya has a Master's degree and works in Southern California. Ryan is getting his PhD from the University of Minnesota in Mathematics after having graduated college with a degree in Mathematics. Haley, the youngest, graduated from college with a

BS in Biology. She works in Northern California. Jayne went on to get a Master of Science in Mathematics degree from Texas A&M University and is now teaching mathematics at the collegiate level.

Jayne got back into tennis in 1998. She was ranked #4 in the Women's 40 and over Singles of the Northern California Section. That is a very good result, considering how difficult it was for me to get my game back and to play at a high level after years of inactivity. Maybe her groundstrokes are just smoother than mine. In any case, that was a fine showing!

Jayne also was in a car accident in April of 2017 where a rock, probably dropped from an overpass, went through her windshield, knocking the rearview mirror into her head. A couple of weeks later she went into the hospital for a CTI scan. Jayne was concerned that she could have sustained a concussion. On April 29th of 2017, a mass, unrelated to her accident, was discovered. An MRI was ordered to get a better look at the mass in her brain and it was revealed to be the size of an avocado. She had to have surgery within a few days to remove the mass. It turned out to be a Glioblastoma Multi-form 4 Grade 4 cancer. This is the most common of brain cancers, but also the deadliest with a 5 percent survival rate after five years. The average patient dies within 12–14 months. As of this writing, Jayne has outlived the average. On January 11, 2019, she had a second surgery to remove a very small tumor that had appeared in the same area. This operation went well. With Jayne's perseverance, we have every have reason to believe that she will live a long and happy life.

My other sister, Nancy, graduated from the University of Wisconsin—Whitewater, which was my alma mater, with a bachelor's degree in Business. She went on to work in the insurance business as an underwriter. She lived in the Dallas area for a while, followed by a short stint in the St. Louis area. She was then assigned to the Chicago office for about a year and a half before settling in the Minneapolis area. In 2004, she married her beloved husband Jason. It was a wonderful wedding that Myra, Rain, and I attended. Nancy and Jason like to scuba dive when they can find the time for a warm weather vacation. Jason is a photographer who now marries couples.

My mother's sister and brother, Fred and Elizabeth, have passed away. My father's sister, Dido, is living in Wisconsin with her husband Jordan. My father's brother, Jerry, is living in South Dakota with his wife Marlis.

Michelle, Myra's daughter, played drums in her high school's marching band. She played for a competition marching band called the Spirit of Sunnyvale as well. For her 16th birthday, we rented a restaurant's large room for the band Sundance to play for our invited guests. Sundance was the group that played at the Sandpiper when I first met Myra. It was a surprise for Michelle. She got to play drums with Sundance, which was fun. After she graduated from high school, she went to New York City to live. We visited her in the early 1990s and even went to the top of World Trade Center. From there, we could look down on planes flying 500 feet below us. Now that was strange.

Michelle ended up coming back to Sunnyvale to live with us when she was pregnant. That was interesting, because she was to come out as gay around that time. Myra and I were happy to have her at home and to get a chance to help raise the child. In 1993, Rain was born. Rain and Michelle lived with us for most of Rain's childhood years.

During this time, she and Rain participated in a number of local stage musicals.

In 2005 and 2006, we went through a very large remodel of both the garage in the back and the house itself. Since the garage was plumbed and had electricity, we turned it into a living quarters and called it our cottage. We remodeled our house to Myra's design. Myra is a fabulous designer and decorator. She spent years collecting ideas from HGTV and would plot out designs on grid paper. When we were ready to remodel the garage and the house, Myra's designs were used. They turned out to be simply fantastic.

Michelle married a woman in 2009 and they lived in the cottage in back of our house for a while before moving to Southern California. Michelle went on to get a degree from San Jose State University and then her Master of Fine Arts degree in Screenwriting from Chapman University in Orange, California.

She wrote a screenplay and entered it into a competition at the Female Eye Film Festival in Toronto, Canada, where she won best low budget screenplay. She was able to fly and be there during the screenings. She also wrote a movie called "The Demon Within." This is a movie of the horror genre, and we were able to find it on Amazon Prime.

In 2017, Michelle's marriage of nearly nine years ended. Although this was a difficult blow for her to deal with, she is doing well.

Rain is a very unique and talented girl. In elementary school, she befriended a boy with severe autism. I was at her school, eating lunch with her one day, when all of these kids came running up shouting "Rain, Rain, Jimmy's in trouble." He was apparently highly agitated and the other kids didn't know what to do. Rain ran over to him and talked to him for a couple of minutes. I could see that he quickly calmed down and I was in admiration of Rain's ability to deal with him.

Rain started performing in elementary school. She was not shy about performing in front of people. In junior high school, Myra and I watched a choir performance that she was in. She had a short solo and her voice was very good. When she was 14, Rain was in the Sunnyvale Community Players' (SCP) junior production of "The Wiz." She played Addaperle, The Good Witch of the North. She told us that she had a solo and I was very concerned. Would she forget lines? Would she sing poorly? Myra and I just didn't know since Rain never sang around us. That night, I was in the audience and Myra was helping back stage. When Rain came out on stage she was playing her part, and then the time came for her solo. She broke into song and I was blown away. She was really, really good! Addaperle was a good part for Rain. At one point, she went and sat in the audience talking to the audience members as a part of the show. SCP's "The Wiz" was a lot of fun.

From then on, Rain participated in many SCP junior shows. She also participated in the Mountain View and San Jose theatres that held junior shows. Rain typically had one of the top characters because of the strength of her voice, acting, and dancing ability. On top of this, she participated in her high school's theater productions. In Rain's final performance of her senior year of high school, she played Toffee, in the show "Zombie Prom." It was not only the lead, but she was to sing 13 songs, most of them solos. She pulled it off with the aplomb of a veteran. Rain was to win three theater department awards her senior year: Outstanding Student Director; Outstanding Musical Performer; and Lifetime Achievement Award. She seemed a little young to get that last award. She was also selected by her high school for their Spirit award. This award honors one male and one female that have their names added to a perpetual trophy. That was quite an honor!

After high school, Rain went to San Jose State University for one year. She then transferred to Chapman University where her mother had gone. After graduating with a degree in Communication Studies, she tried to get an entertainment agent in Southern California, to no avail. Her father had an entertainment agent in New Orleans and he invited her to come live there. He said he would introduce her to his agent. Rain moved to New Orleans and did get accepted by her father's agent. Her father has appeared as characters in a number of mainstream shows. Rain has had acting jobs, but nothing very big yet. We are hoping that she will have a breakthrough soon. Rain now has a boyfriend and they seem to get along very well. After spending a few years in New Orleans, both Rain and her boyfriend have moved to Southern California.

Myra worked for many years in Silicon Valley at companies such as Rolm Mil-Spec, Tandem, and Cisco. She and I have built a wonderful life together. We have now been married for 36 years and she is truly the love of my life! After retiring from Cisco, Myra spent a number of years at SCP producing plays. She served as president of the organization for a couple of years. She has also been a driving force in adopting dogs. We have had three to six dogs at various times over the years, and as many as two cats, as well. We have fostered a number of dogs. I guess you could call us die-hard dog people. We currently have three dogs and one cat. Myra retired in 2009 and I followed in 2017. We sold our home in Sunnyvale and moved to another California city outside of the Bay Area. Myra has spent a lot of time decorating our house to make it our own. Myra's sister Dolores has also moved to our area this year and Myra has spent a lot of time organizing her house. Myra really loves designing, decorating, and organizing. Myra also likes to host family get-togethers for Thanksgiving, Christmas, and a spring or summer get-together. We are not as centrally located as we were in Sunnyvale, but it is good to see the family when we can, especially when Michelle and Rain come to see us.

CHAPTER 61

FINAL THOUGHTS

Almost every passenger who has flown considers what might happen if the plane they are sitting in were to fall out of the sky and rocket toward the ground. What are the odds of surviving a plane crash? Although more than 40 percent of passengers report a fear of being involved in a plane crash, the odds are strongly against it. As mentioned earlier, as of 2015, your odds of being in a fatal airplane crash were about one in 29 million. That means that you would have to board an airplane once a day for over 79,000 years before being involved in a fatal air crash. Even if you're reading this on an airplane while your plane is about to crash, your odds of surviving are quite good. According to a National Transportation Safety Board report of crashes between 1983 and 2000, 95.7 percent of those aboard survived. Much of this is due to improved aircraft safety measures. Even passengers on the most devastating airplane crashes survive at a rate of 76 percent. On my plane, the survival rate was 78 percent. Of course, only 44 percent of us came out without death or injury, and that is not including me among the injured. If you count both planes in my crash, 93 percent survived and only 12 percent were injured.

Retirement living has afforded me the time to write this book. I realize, as I reviewed my crash, that it was much more terrifying than I had remembered. Not unexpectedly, of all of the unusual things that have happened to me in my life, the crash was by far the most unusual. It has had a profound effect on my life. I hope you are never involved in one. I did not suffer from survivor's guilt. I had to get out of that plane as quickly as possible and so did the others. None of us deserved to die in that burning plane. There were all sorts of reasons as to why I might have lived or died, such as how our plane struck the other plane, where I was sitting in the plane, my presence of mind during the incident, how we hit the ground, where the fire started, and many other factors.

I am struck by the fact that if our plane had been able to take off just a little earlier, there would not been an accident at all. Everyone in both planes would be alive and uninjured. If our plane had been a few seconds later or not able to take off as soon as we did, we would have plowed right into the other plane at 160 miles per hour. I suspect that this would have led to the planes tumbling and fuselages breaking into pieces. Of the 138 passengers on board both planes, I believe this would have led to over 100 deaths. So, you see, sometimes our lives hang in the balance of just how the seconds tick off the clock of life.

I am sure that I suffered from PTSD after the incident, and particularly in the first year after the crash. The crash and subsequent fears may have contributed to my later depression. I tend to doubt it, but I cannot be sure. The crash is, however, a constant in my psyche. I know that I was lucky to escape that burning tube of terror and I am very grateful for every additional day that I live.

My life has been very good. I have a wonderful woman as my marriage partner, a great family, and a very good retirement. I am always astounded by how many unusual things seem to happen to me, while recognizing that I have caused some of them. Whenever I was in danger, the Universe always seemed to be with me, keeping me safe! I was never interested in a boring life, and it has not been boring in the least. I can't wait to see what life brings to me next!

AUTHOR'S NOTES AND ACKNOWLEDGEMENTS

Some of the names of those not directly involved in the North Central plane crash have been changed or the last names are omitted. The change of names occurred to maintain the individual's anonymity or because I could not remember the names after nearly half a century.

I wish that I had kept a diary. That would have helped immensely with specific dates and occurrences. Most of the timeframes are pretty accurate, but I like details. The crash details were supported by newspaper articles and photos that I collected immediately after the crash. Of course, there was always the National Transportation Safety Board report of the accident which gave me many of the details used in the book. I was also able to identify many dates through internet research. The Madison State Journal and the Capital Times, Madison's two newspapers, helped me greatly with their articles and photos from reporting on the crash. I thank Chris Lay of Capital Newspapers for giving me permissions to use articles and photos from these two Madison newspapers. I also want to thank Marcia Schiff of AP Images/AP Video for her help in getting permissions to use photos that were taken of the crash site by Associated Press photographers.

This work of recalling so many events in my life has been a true pleasure. I want to thank Walter Hopgood who runs the website www.catastrophecast.com. As mentioned in the book, I discovered that this website had a posting from December 20, 2013 pertaining to my crash. This was done on the 41st anniversary of the crash. In the 17 minute-54 second podcast, Walter narrates the circumstances of the crash. This relatively unknown crash was selected because of the impact it had on all future commercial jet liners. Today all commercial planes have very specific regulations for the escape path lighting used on them. This was a direct result of the North Central plane crash and subsequent fire that I was in. I had thought about writing a book on this subject for many years, but life got in the way, particularly work. Now that I am retired, I had the time to devote to the process.

I also want to thank Lloyd Eastburn for his recounting of the events of the night of the crash and for his insights into the activities in the O'Hare Air Traffic Control tower as they affected both planes.

I thank my fellow survivors for their tales of escape. I truly pray that you were and are able to move on with your lives without too much difficulty. Those who survive such an ordeal know that it is with them all the days of their lives. I want to express my condolences to the loved ones and relatives of those that died aboard North Central Airlines Flight 575. At least some good came out of that crash that has hopefully saved many lives. If any survivors of this crash or other air crashes wish to contact me, I can be reached via the following email address:

EscapingTheFlamesFlight575@gmail.com.

I thank Bob Goodman for his technical help in setting up the formatting/typography. I also want to thank him for his help with the cover design and the back page of the book. I thank David Hardwick, my editor, for his work on correcting many of the mistakes, that I, as an English teacher's son, didn't expect to make. I wish to thank Dan Jacobson for his technical help on all things related to aviation and his time as a preliminary reader. I also want to thank Marty Gunther, Gus Cubillo, and Leslie Cubillo for their preliminary reading of the manuscript and their suggestions for improvement. I particularly want to thank Gus Cubillo for the author's photograph and cover design inputs along with thanking Marty Gunther and Dan Jacobson for their testimonials. I'd like to give special thanks to Bill Lum for his artist's illustrations of the crash wreckage.

I want to thank Carol Sveilich for acting as a path finder and sounding board based on her experience as a published author. I thank Rebecca Newlin for introducing me to Carol and for allowing me to walk in her footsteps as a first-time author.

I thank my fellow rock climbers Kelly McGuire, Kristen Shorette, Scott Sellers, Lisa Stefke, and Shawn Swenson for letting me use their images. I also thank the photographers who took the rock climbing photos used in this book. They are Marissa Christman, Bryan Gohn, Andy Johnson, Bill Olszewski, and Elmar Stefke. I am hoping these photos will let the readers know just how exhilarating this sport can be.

I also want to thank my Aunt Dido Nash for helping me to understand some of our family history, particularly that of my mom and dad. I want to thank my sister, Nancy, for her recollections, and my sister, Jayne, for her contributions to this book. I want to thank Lynn Ulicki for the picture of the 1984 Air Classic runner-ups.

I wish to thank my family for their love and support, in particular my daughter, Michelle, and my granddaughter, Rain.

Last, but not least, I wish to thank my beautiful wife, Myra, for her love through the years and support of my writing efforts.

ENDNOTES

1 NTSB Report Number: NTSB-AAR-73-15, SA-436, File No. 1-0017, Aircraft Accident Report–North Central Airlines, Inc. McDonnel Douglas DC-9-31, N954W and Delta Air Lines, Inc. Convair CV-880, N8807E–O'Hare International Airport–Chicago, Illinois–December 20, 1972–Adopted: July 5, 1973.

2 *The Capital Times* (Madison), Thursday December 21, 1972; Page 4 and 31 by Mike Miller. Photo by Dave Sandell and 2nd Photo by Bruce M. Fritz.

3 *The Capital Times* (Madison), Thursday, December 21, 1972; Pages 1 and 4 (Continued from Page 1 article by Tom Hibbard) Front Page Passenger Photo by Dave Sandell.

4 *Wisconsin State Journal,* Thursday, December 21, 1972; Section 1, Page 1–2.

5 *Wisconsin State Journal*, Saturday, December 23, 1972; Section 1, Page 3.

6 *Wisconsin State Journal*, Thursday, December 21, 1972; Section 1, Page 1–2 by Joseph McBride

7 *Wisconsin State Journal*, Saturday, January 6, 1973; Section 1, Page 9.

8 *Wisconsin State Journal*, Friday, December 22, 1972; Section 4, Page 1 by George Hessellberg.

9 *Wisconsin State Journal*, Wednesday, December 27, 1972, Section 1, Page 2.

10 *Wisconsin State Journal*, Friday, December 22, 1972; Section 1, Pages 1, 2, and 4.

11 https://www.catastrophecast.com. Catastrophecast.com.

12 http://libraryonline.erau.edu/online-full-text/ntsb/air-craft-accident-reports/AAR73-16.pdf. Midway.

13 https://www.ntsb.gov/investigations/AccidentReports/Reports/AAR7314.pdf. Miami.

14 https://www.ntsb.gov/investigations/AccidentReports/Reports/AAR1001.pdf. Buffalo.

ABOUT THE AUTHOR

This is Todd Overgard's first book. The subject of his crash and many other encounters with dangerous situations made for good storytelling. Now retired, he decided to write the book that he had been thinking about for over 45 years. He and his wife, Myra, live in Northern California. (Photo by Gus Cubillo)

Made in the USA
Columbia, SC
28 July 2019